## Critical Perspectives on Canadian Theatre in English

General Editor Ric Knowles

**2005**

volume one *Aboriginal Drama and Theatre*, ed. Rob Appleford
0-88754-792-3

volume two *African-Canadian Theatre*, ed. Maureen Moynagh
0-88754-794-X

volume three *Judith Thompson*, ed. Ric Knowles
0-88754-796-6

**2006**

volume four *Feminist Theatre and Performance*, ed. Susan Bennett
0-88754-798-2

volume five *George F. Walker*, ed. Harry Lane
0-88754-800-8

volume six *Theatre in British Columbia*, ed. Ginny Ratsoy
0-88754-802-4

**2007**

volume seven *Queer Theatre*, ed. Rosalind Kerr
0-88754-804-0

volume eight *Environmental and Site Specific Theatre*, ed. Andrew Houston
0-88754-806-7

volume nine *Space and the Geographies of Theatre*, ed. Michael McKinnie
0-88754-808-3

PLAYWRIGHTS
CANADA PRESS

416-703-0013 • orders@playwrightscanada.com • www.playwrightscanada.com

# George F. Walker

Critical Perspectives on Canadian Theatre in English

volume five

Critical Perspectives on Canadian Theatre in English

volume five

# George F. Walker

**Edited by Harry Lane**

Playwrights Canada Press
Toronto • Canada

**Playwrights Canada Press**
215 Spadina Avenue, Suite 230, Toronto, Ontario CANADA M5T 2C7
416-703-0013 fax 416-408-3402
orders@playwrightscanada.com • www.playwrightscanada.com



Financial support provided by the taxpayers of Canada and Ontario through the Canada Council for the Arts and the Department of Canadian Heritage through the Book Publishing Industry Development Programme, and the Ontario Arts Council.

Canada

The Canada Council for the Arts
Le Conseil des Arts du Canada

ONTARIO ARTS COUNCIL
CONSEIL DES ARTS DE L'ONTARIO

Cover image: Jin-me Yoon, between departure and arrival, 1996/1997. Partial installation view, Art Gallery of Ontario. Video projection, video montage on monitor, photographic mylar scroll, clocks with 3-D lettering, audio. Dimensions variable. Courtesy of the artist and Catriona Jeffries Gallery, Vancouver.
Production Editor/Cover Design: JLArt

**Library and Archives Canada Cataloguing in Publication**

George F. Walker / edited by Harry Lane.

(Critical perspectives on Canadian theatre in English ; v 5)
Includes bibliographical references.
ISBN 0-88754-800-8

1. Walker, George F., 1947- --Criticism and interpretation.
2. Walker, George F., 1947--Interviews. I. Lane, Harry, 1941-
II. Series.

PS8595.A557Z68 2006 C812'.54 C2006-902359-X

First edition: May 2006
Printed and bound by Hignell Printing at Winnipeg, Canada.

To Sue

## Table of Contents

## General Editor's Preface

*Critical Perspectives on Canadian Theatre in English* sets out to make the best critical and scholarly work in the field readily available to teachers, students, and scholars of Canadian drama and theatre. In volumes organized by playwright, region, genre, theme, and cultural community, the series publishes the work of scholars and critics who have, since the so-called renaissance of Canadian theatre in the late 1960s and early 1970s, traced the coming-into-prominence of a vibrant theatrical community in English Canada.

Each volume in the series is edited and introduced by an expert in the field who has selected a representative sampling of the most important critical work on her or his subject since circa 1970, ordered chronologically according to the original dates of publication. Where appropriate, the volume editors have also commissioned new essays on their subjects. Each volume also provides a list of suggested further readings, and an introduction by the volume's editor.

It is my hope that this series, working together with complementary anthologies of plays published by Playwrights Canada Press, Talonbooks, and other Canadian drama publishers, will facilitate the teaching of Canadian drama and theatre in schools, colleges, and universities across the country for years to come. It is for this reason that the titles so far selected for the series—*Aboriginal Drama and Theatre, African-Canadian Theatre, Judith Thompson, Feminist Theatre and Performance, George F. Walker, Theatre in British Columbia, Queer Theatre, Environmental and Site Specific Theatre*, and *Space and the Geographies of Theatre*—are designed to work as companion volumes to a range of Canadian drama anthologies recently published or forthcoming from the country's major drama publishers that complement them: *Staging Coyote's Dream: An Anthology of First Nations Drama in English* (Playwrights Canada, 2003); the two volumes of *Testifyin': Contemporary African Canadian Drama* (Playwrights Canada, 2000, 2003); *Judith Thompson: Late 20th Century Plays* (Playwrights Canada, 2002); the various collections of plays by George F. Walker published by Talonbooks; *Playing the Pacific Province: An Anthology of British Columbia Plays, 1967-2000* (Playwrights Canada, 2001), and other projected volumes. I hope that with the combined availability of these anthologies and the volumes in this series, courses on a variety of aspects of Canadian drama and theatre will flourish in schools and universities within Canada and beyond its borders, and scholars new to the field will find accessible and comprehensive introductions to some of the field's most provocative and intriguing figures and issues.

Finally, the titles selected for *Critical Perspectives on Canadian Theatre in English* are designed to carve out both familiar and new areas of work. It is my intention that the series at once recognize the important critical heritage of scholarly work in the field and attempt to fill in its most significant gaps by highlighting important work from and about marginalized communities, work that has too often been neglected in courses on and criticism of Canadian drama and theatre. In its nationalist phase in the late 1960s and 70s, English-Canadian theatre criticism tended to neglect work by women, by First Nations peoples and people of colour, by Gay, Lesbian, Bi- or Transsexual artists, and by those working in politically, geographically, or aesthetically alternative spaces. While respecting, honouring, and representing important landmarks in Canadian postcolonial theatrical nationalism, *Critical Perspectives on Canadian Theatre in English* also sets out to serve as a corrective to its historical exclusions.

Ric Knowles

## Acknowledgements

Projects such as this are more collaborative and long-term than they are individual and immediate. So I'd like to share the relief of completing this with a number of other people. Ric Knowles, the General Editor of the series, has extended not only friendship but also excellent guidance and extraordinary patience. Present and former colleagues in the Theatre and English programs at the University of Guelph have shared and stimulated my enthusiasm for Walker's work, including especially Ric Knowles, Allan Watts, Ann Wilson, Alan Filewod, Michael McKinnie, Kim Renders, Ajay Heble, Jill Gill, Paul Ord, and Paul Salmon. I personally owe a great deal to the many Guelph students who enhanced my enthusiasm for Walker through our joint studies, in MA thesis work, in dramatic literature classes, and in productions, both at Guelph and in the Love of Louis theatre company, which some of them formed in the late 1990s, primarily so that they could continue staging Walker.

My thanks to the staff of the Archives and Special Collections Division of the University of Guelph Library, and to the staff of the School of English and Theatre Studies, for listening to problems and finding creative solutions. David Murray, Acting Director of the School, kindly provided access to office space in 2005-06. Susan Morgan, Creative Head of Television Drama at CBC, has been especially helpful in providing information and materials relating to *This is Wonderland.* The contributors to this book have been enthusiasts for the project and unbelievably patient with my nit-picking (and my own memory-lapses). Angela Rebeiro has continued to show strong support for the book, and the series of which it is part; and Jodi Armstrong has been an indefatigable and wonderfully enthusiastic copy-editor. I thank them all warmly.

All of the essays and interviews included here are published with permission of the copyright-holders. Ken Gass's "Introduction" was first published in *Three Plays* by George F. Walker (Toronto: Coach House, 1978), 9-15; Chris Johnson's "George F. Walker: B-Movies Beyond the Absurd" in *Canadian Literature* 85 (Summer 1980): 87-103; the excerpt from Robert Wallace's interview "George F. Walker" in *The Work: Conversations with English-Canadian Playwrights*, ed. Robert Wallace and Cynthia Zimmerman (Toronto: Coach House, 1982), 213-25; Jerry Wasserman's "Making Things Clear: the *Film Noir* Plays of George F. Walker" in *Canadian Drama/L'Art dramatique canadien* 8 (1982): 99-101; Denis W. Johnston's "George F. Walker: Liberal Idealism and the 'Power Plays'" in *Canadian Drama/L'Art dramatique canadien* 10 (1984): 195-206; Robert Wallace's "Looking for the Light: A Conversation with George F. Walker" in *Canadian Drama/L'Art dramatique canadien* 14 (1988): 22-33; Stephen

Haff's "Slashing the Pleasantly Vague: George F. Walker and the Word" in *Essays in Theatre/Études théâtrales* 10 (1992): 59-69; Ed Nyman's "Out with the Queers: Moral Triage and George F. Walker's *Theatre of the Film Noir*" in *Australasian Drama Studies* 29 (Oct. 1996): 57-65; D.A. Hadfield's "The Role Power Plays in George F. Walker's Detective Trilogy" in *Essays in Theatre/Études théâtrales* 16 (1997): 67-83; Carole Corbeil's "A Conversation with George Walker" in *Brick: A Literary Journal* 58 (Winter 1998): 59-67; the excerpts from Ric Knowles's "Modernism and Its Containments" and "Aristotle, Oedipus, and the Bible: Forms of Naturalism" in *The Theatre of Form and the Production of Meaning* (Toronto: ECW Press, 1999), 56-58 and 43-49; Reid Gilbert's "Escaping the 'Savage Slot': Interpellation and Transgression in George F. Walker's *Suburban Motel*" in *Siting the Other: Re-visions of Marginality in Australian and English-Canadian Drama*, ed. Marc Maufort and Franca Bellarsi (Brussels: P.I.E.-Peter Lang, 2001), 325-45; the excerpt from Craig Stewart Walker's "George F. Walker: Postmodern City Comedy" in *The Buried Astrolabe: Canadian Dramatic Imagination and Western Tradition* (Montreal and Kingston: McGill-Queen's UP, 2001), 314-38; Marc Maufort's "'Some Kind of Transition Place Between Heaven and Hell': George Walker's Aesthetics of Hybridity in *Heaven*" in *Performing National Identities: International Perspectives on Contemporary Canadian Theatre*, ed. Sherrill Grace and Albert-Reiner Glaap (Vancouver: Talonbooks, 2003), 70-80. The excerpt from Mary Pat Mombourquette's MA Thesis "Walker's Women in the East End Plays" was presented to the University of Guelph in 1990 and Amanda McCoy's "This Is Wonderland" was commissioned for this volume; both are published here for the first time.

## Introduction: Walker and the Critics: "Opening Up the Panel More to See More of the World

by Harry Lane

> I think there is a lot of pressure on playwrights to write structured material. And not just because you deal with an audience that is used to or needs structure but also because theatre is so heavy with tradition and presupposition. (Walker, in Wallace and Zimmerman, *The Work*) [1]

Since 1971, George F. Walker has become one of the most prominent and innovative English-language writers on the Canadian theatre scene, with some 30 stage scripts professionally produced, an extensive career writing for television, radio, and film, and a host of major awards (two Governor General's Literary Awards for Drama in English, three DORA awards for Outstanding New Play in Toronto, and no less than eight Chalmers Canadian Play awards). His work has also inspired a mass of critical commentary and argument, mostly in the form of newspaper reviewing, but including a substantial stream of articles in scholarly journals and a small number of theses and dissertations. This volume attempts to bring together a representative selection of the scholarly articles with excerpts from one of the academic theses and three of the many illuminating interviews that Walker has given over the years, interviews in which he repeatedly reveals his own struggles to come to terms with his work and its reception. Walker's last stage play (at least as this volume goes to press) was premiered and published six years ago, since when much of his writing and production energy has been devoted to various projects in television and film, especially the television drama series "This is Wonderland." In recognition of this shift, the volume also includes an essay on the first season of that series, broadcast by CBC in 2003-04, and issued commercially on DVD in late 2005.

To go back to 1971, in June *Toronto Star* staff writer Urjo Kareda reported on a perhaps typically unconventional performance at Factory Theatre Lab, "a public rehearsal" of George F. Walker's *Prince of Naples.* According to Kareda, Walker's play "was presented in a totally unshaped performance, with the actors still carrying scripts, the furniture arranged at random, and the director [Paul Bettis] shouting instructions to his cast" ("Theatre Lab's"). [2] Kareda captures vividly the sense of unpredictable energy that seems to have typified the company's work. But what I find fascinating is the suggestion in Kareda's review that the partly unstructured spontaneity of the performance may be linked in some way to the vitality with which key qualities in the script were able to emerge: "Here was a play of real vigour and ingenuity," he writes. "The latent strength of Walker's dialogue emerged lucidly, with a crackle that must have been present from the first reading [...] The play is a counterbalance of triumphs and capitulations, a backward-and-forward flow of energies, sparked with some flashes of a wild, inspired humour."

It seems that, when produced more formally, Walker's work presented significant challenges to critics and audiences. In the acutely self-conscious evolution of Canadian drama in the early 1970s, the problem seemed to arise as to how to categorize and therefore how to read work that seemed so distinct from what various critics noted as a national (and perhaps appropriate) trend towards naturalism. Urjo Kareda's introduction to the publication of David French's *Leaving Home*, a kind of review of the entire 1971-72 Toronto season, names four plays as "the most fully satisfying, the most finished new plays of the season": *Leaving Home* itself, along with David Freeman's *Creeps*, Bill Fruet's *Wedding in White*, and Larry Kardish's *Brussels Sprouts*, all fundamentally naturalistic. "Naturalism leads to a useful self-discipline in terms of the material for drama," argues Kareda. "It suggests, but doesn't impose, an author's response to his experience, a method of transforming personally observed information into an artistic order." As Ken Gass notes, the assumption that "Canadian drama" had a "realistic bias" was echoed in Henry Popkin's well-meaning but avuncular survey in *The New York Times* in January 1978, in anticipation of the off-Broadway openings of new plays by Freeman and French.

Gass's Introduction to Walker's *Three Plays* partly reflects his frustration at the limiting power of such assumptions, leading to "the literal banging of one's head against the wall," and his determination to establish that a cartoon-based play like *Bagdad Saloon* can be "violently anti-naturalistic" and at the same time "as Canadian as moose meat."

Arguing that Walker's use of the word "'cartoon' tends to belie its thematic density," Gass reads *Bagdad Saloon* as a metaphor for the 1970s Canadian cultural landscape: "A desert, a place of shifting fashions" dominated by a sense of inertia. So Gass sees Ahrun and Aladdin's futile attempt to create a culture out of other (chiefly American) shopworn myths as an ironic representation of Canada's attempt to reinvent itself through other people's eyes. (Interestingly, threaded through Gass's text is the suggestion of a similarity between Walker's approach to writing plays and Factory Lab's approach to making theatre: Walker's violation of naturalist norms is paralleled by Factory Lab's challenge to Actors Equity rules in the 1972 Works Festival; the inability of critics to understand *Beyond Mozambique* is paralleled by the Arts Councils' unhappiness with Factory Lab in 1974.) Gass's analysis repeatedly focuses on the gains to be made by Walker's anti-naturalist approach to content and structure. While admitting that the formal complexities of *Ramona and the White Slaves* made it elusive for audiences (something Walker himself concedes in his 1982 and 1988 interviews with Robert Wallace), Gass argues that the form of the play, based on the opium nightmare, allows Walker "ample room" to probe the bewildering mind of its title character; in reference to *Bagdad Saloon*, he claims that "the episodic cartoon allows all of Walker's theatrical instincts to break loose." (And Kareda's enthusiastic review of the play in March 1973 celebrated precisely such a breaking loose.)

Chris Johnson's 1980 study, "George F. Walker: B-Movies Beyond the Absurd," published in *Canadian Literature* at the end of Walker's first decade of writing for the theatre, was probably the first full-length academic article published on Walker and has been very influential. Johnson contextualizes Walker's work within what, borrowing a phrase of Northrop Frye, he characterizes as "the 'entire enterprise' of Canadian drama." He distinguishes usefully between the various "Canadian" identities of the work of the main four new "alternate" companies in Toronto at the end of the 1960s (Theatre Passe Muraille, Factory Theatre Lab, Tarragon Theatre, and Toronto Free Theatre), pointing to the more "elusive" and long-term objectives of Factory Lab, which "provided a trade school for Canadian playwrights entirely unprecedented in Canadian theatre history." In turning to Walker's early plays, up to and including the recent *Rumours of Our Death* (1980), he points to an ironic linkage of form to content, "employing a form to question ironically the ideas underlying the form," as an early and ongoing characteristic of Walker's work, both in the early "absurdist" plays and their successors based on the pop-culture conventions of the cartoon. Beginning with *Beyond Mozambique* Johnson identifies "extensive recourse to the raw material of the B-movie," which he argues becomes a "lens" through which the audience could be invited to view Walker's vision of the world.

Using different language Walker suggests something similar in his 1982 interview with Robert Wallace in *The Work*: "in the way other playwrights work out structure, I am working out the reference points the audience needs [...] There are ways that an audience can follow a play other than through plot or two intermissions or whatever." Denying that he writes parody (a point echoed by Johnson and Knowles), Walker asserts: "I tend to like to frame the world, and use various genres to do that. 'B' movies are a generic frame that gives me freedom to jump off in any direction." The "frame" or "lens" serves to provide sufficient reference points to open up meaning, but the writer preserves the freedom to write in response to his imagination.

Johnson's article justifiably became foundational for many future studies of Walker's plays, as in the case of Jerry Wasserman's partly dissenting review article "'Making Things Clear': The *Film Noir* Plays of George F. Walker" and Denis W. Johnston's "George F. Walker: Liberal Idealism and the 'Power Plays.'" While noting that Walker adds "his own distinctive twists" to B-Movie conventions, Wasserman points out that the challenge of "making something of" the raw material of the B-Movie is that it "offers little beyond the slickness of its surfaces," a challenge that Wasserman did not (then at least) feel were always met. However, he sees in *Zastrozzi* "as serious a parodic response to melodrama and revenge tragedy as those genres were to the Romantic and Elizabethan drama that preceded them." (For his more multi-faceted evaluation of Walker's early work, see Wasserman's Introduction to *Zastrozzi* in the 4th edition of his *Modern Canadian Plays.*) Denis Johnston's study of the Power plays also dissents somewhat regarding the structural freedom that Walker claims through using the B-Movie frame. Declaring Walker "a playwright in progress," he sees

*Filthy Rich* as an advancement on *Gossip* because of its "improved dramatic structure": "a much more economical structure […] a single plot line, with twists rather than appendages [and] Walker's more patient exposition of the story." Johnston sees in the third Power play, *The Art of War*, a loss of "the romantic B-Movie lens which gave [the characters'] shenanigans such a roseate glow in *Filthy Rich*"; in the further emergence of Jamie he perceives "the spark of a new idealism."

Walker's transcendence of generic conventions is central to Amanda McCoy's study of the first season of the television series "This Is Wonderland", written by Walker and Dani Romain. McCoy employs elements of the Bakhtinian "carnivalesque" to demonstrate how the series breaks the conventions of the typical television court-room series in politically transformative ways: "'Wonderland' not only gives a voice to those who are normally silenced, but it also destabilizes hierarchies, erasing the barriers between the affluent and healthy and the poor and the sick." McCoy also shows how, within the series, the courtroom drama format seems inadequate to contain the demands and energies of its underprivileged characters: "tension is caused by cases that remain unresolved at the ends of episodes: what happens to the immigrants who cannot find translators, to the juvenile delinquents who refuse help from social services, or to the accused who are jailed indefinitely because of mistaken identity?" As McCoy notes, the series is stitched together by scenes of chaos, both within and on the steps of Toronto's Old City Hall court building: "throngs of shouting, weeping people appear in tightly-framed close-ups. […] The immense, chaotic dissatisfaction of the crowds is a revolution in the making." Noting Terry Eagleton's caution that carnival may be a "licensed enclave" that actually functions as a means of social control, McCoy argues that the case is otherwise in "This Is Wonderland": "The carnival that goes on inside Old City Hall can scarcely be contained, it spills out onto the steps, into the streets."

In his 2001 book *The Buried Astrolabe: Canadian Dramatic Imagination and Western Tradition*, Craig Stewart Walker sees another kind of structural shift in Walker's writing in the East End plays (including *Love and Anger* and *Escape from Happiness*), which, "however much [they] embrace complexity and depict ambiguity […] evince some kind of attempt to move dramatically towards a less morally ambiguous outlook." In his analysis, a key question becomes the degree to which the plays reach beyond moral ambiguity. At one pole, he cites Elizabeth late in *Better Living*—"Political involvement often causes moral confusion. I mean, unless you're mentally rigid"—adding that in the Quinns's domestic situation at least "confusion […] may feel demoralizing, but is less dangerous than moral certainty." In *Beautiful City* Craig Walker seems to observe a kind of not-quite-resolved balance between Gina Mae's "socialist vision" of the future and the skepticism he sees Gina Mae and Paul retaining in the silent shrugs of the play's final moment. However, in *Nothing Sacred*, partly because his reading of Walker's transformation of Turgenev's Bazarov ("from a nihilist to a proto-socialist"), he finds that "the Christ-like overtones of Bazarov's virtually superhuman status are affirmed, for his legacy is to be passed on through his disciples." Walker links Bazarov's "socialist hope" to the unresolved conclusion of *Love and Anger*, in which "though the trial disintegrates, the indictment remains."

D.A. Hadfield takes up the connections to genre explored by Johnson, Wasserman, and Johnston, arguing that such a focus has obscured "an important structural and thematic anxiety [...] about the relationship between art and reality, the power of art in shaping reality, and the question of whose power controls art." As she demonstrates, the semiotics of the plays, programs, and Toronto performances are deceptively complex, revealing a "central concern with how we create reality from what we see and hear," how "malleable" reality is, and ultimately who gets to decide what kind of art we will have in our theatres. Hadfield cites Foucault's observation that "it's a matter not of a battle 'on behalf' of truth, but of a battle about the status of truth and the economic and political role it plays." In the first two Power plays, Hadfield sees this concern flying right over the heads of the reviewers, forcing Walker to make it much more explicit in *The Art of War*, which finally gave Walker his critical success and (dare one say "therefore") its audience success. Responding to L.W. Conolly's summation that *The Art of War*'s "level of seriousness is on an altogether higher plane" (111), she dryly observes: "Beyond the world of the play, artistic victory appears to tilt in the other direction."

Hadfield's analysis is partly about the way the Power plays get opened outward into the world of the audience, something that Ric Knowles also takes up in his 1999 book *The Theatre of Form and the Production of Meaning*, in a brief discussion of Walker's early experiments with modernist forms and in a longer discussion of the "dramaturgy of the perverse." Despite the culturally affirmative ideological work that he sees being performed by Walker's earliest plays, he points to their elements of self-consciousness that avoid folding audiences into their modernist frames. In material developed out of a 1992 article in *Theatre Research International*, Knowles explores the ways in which Walker's plays of the late 1980s, *Nothing Sacred* and *Love and Anger*, "productively pervert" Aristotelian structural principles, as well as such associated assumptions as those of unified character and plot and "the complacent, voyeuristic, oedipal, or ecstatic satisfactions and containments provided by dramatic catharsis." Important in his argument is the point that the dramaturgy of the perverse "typically *foregrounds* the expectations of its audience in order to disappoint, disrupt, or fracture them." Thus the trial scene in *Love and Anger* does not end in reversal or discovery, but in much more ambivalent and complex recognitions. Similarly, in *Nothing Sacred*, Knowles demonstrates how Walker productively perverts the traditional oedipal narrative of Turgenev's *Fathers and Sons*, to enable a shift of focus onto the class struggle.

Picking up on Knowles's concept of the "perverse," Ed Nyman, in his 1996 article "Out With the Queers: Moral Triage and George F. Walker's *Theatre of the Film Noir*," agrees that perversion means more than subversion; rather it is "a pro-active strategy [...] to take control of a system of representation." Nyman points to the deceptive nature of *film noir*, particularly in terms of sexual politics. While it "puts into circulation [...] the unsanctioned male and female," it also repeatedly affirms hegemonic norms of compulsory heterosexuality. And it is this, argues Nyman, that Walker's plays, particularly *Theatre of the Film Noir*, ultimately fail to pervert: "In terms of a very simplistic gender dichotomy of male versus female, the *film noir*'s ideology *has* been perverted. However [...] it becomes clear very quickly that what the play has failed to de-essentialize, de-hierarchicalize, and de-sacralize is the heterosexuality of that patriarchal order." For Nyman, therefore, the ultimate value of the perversity of Walker's plays is that it "demands, itself, to be perverted."

Mary Pat Mombourquette's study of *Love and Anger*, part of her 1990 MA Thesis, works from a Lacanian perspective to argue for a related recognition of heterogeneity and resistance to social containment in the play. Mombourquette points to the figure of Sarah, and to the women who gather around her at play's end, as representing a relationship "based on something other than the immutable hierarchy of power; their relationships are based on the mutable network of pleasure, of human-well-being." While Maxwell wants to create a new society, according to Mombourquette "he can find no clear direction because the systems within which he must work to effect change are invariably hierarchical, designed and retained to transmit power [...] because Maxwell works within social systems, like language, he confronts a closed and vicious circle." By contrast, she sees Sarah as possessing a kind of power that is based on her chosen flexibility and understanding of the impermanence of identity and language. This is echoed, with acknowledgement, in Knowles's observation that "'Character' in this play comes to mean something close to a series of temporarily adopted subject positions that are continually subject to reversal but allow for no final or permanent recognition of an essential self."

Knowles's point about character is echoed in Reid Gilbert's study of two of the *Suburban Motel* plays in terms of post-colonial, psychoanalytic, and speech-act theory. As he argues, Walker's plays "primarily engage contemporary audiences because they interrogate the largely unconscious fears of bourgeois theatre spectators about the tenuous control they maintain on their subjectivity and about that of subjects over whom they hold imperial sway." The protagonists of both plays are trapped, isolated, and controlled from afar (as is the audience on occasion), like colonial Others. Thus, R.J. in *Problem Child* falls into the trap of trying "to take what *feels like* action, to become what *feels like* an independent subject." Questioning Kate Taylor's assertion in *The Globe and Mail* that *Risk Everything* "actually takes the least amount of risk in the series," Gilbert focuses on the figure of Carol, whom he sees Walker investing with a complex awareness of her own status: "Carol simultaneously views herself as 'mother,' knows that such an inscription is illocutionary within the symbolic order, and pierces this act of interpellation with her own desire." Thus he is able to demonstrate that "while the audience is actively engaged in misrecognition of Carol as an autonomous agent (who makes bad choices), Carol herself breaks through this illusion, knowing herself to be the product of an inauthentic structure." Contrary to Taylor's complaint that by staging Michael's "massive erection" Walker ends the play with "a crude sight gag," Gilbert sees it rather as a sign of Carol's power and defiance: "A Mother pointing 'proudly' to a penis that she has caused to become erect and that she intends unabashedly to use for her own pleasure [...] while her daughter (also a mother) blasphemously invokes the name of Helen's chaste God, the Son of the absent Father/Law and His Ever-Virgin Mother."

Postcolonial theory also informs Marc Maufort's analysis of Walker's last stage play to date, *Heaven*, first produced early in 2000. Noting that Walker here breaks the codes of dramatic realism more boldly than ever before, Maufort attributes it to his attempts to translate thematic content into form. He sees the characters, especially the disillusioned human-rights lawyer Jimmy, as struggling with a profoundly troubled sense of "inbetweenness" that he experiences as paranoia and displacement. In addition to its complex confrontations between the codes of comedy and tragedy, the play's boldest dramaturgical feature is certainly a series of fantasy scenes in or related to heaven, which Maufort links to magic realism and argues reflect a hybridity in Walker's dramaturgy that parallels the characters' psychological turmoil. Maufort views Jimmy as "a disappointed white liberal humanist," which does much to explicate the character's divided subjectivity. It is also something that Maufort identifies in Walker himself: "Beyond the dramatic fragmentation of *Heaven* looms the nostalgia of Walker the liberal humanist who laments the impossibility of transcending the throes of postcolonial hybridity." Perhaps it is possible to read Walker's presentation of Jimmy as more distanced, more ambivalent, as reflected in the character's final lines, in which a heavenly stand-up comedy routine breaks down into incoherence and silence: "I mean I guess we'll take just about any fucking excuse to feel good. (*Shrugs.*) Like that helps or something. Like feeling good is the … most important thing … or something. (*Shrugs.*) / *Blackout.* / *The End*" (141).

The uncertain, divided non-ending of *Heaven* (which Maufort perceptively links to that of *Problem Child*) reflects Walker's concerns about endings in his 1998 interview with Carole Corbeil: "When you write these plays, they don't have endings ever. In *Love and Anger* in particular, I'd go Stop! And then I'd go, Oh, there's a bit more! It's really me saying, if the work is getting closer and closer to the bone, then it's the ending which seemed the most artificial […] I try to avoid that by not having endings." He quotes a friend's impatience with an otherwise positive *Washington Post* critic who had problems with his endings: "'The same stuff you liked about his work is why he's having a hard time ending his play […] They're all part and parcel! There are no endings, he's saying that, you can't do that—have that emotional mess—and then go, Aha! But here's the satisfactory ending.'"

The "mess" that Walker's friend describes is also a key element in the acting that Walker looks for in his plays, as he reveals later in the same interview with Corbeil. Recalling earlier comments to Robert Wallace in "Looking for the Light" about "free fall" acting (echoed in Stephen Haff's record of a telephone interview), Walker argues that, partly because of the way he writes, actors in his work need to "commit to the mess, too, before you try and look for solutions of clarity. Take the mess just as far as it will go." In his article "Slashing the Pleasantly Vague," Haff seems implicitly to link Walker's demand for a totally unpremeditated and messy, "free fall" approach to acting to what he describes as "the beginning of a liberation of language into new realms of function" even into silence, as in the final moments of *Love and Anger*. "When coherence and words fail, the complex and indefinite have power by virtue of their mystery which before could be viewed only as threat […] Walker is, in his words, 'letting in some light' on what has been a predominantly dark dramatic world, allowing his plays to 'swirl around' and bring more into consideration."

In "Looking for the Light" Robert Wallace points to contrasting dichotomies of character and scene types in Walker's (then) recent work, such as the contrast between the grotesque theatricality of Junior's encounter with his father in *Criminals in Love*, and his much more naturalistic scenes with Gail in the same play. He notes the common critical objection that such work is "'uneven, is foundering somewhere between the naturalistic and the grotesque." Walker's explanation echoes his frequently repeated assertion for the need to work within a much freer dramaturgical paradigm: "I think the voice, my writing voice, is with them both, trusting the shifts in tone, trusting those extremes more, trusting that these two types can be together, like different colours. In effect, I'm saying that's what the world is like, and I'm opening up the panel more to see more of the world."

(2006)

## Notes

1 Following the practice of earlier volumes in this series, page references and Works Cited listings are not provided for material included in this volume.

2 Denis W. Johnston also quotes this review in *Up the Mainstream* (87), and provides a rich account of the energetic and sometimes "chaotic" programming of the Factory Lab's early years (74-105).

## Works Cited

Conolly, L. W. "Dramatic Trilogies." Rev. of *The Power Plays.* By George F. Walker. *Canadian Literature* 112 (Spring 1987): 110-12.

Johnston, Denis W. *Up the Mainstream: The Rise of Toronto's Alternative Theatres, 1968-1975.* Toronto: U of Toronto P, 1991.

Kareda, Urjo. "*Bagdad Saloon*: Young Playwright Leaps Forward." *Toronto Star* 29 March 1973: 46.

———. "Introduction." *Leaving Home.* By David French. 1972. Toronto: Stoddart, 1985. v-ix.

———. "Theatre Lab's 'Rehearsal' Was an Involving Experience." *Toronto Star* 21 June 1971: 24.

Knowles, Richard Paul [Ric]. "The Dramaturgy of the Perverse." *Theatre Research International* 17 (1992): 226-35.

Popkin, Henry. "Canadian Theater Is Enjoying a 'Naissance.'" *The New York Times* 15 January 1978: D12-13.

Taylor, Kate. "*Suburban Motel* Finale Is More Raucous than Risky." *The Globe and Mail* 19 June 1998: C10.

Walker, George F. *Heaven.* Burnaby: Talonbooks, 2000.

Wasserman, Jerry. Introduction. *Zastrozzi, The Master of Discipline: A Melodrama. Modern Canadian Plays.* 4th ed. Vol. 1. Vancouver: Talonbooks, 2000-01. 257-59.

## Introduction to *Three Plays* by George F. Walker

by Ken Gass

> **ROCCO.** Tell me. Am I amazing? (*Beyond Mozambique* 95)
>
> **AHRUN.** Am I not a king? (*Bagdad Saloon* 22)

Not many prairie landscapes in George Walker's plays. Or, indeed any of those images that one used to associate with Canadian drama. Walker's settings are exotic: Arabian deserts, African jungles, and the seamy ports of Hong Kong. The few Canadian references that do exist, like Lance's preoccupation with wheat in *Beyond Mozambique*, are fiendishly ironic.

Of course, most Canadian playwrights of the 1970s quickly outgrew their self-consciousness with national symbols, but a number of observers found common denominators in the Canadian preference for naturalism (see Kareda, Introduction). Six years later, the *New York Times*, thinking itself very up to date, published an article on Canadian drama by Henry Popkin which also emphasized "the realistic bias of the new Canadian drama [and] its commitment to Canadian subject matter" (D12).

Not much naturalism in George Walker's plays. They are, in fact, violently anti-naturalistic. One might well ask if Walker is outside the mainstream of recent Canadian playwriting.

> **AHRUN.** Style. I think it has something to do with style. (*Bagdad Saloon* 30)
>
> **ROCCO.** European wit? Where did you pick it up? (*Beyond Mozambique* 112)

Walker's early plays, particularly *Prince of Naples* and *Ambush at Tether's End*, show a distinctly European style, a linguistic wit that pays respect to the French absurdists and the English tradition for articulate language. These plays reflect little, if anything, of the Canadian experience. Two years later, when Walker began *Bagdad Saloon*, the frustrations of trying to create an indigenous theatre in Canada had become very real and immediate. Naturalism and conservatism had quickly taken the field—at least in terms of hit shows and public acceptance—and ambitious, personal statements, such as John Palmer's *Memories for my Brother, Part II*, and *Touch of God in the Golden Age* (both of which had a seminal influence on Walker) were totally dismissed and ignored.

After two and one half years of frenetic activity, when the first wave of new Canadian drama burst forth in the 1970s, two images remained in the forefront of our consciousness at the Factory Theatre Lab where Walker's plays were performed. First the realization that the Canadian cultural field was a desert, a place of shifting fashions, lacking in roots or traditions. Second, a sense of inertia, a recognition of the impossibility of change, and the literal banging of one's head against the wall. It is in this context that we must look at *Bagdad Saloon*, which, for all its exotic flavor, is as Canadian as moose meat.

> **AHRUN.** Dramatics. Dialectics. Sub plots. Nothing happening. But with the greatest amount of fuss. Things begin slowly. Divide themselves into scenes. Going madly in all directions. To avoid the problem itself. Inertia. Non action. No action. No play. (*Bagdad Saloon*, 3rd Draft 11) [1]

*Bagdad Saloon* was written during Walker's first trip abroad in 1972, in a large room on Aynhoe Road in Hammersmith, London. While the work is not consciously political or even sociological, it is nonetheless, an apt metaphor for the building of a new Canadian culture. Ahrun, the mad dreamer, obsessed with cult figures and everyone else's fame, creates a structure to house mythic figures from other countries, notably America. He hopes to achieve renown by placing himself in the company of famous people and learning their secrets.

> **AHRUN.** Fame is the artist's only excuse for existence. (57)

> **DOC.** A great man never dies. He doesn't even fade. (28)

The American heroes are all dismantled. Henry (Miller) is a vainglorious fool chasing his own windmills in the form of the Pulitzer Committee. Expatriate Gertrude Stein is a genius, witty and perceptive, but mad, hopelessly mad. Dolly Stiletto is hardly a heroine by anybody's standards, but she goes on dreaming, placing all her faith in her son as the archetypal hero who can reverse all odds. Doc Halliday, for all his bravado, proves to be a frightened schoolboy, still struggling to learn to read.

But the Americans don't worry about their failings. They carry on. "Presume that you are famous and let the world prove you wrong," cries Stein (71). Ahrun desperately wants more. He believes that fame, however fickle, "can create things. Purpose. Glamour. Mystique. [...] Artists. Or folk heroes. [...] [then] Folk-lore (...) [then] More folk-lore [...] and then ..." (55). It is in this terrifying pause that Ahrun realizes the emptiness of his pursuits. What is tragic about Ahrun and pathetic about his associate, Aladdin, is that they can never achieve fame because they worry too much, because they stare at themselves through other people's eyes.

The play and the universe grow progressively out of control. Chaos reigns. Dolly's son, the ultimate hero, the big-time winner, proves to be a grotesque monster-child called Ivanhoe, himself desperately trying to switch careers. In the final scene, Ahrun,

Aladdin, and his servant are buried in cobwebs, while the real mythic figures, fading and rotted, carry on with their banquet, a triumphant toast to style. Ahrun, the man who wanted substance, is no more.

Walker's own style for *Bagdad Saloon* is bold and panoramic, and his description of the play as a "cartoon" tends to belie its thematic density. Walker explored the cartoon form in his previous play, *Sacktown Rag*, an occasionally autobiographical retrospection of life in the slummy side of Cabbagetown in the fifties. The episodic cartoon allows all of Walker's theatrical instincts to break loose—the form is really a celebration of theatre—and certainly keeps naturalistic tendencies and ordinary stage logic at more than arm's length. It offers Walker a sprawling canvas on which to paint his themes and even gives the characters a kind of erratic autonomy to move in and out as they please. The structure of the play is very simple. In the first part, the saloon is artificially constructed, crassly decorated with singing Masonettes, then peopled with cultural artifacts. The second part dismantles the structure and destroys the "culture" in favor of general chaos.

The Factory was filled with chaos itself prior to the *Bagdad* premiere, and nearly collapsed after its mammoth Works Festival in December, 1972, which resulted in a major dispute with Actors Equity. *Bagdad Saloon* came within ten minutes of not making it into rehearsal, but finally the bank yielded, and the show proved an important breakthrough for Walker, paving the way for his next work, *Beyond Mozambique.*

> **ROCCO.** There is a tower growing in the jungle. It is the power of light and the shrewd mind of darkness. It is the culmination of all history and civilization. And it is turning my mind into soup. (*Beyond Mozambique* 113)

In its initial draft, *Beyond Mozambique* also borrowed from the long, sprawling form of *Bagdad Saloon.* But Walker grew dissatisfied with much of it during a workshop exploration of the play and condensed it into a tighter framework. Although very funny, *Beyond Mozambique* is murkier and more obsessive than *Bagdad Saloon*, and marks the beginning of a painful, interior descent for Walker.

Ahrun, at least had the realization that action was only possible within a moral context:

> Morality. [...] The scale of man's shortcomings ranging from greed to petty malice is all defined by the one ultimate evil in him. The ability to destroy his fellows. This obliterates everything. And, therefore, a moral man must act. (*Pause*) Action. One more chance. (*Pause*) Act.... (*Pause*). (*Bagdad Saloon*, 3rd Draft 81-82) [2]

It is too late for Ahrun and he is forced to face his own hollowness. But Rocco, the Italian doctor from *Beyond Mozambique*, is beyond morality. Buried in the deep jungle, the bowels of the earth, he is able to exorcise his conscience by keeping busy with Frankenstein-ish experiments. He is haunted by his past life as a butcher in a Nazi hospital, but his obsession with his own work wins out. Besides, Rocco recognizes in himself a mirror of the world. "There's something about committing crimes against humanity that puts you in touch with the purpose of the universe," he declares (126). He is intent on becoming a force of darkness—more depraved and therefore less dangerous than the Zastrozzi of Walker's later work—but nonetheless a universal force on a par with God and Ignorance.

Yet while Rocco can wryly call himself "the absence of God," (113) he also eventually admits his work is his penance: "It's not glory I'm after. It's redemption" (126).

The other characters are equally haunted and desperate, if less lofty in their obsession. Lance wants to redeem himself in his dead father's eyes; Rita wants to make a non-porno movie; Liduc will settle for a single convert for Jesus; and Olga wants simply to savour her dreams. But it is Rocco who can most calmly face and manipulate the ultimate cataclysm that awaits them.

> **ROCCO:** I have finally destroyed that fucking tower. (126)
>
> **GLORIA:** I can't see no fucking mountain. (*Ramona and the White Slaves* 177)

Like Tom Stoppard (whose writing Walker's most clearly relates to), Walker would probably claim to have no social or political statements to make, and the scintillating writing style would support that claim. Yet all three plays point to a world that is clearly at the point of collapse. What is most frightening about the world of *Mozambique* is its hilarious flirtation with destruction. "I don't understand how you make all this violence seem so gratuitous," jokes Father LiDuc (133), after scenes that include dismemberment and rape. This may reflect some of the darker recesses of Walker's mind—his next play, *Ramona*, grows even darker—but it is also, I think, a concern for a society that has grown out of touch with reality. A social revolution is taking place in the jungle and the neurotic white trash are being driven back into their cages in the final assault of the play.

> **CORPORAL.** "Prophecy is an escape from memory." Now what in the hell does that mean? (130)
>
> **LIDUC.** Jesus doesn't mind losers, but he has no patience with idiots. (128)

While *Beyond Mozambique* is the most direct and clearest of Walker's plays in this trilogy, it was probably the least understood in its first production in 1974. It was negatively reviewed by most critics, and Urjo Kareda, writing in the *Toronto Star*, was simply baffled: "Is this George F. Walker's subversive report to the Canada Council," he asked. The production drew respectable crowds, probably due to the presence of Frances Hyland and Donald Davis in the cast, but the response could hardly be called overwhelming. Even the Arts Councils were unhappy with the production and Factory grants were frozen that year.

Walker became more removed and introspective for a period, and it became difficult for him to write his next play, *Ramona and the White Slaves.* It wasn't just the fact that critics didn't like his work (except for *Prince of Naples*, Walker had grown used to generally weak critical response), but rather it was the realization that he still didn't have a context in which to explore his most important unconventional themes and style. He toyed with the idea of writing novels, where it seemed easier to work in a vacuum. He wrote a first draft of a naturalistic ("I can do it too") play called *Decades.* He and Stephanie Staton (his lady during all this period) bought a truck and travelled to Las Vegas, California, and Vancouver. When I met him in Abbotsford, B.C., a year after *Beyond Mozambique* had opened, he had only written a few scenes of a long, epic version of *Ramona.* The play was, as always, fascinating in its design, but confused and tentative in its approach. We had a very odd conversation about Canadian theatre at the St. Benedictine monastery overlooking the Fraser Valley.

In any case, Walker found a way of dealing with the vacuum, and, in the summer of 1975, wrote *Ramona* in the backyard of an East End Toronto house. On a scene-to-scene basis, I think the play contains his finest writing. Again, he compressed the play into a tighter form than originally conceived, but, with its opium nightmare structure, its short, episodic scenes that jump through time zones, it provided Walker ample room to probe the bewildering mind of its title character. It's not a pleasant play. Though not without Walker's usual ironic humour, it is much less funny than his other works. Ramona is a *man* beyond morals, a vicious bitch goddess, supreme manipulator, whose torments to others are not designed for pleasure or even personal gain. Unlike Olga, she achieves no secret sexual twinges from others' pain, and, despite an overwhelming Catholic background, shows no traces of guilt. In fact, she has moved beyond guilt, through punishment, and into oblivion. She is a Medean figure, a cannibal, who devours her children to keep them at home, and who slices apart the men who have failed her. The play is a dark journey into the soul of a woman who doesn't much like herself, yet who uses drugs to help herself remember her own scars. But she is charming too, articulate and seductive, mirroring too well the society around her. However, it is not the world that is exploding here. The wars taking place beyond Hong Kong seem trivial compared to the clinical destruction of the family unit that Romana brings about.

*Ramona and the White Slaves* creates problems for its audiences, although the essential narrative is revealed unequivocally on the last page: "The story of a family and Miguel's deterioration and how small he became and how he changed disguises" (190). This is the mystery that Detective Cook has been trying to unravel throughout; in the role he is a barometer the audience can relate to. He helps us distinguish reality from hallucination, and past from present. But then the actor playing Cook also plays Sebastian, who turns out to be Miguel. Cook and Sebastian are clearly two distinct characters, but one is less certain about Freddie and Mitch, who are also played by a single actor. Then there is the complication of Ramona and Sebastian suddenly switching roles in one of the final scenes, which, while it provides some clarifying exposition, leaves the audience agape trying to figure out what's going on. Personally, I find this scene glib and overextended, detracting from the rhythm of a cascading series of horrific revelations. But because Walker capsulizes the story so clearly at the end, he may want deliberately to confuse the audience at this point and force us to deal with blurred borderlines.

Some of the fault may lie in the original production, which was, in fact, a difficult first directing assignment for the author. Another production is needed to resolve the question of the final scenes. Nonetheless, the play remains masterful in its use of language, its economy, and its provocative depiction of unnatural human behaviour.

*Ramona and the White Slaves* was also poorly received, and this may have prodded Walker to write two works in a more popular vein, *Gossip* and *Zastrozzi*, both for Toronto Free Theatre. *Gossip* failed in its original production, but six months later proved a surprise critical and popular hit in Seattle. In fact, Walker has had three hit productions in as many months. *Zastrozzi*, which opened in November 1977 at Toronto Free Theatre, was the first Walker play to receive unanimous rave responses, and the revival of *Beyond Mozambique* at the Factory, directed by the author, was also a hit. Either the desert is becoming more hospitable, or audiences may have simply learned to tune in to Walker's unique style.

The publication of these works lends a permanence to the transient nature of their production history. The three plays reflect the most important period in Walker's writing career so far, but, while a distinct unity, the trilogy does not feel complete. Walker is too humanistic to end with Ramona's seductive but amoral final posture. Another grappling with the desert itself seems imminent and will probably find its resolution in a new play, *The Desert's Revenge*, a return to the panoramic form of *Bagdad Saloon.*

It is clear that for all of his dark preoccupations, Walker wants an audience and wants to entertain. To watch George Walker at the opening of one of his own plays is a rare treat. Aside from the endless pacing and peering behind audience risers, as the audience inevitably breaks into laughter, one can see Walker's eyes widen and the face break into a broad, helpless grin.

(1978)

## Notes

[1] Ahrun's words in this and one subsequent quotation from *Bagdad Saloon* are included in the published 2nd edition of the play (Playwrights Co-Op, April 1972), but cancelled in the 3rd draft and omitted from the version published in *Three Plays.*

[2] See Note 1, above.

## Works Cited

Kareda, Urjo. Introduction. *Leaving Home.* By David French. Toronto: New Press 1972. v-ix.

———. "To Begin With, There's This Mad Doctor." Rev. of *Beyond Mozambique. Toronto Star* 13 May 1974: D6.

Popkin, Henry. "Canadian Theater Is Enjoying a 'Naissance.'" *The New York Times* 15 January 1978: D12-13.

Walker, George F. *Bagdad Saloon: A Cartoon. Three Plays* 17-86.

———. *Bagdad Saloon: A Cartoon.* 3rd Draft. University of Guelph Library, Archival and Special Collections: George F. Walker Script Collection: *Bagdad Saloon*: XZ1 MS A003 031. [Hand-corrected copy of *Bagdad Saloon.* 2nd ed. Toronto: Playwrights Co-Op, 1972.]

———. *Beyond Mozambique. Three Plays* 87-135.

———. *Ramona and the White Slaves. Three Plays* 137-90.

———. *Three Plays: Bagdad Saloon, Beyond Mozambique, Ramona and the White Slaves.* Toronto: Coach House, 1978.

## George F. Walker: B-Movies Beyond the Absurd

by Chris Johnson

It is now ten years since the Factory Theatre Lab opened its first season in a makeshift theatre above an auto-body shop on Dupont Street in Toronto. Theatre Passe Muraille had been in operation for two years, and Tarragon Theatre and Toronto Free Theatre were to join the new Toronto "alternative theatre scene" shortly. Together, the four theatres played a major role in encouraging the upsurge in interest in Canadian drama whose impetus we are still feeling. The renewed burst of theatrical activity in Toronto, this time with a distinct Canadian accent, encouraged increased interest in Canadian drama, and a number of Canadian writers who had been exerting their productive energy in a theatrical direction for several years, among them Robertson Davies, John Herbert, George Ryga, and James Reaney, acquired an increased importance in the eyes of those interested in the development of Canadian culture. Encouraged to investigate, scholarly inquiry revealed that there have been in the Canadian literary past a number of playwrights whose work is of more than passing interest. As Northrop Frye notes in his conclusion to the first edition of the *Literary History of Canada,* the deficiency of many individual Canadian literary works has been balanced by the significance of their contribution to the "entire enterprise" of Canadian literature (846-49). With the added efforts of Passe Muraille, Factory Lab, Tarragon, Toronto Free Theatre, and the writers associated with these companies, Canadian drama was seen for the first time as an "entire enterprise," a suddenly more impressive whole whose parts deserved more attention.

The new movement also created a new cohesion, a sense of drama in the fullest meaning of the word, not the isolated work of individual playwrights but a body of work linked by emulation, rivalry, and a shared audience. It is little wonder, then, that the similarities and differences between these companies and the theatrical styles they have espoused have had a profound influence on the generation of Canadian playwrights who have achieved maturity in the decade just drawn to a close. It must be understood that any schematic analysis of what was a fairly complex cultural phenomenon cannot hope to explain satisfactorily the full range of activity, and that this brief summary of the aesthetic preoccupations of 1970s alternative theatre in Toronto necessarily omits mention of exceptions to the general rules, the numerous examples of crossovers and idiosyncratic experiments: none of the theatres under discussion adheres to the rules of a clearly defined "school." Hrant Alianak's whimsical experiments first saw light of day as "seed shows" sponsored by Theatre Passe Muraille, a company with a much clearer sense of social purpose than Alianak has. David Freeman, a playwright whose work is neo-realistic in the manner predominantly favoured by the Tarragon, had his first production at the Factory Lab, whose bias has frequently been anti-naturalistic. George Walker, closely associated with the Factory Lab during most of that theatre's history, has seen three of his last four plays premiered at the Toronto Free. Still, generalizations have their value as rough guides, and some attempt to sort the trees into woods is in order.

Tarragon Theatre, with a standard of finished production generally higher than that of its rivals, had the greatest appeal to a general audience. The neo-realistic, well-made plays which constituted the bulk of the fare offered were easily accessible, and with the familiar conventions, David French and the other Tarragon playwrights showed audiences the previously unfamiliar, Canadians themselves, or at least facsimiles of themselves that audiences were willing, even eager, to accept. "That's us! That's us!" Greg Leach has summarized audience reaction to French's *Leaving Home*. The Tarragon plays have been Canadian by virtue of their content; this, and their accessibility, recommended them to the literary critics, and the Tarragon playwrights were among the first of the new wave to receive widespread critical reaction. By and large the plays were treated as extensions of Canadian literature rather than as dramatic entities, and comment was usually devoted to incorporating the new Canadian drama within thematic patterns applicable to Canadian literature as a whole.

Passe Muraille's approach has been much more theatrical and much more theatricalist. The docu-drama, the form for which the theatre has become best known, goes a step beyond the "Canadianness" of the Tarragon plays in that the depicted reality almost invariably influences the form of the work itself; if the subject is Canadian, the form will be Canadian too. Passe Muraille's distinctly Canadian and highly theatrical style, its influence on writers who have worked with the company, and its influence on theatre groups elsewhere in the country made the organization a favourite subject of theatre critics, and Passe Muraille followed Tarragon into the general critical consciousness.

The Factory Theatre Lab and Toronto Free Theatre, perhaps the most eclectic of the four, were less concerned with Canadian content, and the plays produced by these companies fitted less neatly into the established thematic patterns of Canlitcrit; at the same time, the internationalist theatre style of the plays did not deviate sufficiently from the European avant-garde model to attract the attention of critics of a more theatricalist bent. Here, in short, was the *Tish*-group of Canadian drama, insisting on cosmopolitan values but at the same time asserting the right of Canadians to pursue those values and to be heard while doing so. While Tarragon and Passe Muraille realized their objectives earlier and more fully than did the Factory Lab, the Factory Lab's objectives were more elusive and were pursued through policies designed to produce results over a longer period of time. With its aggressively nationalistic decision not to produce non-Canadian plays, its trading off of production polish for larger numbers of plays staged in a year, its comparative indifference to immediate popular success, and its focus on writing, the Factory Lab and its founding Artistic

Director, Ken Gass, provided a trade school for Canadian playwrights entirely unprecedented in Canadian theatre history. The energetic creative atmosphere, the opportunities to put works to the test, and perhaps above all, the new freedom to fail from time to time, have all produced over the long run the valuable results Gass and his co-workers originally envisaged; the Factory Lab has fostered some of the most intensely personal, formally innovative, and accomplished dramatic writing in the country. It is the purpose of this essay to examine the work of George F. Walker, one of the best of the Factory Lab playwrights, as a first step toward rectifying critical neglect of the company and its writers, and toward assessing the place in recent Canadian drama occupied by Walker and the theatrical movement he represents.

As well as being one of the most accomplished writers to emerge from Ken Gass's laboratory process, Walker is a writer with a long and close connection with the theatre: his first play was produced in 1971 in the company's second season, he was for a number of years the Factory Lab's resident playwright, and he served for a brief period as the theatre's Artistic Director. He wrote his first play, *Prince of Naples*, in response to the Factory Lab's ubiquitous posters calling for new scripts; until then, he had only dabbled in verse and short fiction. The one-act piece, and the full-length play which followed shortly after, *Ambush at Tether's End*, are both clearly the work of a writer new to theatre, of a writer of urban and cosmopolitan sensibility looking to established writers for models in the form new to him.

"Not many prairie landscapes in George Walker's plays," Ken Gass remarks in his introduction to a collection of Walker's plays (9). Indeed not. Or as Walker himself puts it:

> It would be very dishonest of me to attempt to write any sort of rural play. [...] I had been surrounded by things like movies, television—you know "The World at Six," that sort of thing—theatre and literature of all kinds all my life. What did I know about the farmer and his wife?
>
> And yet I was criticized. Everyone kept telling me I should go to the grass roots and that Canadian plays should be naturalistic or historical. Naturalism was very big in Toronto for a long time. I couldn't help thinking that was one kind of theatre, but there were other types of theatre as well. (qtd. in Galloway)

*The Prince of Naples* concerns a relationship familiar to every North American, that of student and teacher, and draws extensively on the perspectives of a contemporary urban world, simultaneously literate and electronic. The work shows its literary ancestry through its form: in its use of language, transforming pat phrases into extended and volcanic passages of nonsense, in its heavy dependence on a central theatrical image, and in its concerted effort to include the audience within the emotional event the characters are experiencing, the play models itself after the Theatre of the Absurd in general and after Ionesco's *The Lesson* in particular. Walker reverses the usual power structure in the educational process, making the young the instructor of the old, to examine a social phenomenon, the cult of the young and the supposedly liberated, associated with the sixties, and in the process questions the new credo of relativity:

> Now the word insane has been reapproached by the wide-eyed armies of time and given a new meaning. The word has been dragged out of the dampness of our mental basement and placed high on the clouds of our consciousness. (*Prince* 76)

The method of employing a form to question ironically the ideas underlying the form became characteristic of Walker's work.

*Ambush at Tether's End* was Walker's second exercise in the theatrical techniques of the Absurd: this time, the most important model appears to be Samuel Beckett's *Waiting for Godot.* The central character in the play is a corpse (an echo of Ionesco's *Amédée, or How to Get Rid of It*), a poet-philosopher who has hanged himself and who has left a series of notes attacking the values of his friends, challenging them to confront "reality" as he has with a "definitive act" equal to his. While there are similarities linking the friends to Beckett's tramps (Mullaly correctly identifies rhythmic similarities in their speech [53]), Walker has localized the situation, and has made from the dichotomy depicted by Vladimir and Estragon a more North American opposition of obsessions, those of the ambitious businessman and the sexual athlete. If those who wait are diminished, so too is that for which they wait. Max, the moralizing corpse, endangers his own authenticity through his posthumous showmanship, and the philosophical life is discredited by the dead man's petty rivalry with a colleague. While Galt and Bush are, predictably, destroyed by the dilemma in which they find themselves, there is little to recommend an alternative to their views if Max is the representative of that alternative. Walker sees both the society he satirizes and the modish and pseudo-romantic challenge to that society as inadequate, and in the play constructs a theatrical model of the intellectual quandary in which many of his generation found themselves.

***

The influence of the Theatre of the Absurd can be seen in many of the plays produced in the Factory Lab's first few seasons, and several critics were quick to identify their derivative nature. In his review of *The Factory Lab Anthology,* in which *Ambush at Tether's End* appeared, Edward Mullaly writes:

> Twenty-five years ago the enunciation of man's absurd situation might have constituted a positive statement. But a similar inability to discover or point out shapes and structures today no longer constitutes experimental, or even interesting, drama regardless of the country in which it is written. (51)

Of Walker's play itself he asks "why Walker has spent his time on a script Beckett had already written with much greater discipline, intelligence, and skill" (53). While Walker's early efforts are in many respects undergraduate exercises, few saw at the time that they are superior undergraduate exercises, and that in turning the form against its content, Walker avoided slavish imitation.

The Theatre of the Absurd has remained largely a European phenomenon: American playwrights have had as much difficulty transplanting its insights and techniques to a North American *milieu* and audience as have had the Canadians Mullaly criticizes. Martin Esslin attributes the difficulty to history:

> [T]he convention of the Absurd springs from a feeling of deep disillusionment, the draining away of the sense of meaning and purpose in life, which has been characteristic of countries like France and Britain in the years after the Second World War. In the United States there has been no corresponding loss of meaning and purpose. (266)

While the statement is undoubtedly less true than it was when it was first written, it is significant that most of the American playwrights whose work had close affinities to the European avant-garde of the fifties and early sixties have subsequently developed in different directions. Thomas Porter advances a more commercial explanation in *Myth and Modern American Drama.* While mainstream American drama consistently portrays the failure of the American Dream, that which has maintained the illusion of "meaning and purpose," the American theatre-going public has an aversion to the next step, a dramatic form which not only discusses but reflects the disintegration of the Dream. In consequence, American attempts to transfer the technique as well as the message have been stillborn (255). The American playwrights who have most successfully communicated to an American audience those insights usually associated with the Theatre of the Absurd have been those, like Jean-Claude van Itallie or Sam Shepard, who have taken particular care to couch these insights in an American idiom, who have employed the disjointed nature of American popular culture to display a fragmented theatrical vision of lost "meaning and purpose." Shepard, whose work is most clearly relevant to a consideration of Walker's, has proven particularly adept at employing the trivia of American society as a means of both celebrating the vulgar vitality of that society and suggesting an emptiness beyond.

In Walker's third play, *Sacktown Rag,* he draws on North American pop culture in a manner somewhat similar to Shepard's, and in turning to more autobiographical subject matter, discards some of the literary self-consciousness which intrudes in the earlier plays. The structural technique is that of the cartoon: the schoolboy protagonist experiences the traumas of growing up in a world sometimes realistic and sometimes drawn in the lurid colours of the comic strip. While the caricatures of parents and teachers sometimes have the gleeful and scatological energy of schoolboy graffiti, Walker does not entirely trust his conventions and chooses to explain them away with an unconvincing memory frame: the play subsequently loses the impact of the cartoon without gaining enough in psychological insight to compensate. It is probably the least satisfying of Walker's published work.

In *Bagdad Saloon,* first produced in 1973 and subtitled "a cartoon," Walker does not dilute his pop art conventions: the result is a bawdy, sprawling collage of short scenes, music, and *coups de théâtre*. The cartoon figures are less personal than the graffiti of *Sacktown Rag*; characters drawn from American high and low culture, Gertrude Stein, Henry Miller, Doc Halliday, have greater resonance, and extend the implications of the piece beyond itself.

The incident which precipitates the action of the play is the kidnapping of the American legends by a pair of improbable Arabs who want to learn the secret of mythic immortality. The attempt, of course, is futile: Halliday and Miller are frauds, and Stein, while she has visions, proves incapable of communicating what she sees. The American saloon is grafted onto fabled Bagdad, and Aladdin decks himself out as a dime store cowboy in pursuit of a new and neon mythology, even while the efficacy of any myth in staving off the chaos is put in question:

> **AHRUN.** Fame is a fickle commodity. Not bad, mind you. Just fickle.
> **DOC.** So what?
> **STEIN.** Exactly.
> **AHRUN.** It needs to be guided, so to speak. And if it's guided in the right direction, it can create things. Purpose. Glamour. Mystique. (*Pause*) Artists. Or folk heroes. All things which we find very scarce around here.
> **STEIN.** What happens then?
> **AHRUN.** Folk-lore.
> **STEIN.** And then?
> **AHRUN.** More folk-lore.
> **STEIN.** And then?
> **AHRUN.** And then ... and you can—and then there's always ...
> **STEIN.** Yes?
> **DOC.** What?
> (*AHRUN shakes his head violently. Turns. Leaves.*) (55)

So much for identity, Arab, Canadian, or otherwise.

As Gass points out in his introduction, the first movement of the play constructs the saloon and decorates it in all its crass glory, while the second movement destroys and discredits the structure (11). Unfortunately, the process is unduly protracted and Walker is often distracted by his fascination with the decoration; the piece is theatrically inefficient. Still, in *Bagdad Saloon* Walker shows increased control of his new medium, and develops further the talent for stage metaphor revealed in the earlier plays: the image of the all-American hero, sportsman, and pop singer as pathetic, speechless grotesque is an image that lingers long after memories of the irritating meanderings have faded.

***

It is a commonplace that, particularly in matters of structural convention, theatre has been drawing for the last two or three decades on popular electronic forms, especially film, reclaiming the debt that art form owes theatre in general and August Strindberg in particular. Walker has not been the first Canadian playwright to borrow from cinema: Ryga's "liquid dramaturgy" owes as much to film as it does to the folk song (Hay 6), and James Reaney cites Walt Disney as an important influence (see Woodman 17-18). The older playwrights, however, use cinematic devices to shape the presentation of their vision of the world whereas for playwrights of Walker's generation, the vision itself is frequently filmic.

> Like so many of my generation, my mind is sort of a media garbage bag sometimes. We're all so heavily influenced by television and movies and you don't have to be very perceptive to see it coming out in new plays. The dilemma for me was not to rebel against the problem—it is, after all, a fairly central reality—but to assimilate it and make something of it. (qtd. in Fraser)

As Walker suggests, the influence is to a certain extent involuntary, the result of a lifetime's exposure for the generation which grew up with television and whose dreams are, in effect, movies. The process of "making something of it" has involved becoming aware of this mode of thought as just that, an artificial construct rather than part of the natural order (Esslin identifies the post-war generation's frequent inability to make that distinction in the postscript to the revised *The Theatre of the Absurd* [378-82]); it has also meant exploiting the dramatic possibilities of a contemporary pool of shared understanding, which becomes the basis of a coherent (if not necessarily logical) set of social assumptions to which the social act of theatre can be addressed.

Obviously film is a richer source of theatrical convention than is the cartoon, and provides fuller access to the popular pool of understanding. It also provides, especially through the so-called B-movies, a rich source of images, plot models, and a set of stock characters not unlike those used in melodrama or Commedia dell'Arte, an iconography available to the contemporary playwright to be employed as he sees fit. While Walker uses a number of cinematic structural devices in *Bagdad Saloon*, he makes comparatively little use of filmic iconography; *Beyond Mozambique* (1974) marks the beginning of extensive recourse to the raw material of the B-movie, material characteristic of all his subsequent work. In employing stock characters and situations as the vehicles for insights and ideas beyond the capacity of the popular form from which they were drawn, Shepard in *Mad Dog Blues* or *Angel City* and Walker in *Beyond Mozambique* and *Ramona and the White Slaves* follow well-established theatrical practice: Beckett and Ionesco draw from music hall and film comedy; Pirandello, Chekhov, and Ibsen drew from melodrama; and, of course, Molière made use of the characters and conventions of Commedia dell'Arte.

The B-movie also provides an ironic mode, an element acquired through the almost accidental manner in which the older B-movies were reintroduced into the mainstream of popular art through late-night movies on television and hence into the imaginations of the generation shaped by television. In this way, trivial work which would otherwise have perished, as do novels unworthy of reprinting or plays not worth reviving, lead an extended life; the extension, the survival of artifacts meant to be disposable, frequently leads to levels of meaning not intended by their creators. The

B-movies of the forties and fifties present a vision of life so simple and naive that the effect is comic, while the rapidity of shifts in popular taste gives the films a quaintness which emphasizes the naiveté and heightens the comic effect.

In adapting the world of the B-movie for the stage there are two dangers. The first is that an audience might accept that world at face value, despite the integral irony of a topical perspective out of context. The second pitfall is the temptation to revel in the exuberant awfulness of it all: the result, here, is usually described as "camp." Tom Cone's *Shot Glass* and Hrant Alianak's *The Blues* are examples of plays which duplicate the mood and rhythms of old B-movies very accurately indeed, but which offer almost no perspective from outside the worlds they depict, which remain satisfied with accidental irony, and which therefore succeed as anachronistic replicas, camp artifacts, rather than as original works of art. In *Beyond Mozambique* and subsequent plays, Walker circumvents the perils through the addition of elements from other modes, hyperbole, and explicit comment on the theatrical context.

*Beyond Mozambique* is a jungle movie, but contrary to the opinions of several first-night critics, it is not just a jungle movie. Set on the porch of a decaying colonial mansion in the jungle, the play throws together six disparate characters, in the best "ship of fools" tradition, and allows these figures, or "masks" as Richard Horenblas describes them (8), to enact for us the decline and disintegration of western civilization; while its mode is that of the B-movie, its content is not: technology does not triumph over nature, white heroines are not pure, white horses are not all-powerful, and while the embattled whites are not overwhelmed by the forces of "savagery" drumming in the bush, they do succumb to the chaos within, and it is the drumming of that threat which provides the play's rhythm and central theatrical metaphor.

The play's central character, played by Donald Davis in the original production in 1974, is that most twentieth-century of archetypes, the mad scientist. Rocco combines the familiar B-movie archetype and hints of concentration camp "medical experiments," sadism disguised as a quest for knowledge, or, perhaps, the quest for knowledge undisguised; he is both the historical nightmare and the popular rendition of the obsessions in part responsible for those nightmares: in the face of impending disintegration, he can think only of pressing on with his experiments and of acquiring the necessary subjects. While he is horrifying, Rocco is, in Walker's wry view, the most positive character in the play; he has a Kurtz-like integrity which compels him to define, to defy chaos even if in a perverse way, a drive often expressed in gloriously B-movie lines: "There's something about committing crimes against humanity that puts you in touch with the purpose of the universe" (*Three Plays* 126). Parody makes the line funny; history, and the terrifying possibility that Rocco may be right, given an Absurdist vision of the universe, make it not funny.

Rocco is accompanied by the requisite hunch-backed assistant, Tomas, who is primarily responsible for acquiring the experimental subjects and initiating a one-man crime wave. Tomas says very little, and much of that in Greek (a sardonic combination of classical heritage and bestiality personified), but his presence brings onstage a manifestation of the savagery by which the central characters feel themselves threatened, and makes explicit the erotic and racist implications of all those glistening dark bodies in B jungle movies. As the whites decline, non-white Tomas ascends, expropriating for himself the style and trappings of power. Later in the play, we encounter a third B-movie personage, the failed priest; again the element of parody is present, as LiDuc does not go to the ends of the earth to redeem himself, but has been sent by a Church which sincerely hopes he will never be heard from again. His presence makes possible the introduction of the pseudo-philosophical observations so characteristic of the B-movie as a form, and which Walker gleefully deflates and redirects: "Jesus doesn't mind losers but he has no patience for idiots" (128).

To these refugees from a jungle movie, Walker adds figures from other worlds, but worlds no less threatened by the surrounding chaos. Olga, Rocco's wife, is obsessed with the world of Chekhov's plays to the point where she believes that she is the character of the same name from *Three Sisters*, complete with a sentimental attachment to the artistic traditions of the *ancien regime* (represented in the play by a treasured Renoir which she employs as a talisman against the forces of the jungle), a determination to preserve social form at all costs and the obligatory yearning for Moscow. In the original production, the part was played by Frances Hyland, further heightening the effect created by introducing high culture into flamboyant pop. The introduction of a Chekhovian character points the pattern of non-communication and obsession in the piece, gives an added significance to the manner in which characters are isolated from each other, and adds a dream-like memory of bitter-sweet against which Walker can contrast his more garish effects.

Corporal Lance, formerly of the RCMP, brings a distinctly Canadian contribution to the model apocalypse; we, too, get a share in the fall of the West. The Corporal is the only explicitly Canadian character in Walker's work (although the unpublished plays, *Gossip* and *Filthy Rich*, are nominally set in Toronto) and it is a reflection of Walker's views on what Canadian theatre ought to be that the character is a very crafty parody: the Corporal is inept (natives have dismantled his motorcycle and he can't put it together again), naive, apparently clean-living, and very Canadian—in the grip of malarial hallucinations, he sees wheat. The character is a good example of Walker's growing ability to manipulate audience expectations. The Corporal is at first merely a comic Mountie, who, as we would expect, fails to understand what is happening in the sophisticated world of decadent allusion, worries about not having anything formal to wear but his scarlets ("Am I over-dressed?" [96]), and gives his wholesome all to the battle against subversion. But this quintessentially Canadian joke, which makes possible the uniquely Canadian pleasure of being self-deprecatory and self-congratulatory simultaneously and which therefore neatly disarms a Canadian audience's defence mechanisms, acquires an uglier, more sinister quality as the play progresses: he is so distressed by misery that he puts to death all who suffer, hence making his Canadian wholesomeness an agent of the final destruction. The acute but unkind comment about our national personality is administered while we are still distracted by the reassuring cartoon.

The last of this stranded crew of expatriate whites is both of the world of B-movies and not of that world, thus providing a bridging device and a means of comment. Rita is a porn-movie star engaged in jungle smuggling operations in an attempt to raise the money to finance a legitimate movie and realize her dreams of respectable stardom: "This one is going to be a classic. It'll have sex. But it'll be sex with class" (106). A classic definition of the romantic B-movie, or, for that matter, B jungle movies. Rita is the character most fully aware of the theatrical and cinematic elements of their plight, and the one most given to consciously dramatizing the situation; through her, Walker adds to the devices of hyperbole and film the technique of explicit comment which makes *Beyond Mozambique* more than an exercise in nostalgia and parody:

> Sometimes I just pour myself a stiff gin and lean against that big tree outside my tent and just let that sun sink slowly down into the ground while I shake the ice cubes around in the glass. And when I do that I get so deeply into Rita Hayworth I could just about die. (107)

We all play our roles to the death. Rita also prepares the way for the final moments of the play in which the characters become aware of the audience, either making us the drummers or including us within the circle surrounded by the drummers, and so involving us in this last moving picture show before the final darkness descends.

***

*Beyond Mozambique* is a much more disciplined play than is *Bagdad Saloon*, evidence that Factory Lab's policies were paying off; some of the original writers were dropping away while others, like Walker, pushed doggedly on, learning the language of the theatre. The comparatively poor showing of much of Canada's earlier drama can be attributed to the extremely high proportion of first plays: the early 1970s was one of the few times and the Factory Lab one of the few places allowing a playwright progression from production to production. *Beyond Mozambique* has tighter focus, and a clearer sense of direction, in part created by Walker's continued progress in the creation of the single, unifying stage image, the device which gives Theatre of the Absurd much of its trenchant force. The split between Walker's manic sense of humour and his more serious concerns is effectively healed; *Beyond Mozambique* is splendid black comedy, combining the comic and the grotesque to produce Jonsonesque social comment. And Walker completed, in this play, an important step toward developing an efficient personal style. In his perceptive discussion of James Reaney's plays, Ross Woodman notes that in order to progress from the early pastoral comedies, Reaney needed to develop a "lens" through which his personal vision could be viewed by an audience (48-49); in Reaney's case, the necessary "lens" was provided by childhood games, rituals, and rhymes. Walker, too, needed a "lens," and in *Beyond Mozambique* he discovered that his lens was the B-movie. When watching a Walker play, we, like Leonard Cohen's Nancy, see "the late late show / through a semi-precious stone" ("Nancy"). The world revealed is eerie, often beautiful, the ordinary made extraordinary by the unnatural hues and the lateness of the hour.

Having used this lens to bring social comment into focus in *Beyond Mozambique*, in *Ramona and the White Slaves* (1976) Walker directs his new instrument on the problems of characterization, an area of dramatic endeavour notoriously weak in much Canadian drama. Set in what is apparently a brothel in a turn-of-the-century, impossibly decadent and chaotic Hong Kong, the play shows us the Madam/Mother, Ramona, and her convoluted relationships with her daughters, their lovers, her crippled son, and a man who may be her pimp, her missing husband, or both. Two frameworks are provided: the piece begins with Ramona's opium dream in which she is raped by a lizard—and there is a strong possibility that the entire play is an opium dream (a drug-induced state of mind is another "lens" to which Walker sometimes resorts)—while commentary is provided by a detective ostensibly attempting to solve a murder, one of many, which occurred in the street outside the brothel. The detective (a device Walker also employs in *Gossip* [1977], and *Filthy Rich* [1979]) has a long history as a useful dramatic device, and in addition provides the B-movie lens. Cook's inquiries do not produce the answers he sets out to find, nor do they reveal much biographical information about Ramona, for most spectators guess early in the play the bizarre secret of the ex-nun's history. The search, however, takes us through a tour of Ramona's psyche, the obsessions which compel her to devour her children and which make her simultaneously a powerful and compelling figure, a B-movie Medea. Her character provides one of the most rewarding roles for an actress in Canadian drama, a striking presentation of the mother/whore dichotomy so central to Western erotic fantasy, and the play makes an extraordinarily effective use of eroticism.

Walker's growing skills as a social satirist and his developing expertise in portraiture are both brought to bear on *Zastrozzi* (1977). After a period of personal crisis and discouragement, which Ken Gass documents in his introduction to *Three Plays*, Walker had begun with the preceding play, *Gossip*, to alter his tactics somewhat, to make his plays "more generous" (qtd. in Fraser). *Zastrozzi* is certainly more accessible than all but his earliest plays, and this, in combination with Walker's continued growth as a playwright, has made *Zastrozzi* his most popular work. The play is, unabashedly, a melodrama, and is subtitled as such. It pits good against evil in a plot taken from Shelley's novel, but a note in the Playwrights Co-op edition of the play informs the reader that Walker worked from a description of the novel: therefore the play is not really an adaptation of the original work. In the context of this discussion, it is important to note that there is certainly as much Errol Flynn as there is Percy Bysshe Shelley in Walker's play, and that Walker is continuing to make use of his B-movie lens.

As William Lane, the director of the original production, implies in his introduction, *Zastrozzi* is, in addition to being a melodrama, a contemporary (and tongue-in-cheek) morality play; Walker evidently believes that morality plays are rare in contemporary theatre and ought to be supplied, but is also aware that a contemporary audience is unlikely to accept a naked statement of central propositions: our defensive objectivity or superficiality or materialist disbelief must be circumvented through giving us the opportunity to laugh. "The real moral centre of the play is Zastrozzi himself—the very one who never has a moral crisis" (Lane 5). Zastrozzi, in fact, constitutes the moral centre through his implacable desire to follow the dictates of a kind of morality to that point where morality annihilates itself. "Mankind is weak. The world is ugly. The only way to save them from each other is to destroy them both" (*Zastrozzi* 12). This is a logical extension of the thinking of both fundamentalist Protestantism and the Playwrights of the Absurd. In the plot, Zastrozzi is the play's villain, the master criminal of Europe, and the adamant pursuer of his mother's murderer, a man turned saint or fool by the magnitude of the act. Within the play's metaphorical structure, Zastrozzi is the principle of order, standing as the last bastion against the coming of a new, liberal, "pleasantly vague" world being born at the turn of the century, the time of the play's events and the beginning of our own era. As William Lane observes:

> Zastrozzi is already a figure out of his time. He comes on like some medieval nightmare, wielding his sword and dagger as though they were still the most lethal weapons on earth. [...] Zastrozzi's attitude is mercilessly aristocratic. His foe is the new middle class with its shiny new liberal education and its fancy for art. (4)

He is, in short, "the master of discipline," the one who takes it upon himself to supply an absolute, a means of assuring that everyone is answerable.

Evil has great stage presence, and given the theatrical advantages ever afforded the villain, it is inevitable that the eponym seizes and holds the attention, and in some ways, the sympathy of the audience (after all, the murder of a mother is difficult to forgive, even allowing for extenuating circumstances and the fact that the lady herself may have been a killer). Walker himself has expressed some concern over the implications of the attraction a figure such as Zastrozzi commands, compared to the evidently pallid alternative, Verezzi the guilty saint:

> There's been a tendency to think of him [Verezzi] as moronic. I think that's just a reflection of our own age. We cannot accept God, obsession or goodliness, when in fact, a Verezzi has his own power. [...] It's a sign of our times that we tend to think of Verezzi as a fool, and Zastrozzi as a charming evil villain who's more in touch with reality. Well, maybe he is, but I still think there's room in this world for people like Verezzi. At least I hope so. (qtd. in Hallgren 24)

Walker is surely leading his interviewer down a garden path. He deliberately presents the B-movie hero-in-white in such a way that contemporary cynicism cannot fail to judge the character a fool. The man whom Zastrozzi has pursued for three years cannot recognize the danger he is in, choosing instead to fantasize that he is a sort of messiah, complete with invisible followers; most telling stroke of all, he is a sexual flop, and we certainly don't want to identify with that. At the same time, Walker puts into the mind and mouth of a character we are sometimes invited to despise sentiments with which we know we ought to agree. At first glance, *Zastrozzi* seems to run contrary to Walker's usual practice of using a form to undermine the mode of thought behind the form: for the play, like melodrama and melodramatic B-movies, makes a clear distinction between good and evil, and gives each side the formalized statements of faith or anti-faith. However, by giving to the villain a passion for order and definition in some respects attractive to the inhabitants of chaotic times, as well as many of the best lines, and by giving to the putative hero qualities which we know cannot stand up to current events or intellectual trends, Walker encourages the wry and condescending smile with which we customarily respond to melodrama (unless it has been updated with the contemporary trappings of TV social drama) and with which we reject the melodramatic world of good and evil revealed. Walker's skilled evocation of the double response leads us into an old-fashioned examination of the nature of good and evil; again, the theatrical hand is quicker than the eye of the audience, who thought they were just watching swashbuckling melodrama and parody of swashbuckling melodrama.

Melodramatic simplicities are further complicated by Victor. In some ways, Zastrozzi and Verezzi are opposites: Zastrozzi is a realist and Verezzi is an idealist. In other ways, they are similar; both shape their lives with absolutes. In this respect, and others, both find their opposite in Victor, servant to Verezzi and failed priest, who, in order to keep a promise does his utmost to protect the victim from the destroyer. Realistic, materialistic, pragmatic, Victor commands respect for his decency, resourcefulness, and courage. It is here that Walker's growing powers of characterization are most impressive, for despite all his decencies (and decency is notoriously boring on stage), Victor is an interesting character; he is the one who, as Lane points out, has the moral dilemma, and he responds to it in a manner with which most members of the audience would agree. He calls a madman a madman, acts instead of hypothesizing, and, alone among the characters, is possessed himself of a sense of humour. We identify with him; he is like us. And like us, he is wrong, and the error results in his death. His secular faith also has its limitations, and his balance, his moderation, is ultimately his undoing.

We therefore agree intellectually with one character, feel we ought to respond spiritually to a second, and identify most closely with a third. While B-movie conventions would lead us to expect an either/or proposition, we are given three poles, and ambivalent poles at that. Walker uses the rest of the cast of stock characters to extend the central issue, and to comment upon it. An assistant villain is present not only to facilitate the plot in the usual manner, but to demonstrate the difference between ideological evil and mere thuggery. The presence of a villainess and a purer-than-white heroine gives a sexual shape to the contest, reducing the cosmic struggle to "naughty" *vs.* "nice," and at the same time adding a strong strain of eroticism to help bring the point home, to bed. Zastrozzi's imaginary seduction of Julia is a very compelling scene indeed.

***

The values which emerge from Walker's work seem to be those of a small-"c" conservative, the technical trappings of the *avant-garde. Zastrozzi* ultimately asserts that evil does exist, is not the product of environment, and must be confronted. In *The Prince of Naples*, the easy assumptions based on a facile acceptance of relative values are pilloried, and *Bagdad Saloon* dismantles a system of value based on the publicizing of subjective fantasy. Walker is a champion of language and definition, a concern that has increased as his career progressed, and he rejects naturalism, in part, because it has forgotten how to reach areas of human experience accessible to older dramatic forms. In this, he resembles Eugène Ionesco, who claims not to be of the *avant-garde* at all; Ionesco dismisses much recent drama, finding "Ibsen heavy, Strindberg clumsy, Pirandello outmoded," and wants in his own work to return to the theatre of the Greeks and the Elizabethans, a larger than life theatre "concerned with the human condition in all its brutal absurdity" (qtd. in Esslin 164-65). That is what we are left with at the end of *Zastrozzi* as the villain surveys a positively Jacobean heap of corpses, enjoying his impersonal Greek blood revenge. The form is contemporary but the clash of forces therein depicted is an old and vital one.

While *Zastrozzi* is a continuation of Walker's earlier thematic explorations (there are, for instance, striking similarities between the obsessions of Rocco and those of Zastrozzi) and of the playwright's technical development (the manner in which Victor is employed to manipulate audience expectations differs from the way in which the Corporal was used only in that the technique is elaborated in the later play), it is at the same time a meticulously constructed and highly successful piece of entertaining theatre: to be truly successful, parody must be as skillfully constructed as that which it parodies, and in this respect *Zastrozzi is* a literary in-joke—poker-faced, Walker demonstrates that he is perfectly capable of writing a well-made play, and does so without sacrificing his personal, non-documentary vision.

This new concern with "generosity" is evident in Walker's other recent plays. *Gossip* and *Filthy Rich* appear to be detective B-movies, and can be enjoyed at that level, but they are really contemporary comedies of manners, high comedy revived. *Rumours of Our Death*, first produced in 1980 and published in *Canadian Theatre Review* 25, is, on the surface, a Ruritanian romance-*cum*-spy movie, and was given punk rock treatment in the original Factory Lab production, but it introduces politics through a tantalizing political fable which at times seems to apply to Canada, and at others (no doubt as a result of the playwright's intention) snatches the easy and national answer away by interrupting the pattern. Walker is using popular forms, primarily B-movies, as a means of exploring old dramatic verities, rather as John Gray does in *Billy Bishop Goes to War*, as Maynard Collins does in *Hank Williams: The Show He Never Gave*, and as the Hummer Sisters do in their video-theatre-rock-and-roll extravaganzas.

The man who appears to be among Canada's most abstruse and esoteric playwrights has, in fact, a thorough grasp of populist techniques, and can use the forms: of popular theatre as both popular vehicle and as a means of sharing with a broader audience a more demanding dramatic view. In this ability to speak to a more general audience, Walker resembles the populist docu-dramatists of Passe Muraille or the Tarragon playwrights, who address a popular, middle-class audience within the conventions it knows best, and in the process, he gives them some penetrating analyses of themselves. The tendency to commercialism in recent Canadian drama and commercialism in the artistic policies of many Canadian theatres has been decried, as it should be, but commercialization should not be confused with a movement underway in Canada for some time, a movement whose aim has been to take theatre to a larger audience, abandoning the coterie audiences of the regionals and attempting to reach instead an audience previously unaccustomed to attending formal, legitimate theatre. The venture, should it prove successful, could help to change the status of theatre as mere social status symbol, to which it has unfortunately so often been relegated in twentieth-century North America, and to restore to the theatre the power of broad appeal which has traditionally given drama an edge over other literary forms. This increased ability to reach out to an audience is one of the directions which theatre has taken in response to Esslin's question, "After the Absurd, what?" And it is a direction to which Canadian drama has been a major contributor. Seen in the context of these larger movements, Walker and the Factory Lab are not mavericks at all, but the source of one of the most theatrically potent streams within the new Canadian drama.

(1980)

## Works Cited


Cohen, Leonard. "Nancy." *Leonard Cohen: Live Songs.* Columbia Broadcasting System, 1973.

Esslin, Martin. *The Theatre of the Absurd.* Rev. ed. Garden City, NY: Doubleday, 1969.

Fraser, John: "Walker Turns to Murder with Comedy." *The Globe and Mail* 19 April 1977: 16.

Frye, Northrop. "Conclusion." *Literary History of Canada: Canadian Literature in English.* Gen. Ed. Carl F. Klinck. Toronto: U of Toronto P, 1965. 821-49.

Galloway, Myron. "George Walker—Resolving the World's Chaos." *Montreal Star* 3 March 1979: D9.

Gass, Ken. Introduction. *Three Plays: Bagdad Saloon, Beyond Mozambique, Ramona and the White Slaves.* By George F. Walker. Toronto: Coach House, 1978. 9-15.

Hallgren, Chris. "George Walker, the Serious and the Comic." Interview with George F. Walker. *Scene Changes* 7.2 (March/April 1979): 23-25.

Hay, Peter. Introduction. *Sunrise on Sarah.* By George Ryga. Vancouver: Talonbooks, 1972. 5-7.

Horenblas, Richard. "Playnotes." *Scene Changes* 3. 10 (October 1975): 8.

Lane, William. Introduction. *Zastrozzi, the Master of Discipline: A Melodrama.* By George F. Walker. Toronto: Playwrights Co-op, 1979. 3-6.

Leach, Greg. "Tarragon's Trademark Was Script Development." *That's Showbusiness* 4. 24 (January 1976): 1.

Mullaly, Edward. "Waiting for Lefty, Godot, and Canadian Theatre." *The Fiddlehead* 104 (1975): 51-54.

Porter, Thomas E. *Myth and Modern American Drama.* Detroit: Wayne State UP, 1969.

Walker, George F. *The Prince of Naples. Now in Paperback: Six Canadian Plays of the 1970's.* Ed. Connie Brissenden. Toronto: Fineglow Plays, 1973. 61-102.

———. *Three Plays: Bagdad Saloon, Beyond Mozambique, Ramona and the White Slaves.* Toronto: Coach House, 1978.

———. *Zastrozzi, the Master of Discipline: A Melodrama.* Toronto: Playwrights Co-op, 1979.

Woodman, Ross. *James Reaney.* New Canadian Library: Canadian Writers 12. Toronto: McClelland, 1971.

## From "George F. Walker" in *The Work: Conversations with English-Canadian Playwrights*

by Robert Wallace

**Wallace:** We don't get the opportunity to see your work done a second time very often. Recently, I saw *Gossip* done by the University Alumnae Drama Club in Toronto. I had seen the original production, and I liked the amateur one better. It was a more musical, less grotesque approach to the play that I thought was more appropriate. Why don't we see your plays a second time more often?

**Walker:** People just don't want to do them, I guess. Or the ones who do want to do them don't have the resources. I mean, usually the ones who do them the first time want to do them again. I agree, by the way, about *Gossip*. It was much better in the amateur production. It had an edge. That's a play that I'm genuinely uncomfortable with anyway, but I never was able to tell why because the first production missed the mark. Generally I think Artistic Directors are timid and don't go back and take another look at things. We haven't developed confidence in our repertoire—we suffer from the Dixie Cup syndrome: constantly in search of the new and exciting. Real confidence is to let the work settle and take another look at it, challenge it again. It might not work out. A play that looked good the first time can show its true colours the second time around, for better or worse I guess. Artistic Directors just don't have the confidence in Canadian material to take that kind of risk with it.

**Wallace:** Are there any of your plays besides *Gossip* that you think need a new production to achieve their potential?

**Walker:** *Ramona and the White Slaves* needs a second production. I did it myself the first time and I didn't do it very well at all. Although the acting was just terrific, it wasn't properly conceived in terms of design. And the script needs work. I think I was on to something in that script and I'd certainly like to take another look at it. But I need a director. And because of the nature of this particular play I don't think it's likely to get a second production in Canada. It might get one somewhere else. I'd like to see all my plays done again because I'd like to take other looks at them. But some like *Ramona* need a second production.

**Wallace:** Why does the nature of this work inhibit a second production? What is so "particular" about it?

**Walker:** Well, if my work is out of the mainstream, I think this is way, way out of the mainstream. Its rhythms are different. I think it's experimental in that sense; it's not very easy to define what it is. And I think in our culture—a fairly timid culture—things generally don't get done or done a lot unless they are very easy to define. The paradox is that even if you want to define something to yourself, which I'd like to do with this play, you don't get a chance to do it. It's not so much the content that's different; it's the approach and the style of the play. I can only talk about the rhythms of it … it's sort of like a personal point of view, I suppose. It doesn't have a lot of plot, and it is not easy to get there. For me as a writer it would really be interesting to have a director do a new production. Because I think I was on to something that I think I shied away from after that.

**Wallace:** Which was what?

**Walker:** I don't know exactly. There there was an almost subconscious writing going on with *Ramona*; it had the rhythms of dreams and things like that, a way of telling a story without inserting a plot, doing it a lot with imagery. I had the feeling I was on to something that I never could verify. And because of its reception I shied away from it again.

**Wallace:** It wasn't received too well, either by the audience or the critics. Would you agree that your work has become more mainstream and less experimental since *Ramona*?

**Walker:** Well, it did for a while, I think. But with *Theatre of the Film Noir* and the work in progress, it's moving back more towards … well, I'm comfortable with experiments again. I'm closer now to what I think my voice is. Which is just the way I see things, and the way it comes out in theatre.

**Wallace:** How important is it for you to feel free to experiment with structures that are less accessible to a mainstream audience?

**Walker:** I think that is of the ultimate importance. Because I think I'm what I've heard described as a "writer of the imagination." There's supposed to be two schools in modern playwriting right now: the realists and the writers of the imagination. I need to have total freedom to explore my voice and themes and, through that, theatrical structure. But it's got to bend. It has to change with the voice. I mean, I have respect for Chekhovian structure and everything that he and Ibsen did. But you can't necessarily put your voice into that structure. It's important to have total freedom in writing. But you also need an audience. You can't just go racing off without them. You have to sort of go along with them and hope that someone down the line is open to these things as well. Basically it ain't my job to write plays that other people are writing. I feel I should write the way it comes out. And sometimes it comes out in ways I don't understand. I don't understand the structure of *Rumours*, for example. I mean, I don't understand it well enough to explain it. I understand it intuitively. I understood what was going on as it was coming out; for example, I knew that this play was totally too sparse to be dramatically presented. And yet I couldn't find any other way to write it. It came out almost in monosyllabic phrases. I said this is not right, this is not what you see on the stage, and yet it seemed to be the voice of the play, and the voice of the people in the play, the voice of the play's world. And I had to go with it and find the structure. Which again was sparse and almost epigrammatic in the way the scenes developed. I didn't know if it would go. I'd never seen anything like it on the stage.

**Wallace:** It did go. Not with the critics, but with the local audiences who kept it running for months. Did you learn from that process that you can go with your own voice and still get an audience?

**Walker:** Yeah. I'm still working out the relationship between a writer and his audience. And it's really complex, you know—what they expect from me and what I expect from them and what we're going to give each other ... I've never felt it's just up to me to give to them. It's certainly up to them to give stuff back, to take a step or two with me—and not to expect Chekhov. And not think that if I do something that I've made a mistake because I was trying to do Chekhov. At the same time I do feel a responsibility not to pretend that they are not there. And therefore certain reference points are needed. Those are the ones I guess I am working out. In the way other playwrights work out structure, I am working out the reference points the audience needs. There are ways that an audience can follow a play other than through plot or two intermissions or whatever. It's really complex. I mean, searching for those points must never get in the way of writing right from the source, I mean as it comes out of you. But it is something that I've become increasingly aware of.

**Wallace:** Chris Johnson has suggested you're a populist playwright, that throughout your career you've utilized so many different forms that you've proven you can appeal to a wide variety of audiences. I think I might agree because although you could typify the *Rumours* audience as a sort of cult, the *Gossip* audience looked entirely different; it was definitely middle-aged and, to all appearances, middle-class. It would seem that in Toronto you are striking a fairly wide variety of the theatre-going public. Yet we don't hear of your plays being done elsewhere in Canada. Do you have an explanation for that?

**Walker:** Only the one I can pass on from Ralph Zimmerman, my agent. He says that audiences don't have any trouble with my work, with a couple of exceptions. But Artistic Directors are timid about taking the first step because the work's not naturalistic, not what they are used to seeing from most Canadian playwrights, the ones that they took their earlier steps with. In terms of being populist, I just know that audiences don't usually have any trouble at all. Critics have more trouble than audiences. And I think that's only because they have to take notes. The work tends to go fast and it gets frustrating when you have to take notes and watch at the same time.

**Wallace:** Do you ever find yourself holding back with a play? Or do you really let it come out the way it wants to?

**Walker:** Sometimes I think I consciously inhibit myself. And sometimes that's good. I have a real love for low comedy which I have to hold back on sometimes.

Someday I'm not going to hold back, I'm going to write a really low comedy that has its roots in burlesque and stuff like that. I also have a love of the literary and sometimes I consciously hold back on that. But the rest is a sort of an unconscious holding back. It deals with stuff being written as it is being written. Like sometimes I look back and think, my God, that's structured and I wasn't looking for structure; I was looking to let the characters speak in this world. I think there is a lot of pressure on playwrights to write structured material. And not just because you deal with an audience that is used to or needs structure but also because theatre is so heavy with tradition and presupposition. I think playwrights consciously or subconsciously bend to that. I'd like to find out how much I do and then not do it sometime, just to see what happens. Because I think that just about anything is possible in theatre.

**Wallace:** I think the love of the literary comes through in your work and the love of low comedy. A lot of other loves or, at least, interests also emerge. Much has been made, for example, of your interest in "B" movies. Could you talk a little bit about that?

**Walker:** I'll take the opportunity to say right now that I don't write parody. I don't think I've ever written a parody. I saw in "B" movies a horror and an ugliness that was only hinted at. I don't know why, but in Hollywood or wherever these movies were made, perhaps because they were low-budget, people felt the freedom to suggest the horror but they never went all the way. *Beyond Mozambique* expresses what I think those jungle movies were really all about—the ugliness, the imperialist quality, the desperation of the characters, placed in a theatrical setting. I tend to like to frame the world, and use various genres to do that. "B" movies are a generic frame that gives me freedom to jump off in any direction that I want to or that the characters will take me. *Mozambique* is a jungle movie and *Filthy Rich* is a detective story, but they are both about other things, about other characters.

**Wallace:** And *Theatre of the Film Noir*?

**Walker:** *Theatre of the Film Noir* is a murder mystery set in Paris just after the war about sexual and political intrigue. It is *like* a Film Noir. I wasn't aware that it actually had a plot and that it was a murder mystery until after I finished working on it. Then I realized that that's what it was. In many ways it's like *Ramona*: it has rhythms of a dream but it deals mostly with character—specific characters in a specific situation in a specific world, which is basically what I write, I think.

**Wallace:** It also is episodic, as are all your plays. Is this also a result of your interest in "B" movies?

**Walker:** Perhaps. But it also reveals how I look at the world. I mean, I see things like that. I see that's how life proceeds—episodically and arbitrarily. And that, in fact, the unnatural theatrical structure is the three-act play, the structure which says that life proceeds in a neat form. I think things seem to stop for no apparent reason and start quickly again and sometimes half-way through. And we don't always start at the beginning; sometimes we start in the middle and we don't always have a satisfactory climax.

When I write, I don't plot out, I don't plan. I have general notions and, usually, strong ideas about the characters, and I sort of put them in the world and let them take control, or try to let them take control. It sounds a bit arch, but if you are not satisfied with the conclusion of one of my plays, blame the characters. If it's working for me, they are more responsible for that than I am. They brought it to an end. Not me. There's an inevitable question people ask of playwrights. As you know, they say, where's your voice? Which one of the characters is you? Or what do you believe about this? What's the answer? I mean, if you've written five or six characters into a play, and they are all speaking for themselves, as I think they should be, then it's very difficult to find what the playwright thinks. What's important is that the characters express themselves honestly and that the conflict is expressed honestly among them.

**Wallace:** In another interview you acknowledged the influence of the electronic media on your sensibility. Actually you described your mind as a media garbage bag and you said you wanted not to confront the influences, but to assimilate them (see Fraser). Have you achieved that?

**Walker:** Well, first of all, that was an assumption, that statement. I just assumed that that must be the way I was. Given the way I was brought up and the way that we were all brought up, just the amount of information coming in, the influence is there. Up until maybe the Sixties, you would have been confronting that, or trying to avoid that if you were trying to write well-made plays, putting in classical reference points rather than dealing with bad movies and other themes that were so much a part of how you were brought up. I don't know whether I have been successful, but I'm trying to find my way through it. I'm not trying to reproduce those influences. I'm trying to fight my way through the chaos of what, in fact, has been garbage and what, in fact, has been worth saying about things that concern me, using those forms to write, say, a political play which is not obviously a political play but which makes people think about politics. And to do it in the form of a "B" movie because that was what influenced my brain when I was young. We're living in a rather messy culture full of foul stuff and so I guess it's a matter of sorting out the good from the bad, the garbage from the worthwhile.

**Wallace:** It's interesting to hear you use the word "chaos," because the vision that comes to me through all the humour and mix-ups in your plays, is, finally, just that, of the world spinning out of order. Yet there do seem to be fixed points in this disorder and, often, these take the form of evil. I'm thinking of Rocco, or Ramona, or Zastrozzi. What is the place of evil in your work?

**Walker:** Well, it's there in the world that's spinning out of control. In fact, evil makes the world spin out of control. Well, by "evil" I mean destructive elements, seductive destructive elements. It's there. It's an obsession of mine. I can close my eyes and say that I do see the world in terms of good and bad. I have a very simplistic, moralistic vision. Evil is the threat that I put in the plays, the threat that I feel and therefore must express in moral and spiritual corruption and people trying to fight their way out of it, or else succumbing to it. And they do it in various ways. Sometimes they do it by telling jokes to stay alive. That's how I feel, how I act, I guess.

**Wallace:** Bill Lane discusses *Zastrozzi* as a contemporary morality play (Lane 4-6). Is there a strong moral impulse behind your writing? Do you want to write plays that incite people to change the world or reform their lives or confront the powers of destruction?

**Walker:** No. I have a strong impulse to express the things that are on my mind in a way that is natural to me, in a theatrical form. I want to share points of view with people. But I don't have anything to teach. I don't have any wisdom. And if I do, it is no more than anyone else. If I ever get any I'll pass it on, for sure. I won't hoard it. I do have energy, I think. And alertness. And I try to pass that on. And a sense that humour is a survival mechanism, which is said so often about people who write comedy. I try to put evil at arm's length, somehow. And the letters—some lovely letters we got from people on *Rumours*—were just about that. Because it was a play about the neutron bomb, as much as about anything. And people would write us letters saying thank you for writing a play about the madness, the utter madness of the neutron bomb, and allowing us to put it at arm's length—all this political and economic and potentially cataclysmic stuff. Thanks for helping us laugh, not giggle, but laugh. I guess that's what I'm trying to do. Do it for myself. It's not therapy. I'm not trying to purge. It's a survival mechanism. One of the ways of making the world less chaotic, I guess, is to show that it *is* chaotic.

**Wallace:** You've said in the past that if there's a common concern in your plays, it's obsession. And you've just said that evil is a personal obsession. How does obsession figure in your plays, evil or otherwise?

**Walker:** People focus on something. Not necessarily out of will, but because they have been driven to that point. I think that everybody alive has an obsession, to varying degrees. That's what I focus on in the characters. Sometimes I replace what is normal dramatic conflict with conflict between two obsessions. Or I focus on one person's obsession and nothing else. Or on a conflict between nothingness and obsession. It's sort of how I see people, as obsessive strong beings. To all those people who think I write defeatist themes, I don't feel that I write defeatist themes. I write about strong people. If we take away the banal, we're left with strength. I guess that if I was a teacher, and if I was using writing as a way of teaching people, I wouldn't teach by putting up signposts and making statements; I would teach by exorcising the banal. By trying to ignite the imagination.

**Wallace:** Some people see your plays as social satire. Chris Johnson discusses *Beyond Mozambique*, for example, as the welding of the comic and the grotesque into a type of Jonsonesque satire. Do you consider yourself a social critic or satirist?

**Walker:** We are all, I think, social critics of our times or we are asleep. To write anything is to be a critic of the times. But I don't start off with any answers. If I don't like something, I take a shot at it, I suppose. But …

**Wallace:** It's not so much that you suggest answers in your work, but that you reveal problems. There appears to me an implicit hope that people will have the good sense to want to change their condition, whether it be to stop the neutron bomb or defend themselves against the power of evil growing in the jungle. It's the hope implicit in knowledge. Do you think I am going too far with this?

**Walker:** No. I think you are right. I guess I do want to change the world. But I won't teach anyone how to do it. I am teaching myself. We will change it together. The type of satire which thinks it has all the answers, I don't understand and I don't write. But I am alert and concerned and angry—and the work is getting angrier—never defeatist, I feel, but angry. Yeah, I want to change everything.

**Wallace:** Are you writing within any tradition?

**Walker:** Maybe. In a larger world view. Often I've lost sight of it, because the main thrust of Canadian writing has been naturalistic. Often I've felt I was writing in limbo. I like writers who take risks and who lead me somewhere. Not, again, to teach me, but to transport me, writers who make me alert, who make me think, who strike my imagination. I like some of the work of Edward Bond and Peter Barnes—one in particular, *Bewitched*, because it is colossal; it's about history and politics and yet it's a great farce, a structure that I can't even describe. I particularly like the early work of John Palmer, because he transports me. I'd know I was in a theatre when I was watching Palmer's work, yet I would be transported to another place at the same time. That ignited my brain and made me think. I didn't come out of the theatre with answers, but I came out alive and alert. I think that's what theatre should do, first and foremost: keep you awake.

**Wallace:** You've been compared to Tom Stoppard and you've also been discussed in relation to the Theatre of the Absurd. Do you consciously work with techniques that relate to traditions other than Naturalism, or are you just coming to them on your own?

**Walker:** Just coming to them on my own. Starting to write plays in Canada, as you know, was starting from nowhere, really. We had no tradition that we could hold fast to. Certainly I wasn't aware of any tradition. The second live play I saw was one of mine. So out of ignorance more than anything, I just started to write. And theatre for me was, literally, an empty room; you filled it up with what you thought and did. How is something I'm still arriving at. I'm not conscious of working in any particular way. When I have tried to, my experiments have been in Realism, which for me is an unnatural writing style. It's not how I see the world. How so-called realistic or naturalistic writers portray the world is false to me. Their work never acknowledges that fact that you are in a theatre; it always requires you pretend. That, for example, is the way that O'Neill writes, which I can't abide. Forget all the great stuff about his work, the wonderful poetry and the scope. His characters carry their history around on their backs like a knapsack and then bring it out when it suits the dramatic structure of the play. That, I think, is more arch than any Absurdist drama.

**Wallace:** I think we tend to confuse Naturalism and Realism. I mean, Brecht maintained he was writing realistic drama, even as he drew complete attention to the theatre as artifice. Certainly external reality is not the only reality. I mean, consider the reality of dreams; it's not so accessible, but it's just as meaningful to most people. Yet trying to communicate that type of reality as I think you do in *Ramona* can be very difficult when you're dealing with audiences more accustomed to Naturalism. Do you think this might be why your plays receive more notice outside of Canada, in centres where theatre has a much longer history?

**Walker:** And where they're comfortable with a lot of styles other than Naturalism? Yeah. I think a message went out to Canadian playwrights in the early Seventies that Naturalism was the way to go because of our rural tradition and because it was modest. And we should be modest because we were just starting out and we had a lot to learn and we should write one-act plays modestly, and then we should write longer plays modestly, and then when we grew up we could do whatever we wanted. Well, I guess I never wanted to be modest. I just wanted to try stuff. It would have been really wrong for me to write rural dramas, since I was brought up in a very large North American city. I am Canadian. I know I'm Canadian because when I travel to other parts of the world, even to the United States, I feel different. But I'm an urban Canadian. And I had to let what came out express what was me.

**Wallace:** We talk a lot about regionalism in Canada—the Maritimes, the Prairies, and so forth. I wonder if there isn't also the Urban region, "Urbania," as Des McAnuff called it in an early play. Do you ever feel that you are a regional playwright in that sense?

**Walker:** Yes, I do. And a minority playwright. I'm a minority regional playwright. I think what you've just said is perfectly valid. But though we bring into the region of Toronto plays from right across Canada which express many points of view—geographical, philosophical, whatever—it doesn't seem that the process is reversed. I don't think there is any lack of generosity on the part of Toronto; it opens itself to lots of theatrical expressions, and it has to do even more if it wants to be a major theatre centre. I don't know why the process isn't reversed. Deep down I don't think that people in rural centres would have any trouble with plays by people who write in the city. I think they just don't get enough of them, that's all.

**Wallace:** Have you ever been produced in a Regional Theatre?

**Walker:** In the United States. And once, I think, in Vancouver. I think the Arts Club is Regional, and *Gossip* was done there. By the way, that's the typical choice if you are going to do one of my plays. Not the best by a long shot but …

**Wallace:** Obviously Canadian theatre is experiencing a very fast evolution, and so are you. Do you see yourself running parallel to the changes in Canadian theatre or are you developing differently?

**Walker:** I felt I was running parallel for the first five or six years. Certainly in terms of developing the work, which was the primary concern of theatre here, to develop new work. Although I'm still developing new work, I worry that in Canadian theatre that is no longer the primary concern. The search for products, for commercial viability, are important things for a vital theatre; nevertheless they tend to relegate developmental work to the back burner. And for a playwright that's not good, no matter what kind of play he writes. I think I am not part of that trend. Of course I might accidentally write a play that is commercially viable, *Zastrozzi* or *Gossip* are possibilities there. But mostly I'm concerned with just continuing to write and to create a body of work. That becomes increasingly difficult, you know, because the resources aren't there for theatres to develop work and take risks. The adventurous spirit is not there in the way that it was. It can come back, I guess. I diverge there, I think.

**Wallace:** How important is it for you to be done outside of the country?

**Walker:** I don't go seeking acknowledgement from other cultures in order to justify my existence. But it's nice that it happens; there are human beings in other countries and it's nice to know that they are seeing your work and that there's some kind of communication going on. For the longest time I felt that being a playwright in Canada was really an illegitimate thing to be. It was not very confidence-making. I feel more confident now. And I think that from confidence can come better work.

(1982)

## Works Cited

Fraser, John. "Walker Turns to Murder with Comedy." *The Globe and Mail* 19 April 1977: 16.

Lane, William. Introduction. In Walker, *Zastrozzi* 3-6.

Walker, George F. *Beyond Mozambique. Three Plays by George F. Walker.* Toronto: Coach House, 1978. 87-135.

———. *Zastrozzi, the Master of Discipline: A Melodrama.* Toronto: Playwrights Co-op, 1979.

## Making Things Clear: The *Film Noir* Plays of George F. Walker

by Jerry Wasserman

George F. Walker may not be our best playwright (although in fact he *may)* nor even our most original, but he is surely our most distinctive. The exotic locales of plays like *Bagdad Saloon, Beyond Mozambique, Ramona and the White Slaves,* and *Zastrozzi* are matched by compulsively baroque plots and characters arrayed across a spectrum ranging from the mildly demented to the seriously deranged. As unlikely as one is to find any prairie landscapes in these plays (see Gass 9), one is equally unlikely to find an inelegant line. The pop metaphysics of Ahrun or Rocco or Zastrozzi thicken with the wonderful balance of Walker's phrasing and the characters' passionate commitment to the kind of truth that shatters lesser men: "I am what I am. The force of darkness. The clear sane voice of negative spirituality. Making everyone answerable to the only constant truth I understand. Mankind is weak. The world is ugly. The only way to save them from each other is to destroy them both" (*Zastrozzi* 12). In Walker's sure rhythms Zastrozzi's post-romantic nihilism manages to be both comic and provocative. One could hardly mistake these lines for the work of any other Canadian dramatist.

In *Zastrozzi* especially, Walker mapped out his own unique theatrical territory: a loose alliance of nineteenth-century melodrama and Jacobean revenge tragedy ruled over by a triumvirate of equal parts Nietzsche, Artaud, and Marx (Groucho, of course). The play has just the right note of flippancy, but ultimately it is as serious a parodic response to melodrama and revenge tragedy as those genres were to the Romantic and Elizabethan drama that preceded them. "Remember that as you go through life there are only two things worth knowing," Zastrozzi advises his colleagues in crime: "The first is too complex for you to understand. The second is that life is a series of totally arbitrary and often meaningless events and the only way to make sense of life is to forget that you know that" (55). Here we are at the thematic centre of Walker's recent work. Chaos and meaninglessness—but chaos in particular—rule the day. The hero is he who, because he cannot forget, must restore order, impose justice or, if necessary, invent meaning.

*Gossip, Filthy Rich,* and *Theatre of the Film Noir* all have their roots in the B-movie. Chris Johnson subtitled his seminal 1980 article on Walker, "B-Movies Beyond the Absurd," arguing that Walker's use of the B-movie paradigm beginning with *Beyond Mozambique* enabled him to escape the limitations of the Theatre of the Absurd which had circumscribed his earlier work. In the three plays under discussion here, the chaos and pointlessness symptomatic of absurdity are made to answer to archetypal cinematic justicers: the investigative reporter, the private eye, and the chief inspector. Walker is a master at mimicking the conventions of the genre, its tones and clichés, adding always his own distinctive twists along the way. But the problem is that unlike the stylistic sources for *Zastrozzi*, the B-movies' raw material offers little beyond the slickness of its surfaces. Walker has described his own mind as "sort of a media garbage bag" and said he chose to deal with the inevitable influence of TV and movies by trying in his plays to "assimilate it and make something of it" (qtd. in Rubin and Cranmer-Byng 183). Unfortunately, there is only so much that can be made of such thin stuff, especially when drawn out over three plays. That's the bad news. The good news is that even second-rank George Walker is very good, suffering only in comparison with his own work at its most inspired.

All three of these plays are darkly comic murder mysteries, a genre Walker had begun exploring in *Ramona and the White Slaves*, written in the same year as *Zastrozzi* and *Gossip* (1976). But the murder plot and detective are subordinate elements in *Ramona*, a play so richly textured in its opium-induced grotesqueries as to be virtually impenetrable. For *Gossip*, Walker concentrated instead on a familiar kind of B-movie storyline with familiar kinds of B-movie characters and a rapid-fire sequence of cinematic clichés. The result is a stylish piece with an extremely clever plot, very funny, and easy to get at. With its *film noir* overlay of sex, cynicism, and urban corruption, its echoes of Dash Hammett and Raymond Chandler, and its evocations of Bogart and Bacall, it isn't hard to see why the play has had such popular success. Yet aficionados of Walker's drama can't help but be a little disappointed that *Gossip* is so unambitious, even if self-consciously so. Its opening line is a toast "To minimal art!"—as if the playwright were warning us of the aptness of his title for a play with the insubstantiality of gossip.

What substance the work has is provided by Tyrone M. Power, the hardboiled political reporter who begrudgingly enters the world of the gossip column in his assignment to find out "who killed Bitch Nelson," a useless socialite. Power is middle-aged, balding, and shabby—the antithesis of his Hollywood namesake. And he is a confirmed nihilist. The most frequent words in his journalistic vocabulary are "cataclysm," "anathema," and "armageddon." He firmly believes that "civilization is sinking into the slime." Yet despite the fact that no one he meets in the course of his investigations does anything to obviate his pessimism, he obsessively keeps after the truth. He refuses as well to be sidetracked by the vamp ("a cross between Gertrude Stein and Jane Fonda" [19]), who assures him that "truth is a relative commodity beyond your grasp" (43). At the play's end Power has lost the woman he loves, pinned the murder on his only friend, and watched his dog die. Still, he has pursued truth into the darkest corners of his world and salvaged something of it at least.

*Filthy Rich*, written in 1978, is a sequel to *Gossip*; and though not without its own virtues, it is not as good a play. It relies heavily on rhetoric and exposition, a plot distinctly reminiscent of *The Big Sleep* and a character study out of *Casablanca*. We rejoin an even more cynical, whiskey-soaked and now maudlin Tyrone Power who has left his newspaper job for a life of "obscene neutrality": "I'm a cynic. Get it? A cynic doesn't get involved with anything [...] I'm not happy. But I'm immune" (16). Cast in the role of private eye in spite of himself, he is dragged out of his inertia back into the world of criminal intrigue and political corruption. It is the familiar Walkeresque landscape in which distinctions between truth and falsehood, guilt and innocence, necessity and expediency all blur. We are reminded of this on nearly every page of script: "We live in troubled times. Morality is a foggy foggy concept" (28); "nothing makes sense" (52); "life is a series of apparent coincidences contrived by mysterious forces" (13); "the whole world's nuts" (26). This time our unwilling hero doesn't have the impetus or energy to reassert sanity on his own. A watered-down Zastrozzi losing his "power," he needs the help of a younger man. Jamie ("I am a positive force") temporarily recharges Power's ethical batteries, though his own motives are pure greed and ambition, and Power does come through finally with that curious integrity so typical of Walker's protagonists. His summing up is characteristic as well:

> **POWER.** Isn't that something. That's ... that's that's ... You know what life is. Life is–
> **JAMIE.** Ah, who cares?
> **POWER.** I do.
> **JAMIE.** Well that's something at least.
> **POWER.** Yeah.
> **JAMIE.** Not much though.
> **POWER.** No. (69)

In *Theatre of the Film Noir,* his most recent play to date, Walker explores much of the same generic territory. But with a shift away from an American setting and strictly "cosmopolitan" style, he seems to have found once again those bizarre imaginative resources which gave his earlier work so much of its uniqueness. Combining the kitsch depravity of *Ramona* with the relative accessibility of *Gossip, Theatre of the Film Noir* is the most interesting of these new plays (though it certainly does not warrant the rave notices it received upon its Toronto premiere). The setting is liberated Paris, 1944. Though the war has ended there, its consequences have not. "Behaviour has no recognizable pattern. Morality is a question of circumstance. And guilt a matter of degree" (1). A murder has been committed and Inspector Clair has been put on the case. His name defines his function: "I'm going to begin specializing just in making things clear" (1).

Borrowing atmosphere and images freely from his own earlier work, Walker brews up a skillful blend of sexual perversity, paranoid fantasy and *film noir* convention, lacing it all with the kind of tight suspense plotting at which he has become very good indeed. This is not just a parody but a distillation. Such stock props of the genre as cigarettes and chocolate bars are completely revitalized. Both the Nazi and American soldiers are finely crafted variations of their stereotypes (the Nazi in fact dies cursing clichés), as is Lilliane, the tough but vulnerable beauty who does what she must to survive. Bernard, the psychotic coward, is an original, though clearly in the tradition of Walker's demented would-be visionaries. And even Inspector Clair's rather unorthodox method of putting things in order at the end takes us back to

Walker's fascination, in his very early plays, with such archetypal pop justice figures as Gary Cooper in *High Noon* and Doc Halliday.

Finally, however, the theme of this play is survival. Lilliane will always find some men to bring her things, and will survive the war to become "one of this country's more successful film actresses" (50). Bernard will always live on, says Inspector Clair, "in the film that runs inside my head." And certain images that survive on celluloid will find their way back into our culture, recycled once more via Walker's theatrical art. It is only one of many ironies regarding George F. Walker, Canada's most distinctive playwright, now in residence with Joseph Papp in New York, that his play about the Americanization of the post-war world uses as its central metaphor that most fundamentally American of art forms to develop the most quintessentially Canadian of themes.

(1982)

## Works Cited

Gass, Ken. Introduction. *Three Plays: Bagdad Saloon, Beyond Mozambique, Ramona and the White Slaves.* By George F. Walker. Toronto: Coach House, 1978. 9-15.

Johnson, Chris. "George F. Walker: B-Movies Beyond the Absurd." *Canadian Literature* 85 (1980): 87-103.

Rubin, Don, and Alison Cranmer-Byng, ed. *Canada's Playwrights: A Biographical Guide.* Toronto: CTR Publications, 1980.

Walker, George F. *Filthy Rich.* Toronto: Playwrights Canada, 1981.

———. *Gossip.* Toronto: Playwrights Canada, 1980.

———. *Theatre of the Film Noir.* Toronto: Playwrights Canada, 1981.

———. *Zastrozzi, the Master of Discipline: A Melodrama.* Toronto: Playwrights Co-op, 1979.

# George F. Walker: Liberal Idealism and the "Power Plays"

by Denis W. Johnston

It is a commonplace observation that an enormous number of new Canadian plays and playwrights have appeared since 1970, nurtured by various federal funding agencies whose years of greatest largesse coincided with the rise of Toronto's so-called alternate theatres. Of these new playwrights, George F. Walker is perhaps the most prolific. At least fourteen of his plays have been produced in Toronto since 1971, mostly by the Factory Theatre Lab, with which he has been so closely associated throughout his career. Walker was hardly an overnight success: his early plays were rather slow and obtuse, and received "generally weak critical response" (Gass 13). More recently, however, Walker's plays have attracted a great deal of attention beyond the confines of Metro Toronto. Although published production histories are sketchy, *Gossip* has been produced in several American cities, *Zastrozzi* has been produced in England and in Australia, and Walker himself served a stint as playwright-in-residence with Joseph Papp in New York.[1]

By 1980, then, Walker had earned the ironic grand prize of Canadian arts and letters: fame abroad and obscurity at home. As Martin Kinch put it, Walker seemed "well on his way to becoming a celebrated and successful American playwright" (qtd. in Wallace and Zimmerman 346-47). Despite the attention that his plays have attracted in some quarters, along with varying measures of critical and popular acclaim, they have been ignored by Canada's larger regional theatres. Considering that Canada Council funding demands a certain proportion of Canadian plays, this indifference to a major new native talent is somewhat disconcerting, although hardly unfathomable. Walker's esoteric early plays and his long association with the radical Factory Theatre Lab placed him well outside the mainstream of the Canadian theatre establishment. And his writing style, while changing through the years, always remained far from the orthodox "Canadian naturalism" which spread to the regional theatres from Toronto's Tarragon Theatre and its successful productions of Freeman, French, and others. As the Factory's Ken Gass drily remarked, "Not many prairie landscapes in George Walker's plays" (Gass 9). The early plays especially seem defiantly uncommercial, as if brandishing their impenetrability as the badge of an artist, and generally did not invite a second production anywhere. However, the Factory gave Walker precisely what a beginning playwright needs most: production after production. Without this opportunity, it is unlikely that Walker could have persisted beyond his early explorations, finally developing his own distinctive style and an audience which appreciated it.

Chris Johnson's excellent article, "George F. Walker: B-Movies Beyond the Absurd," analyzes his early plays in terms of both their dramatic ancestry and the context of Toronto's alternative theatre scene where they first appeared. Borrowing heavily from the European absurdist tradition, both *The Prince of Naples* (1971) and *Ambush at Tether's End* (1971) contain little character development and less plot line, floundering in a quasi-literary style that was already passé. In *Sacktown Rag* (1972), Walker "discards some of the literary self-consciousness which intrudes in the earlier plays" (Johnson 92),[2] drawing on his own bizarre perceptions of growing up absurd in Toronto. He also juxtaposes third-person commentary and cartoon-like stylization with elements of realism, exploiting his own awareness of cinematic techniques and his ebullient sense of humour which characterize his later work. In *Bagdad Saloon* (1973), explicitly subtitled "a cartoon," Walker continues to broaden his vocabulary of anti-realistic devices, while moving closer to his Canadian roots. Although peopled with Arabs and Americans, this play deals with a quintessentially Canadian theme: the adoption of American mythic heroes by a society which hasn't developed any of its own. While *Bagdad Saloon* still lacks any character development or cogent plot, it also shows Walker's progression toward themes of more widespread interest, and toward graphic theatrical rather than literary images.

In *Beyond Mozambique* (1974) Walker uses the B-movie rather than the cartoon as his stylistic model for a prematurely decaying society. As in each of his previous works, there is an obvious improvement in his handling of the theatre medium and an obvious progression toward a writing style distinctly his own. While *Sacktown Rag* and *Bagdad Saloon* had a kind of flamboyant energy which shone through some awkward theatricality, the panache of *Beyond Mozambique* is integrated with the style of the play. Instead of discreetly drawing on his awareness of pop culture in an intellectual way, Walker frankly revels in it. Instead of struggling with his technological upbringing, he begins to put it to use:

> Like many of my generation, my mind is sort of a media garbage bag sometimes. We're all so heavily influenced by television and movies and you don't have to be very perceptive to see it coming out in new plays. The dilemma for me was not to rebel against the problem—it is, after all, a fairly central reality—but to assimilate it and make something of it. (Fraser)

In *Beyond Mozambique*, Walker mixes high art with low pop culture: images of Chekhov and Victor Hugo share the stage with Rita Hayworth and Nelson Eddy. He indulges in his gift for outrageous epigrams: "Jesus doesn't mind losers," says a failed priest, "but he has no patience for idiots" (*Three Plays* 128). The plot careens along with more energy than direction, but finally there is a sense of it moving somewhere. If the ending dissipates in a welter of sexual perversity, gratuitous violence, plagues of insects, and jungle drums, the problem is one of control rather than creativity; at last Walker had reached the point where he had something to be economical about! Four years after its first production, *Beyond Mozambique* was the first of Walker's plays to be re-mounted, and the first one to merit it.

*Ramona and the White Slaves* (1976), a kind of opium dream set in Hong Kong after World War I, represents a watershed in Walker's career. Published in a volume with *Bagdad Saloon* and *Beyond Mozambique*, *Ramona* resembles its companion pieces in its exotic setting and its characters brought together from a variety of times and places. This play too is imbued with mutilation and eroticism, but in a much less gratuitous way than in *Beyond Mozambique*. The characters have more depth than in any of his preceding plays, and there is no recourse to easy laughs to alleviate the tension. Gass notes that Walker had grown "removed and introspective" (13) before completing *Ramona*, and nearly abandoned playwriting altogether. When he returned to the Factory, he returned as a more accomplished man of the theatre, back from a period of travel and turmoil. He began to direct his own plays, and to gather around him a solid corps of competent actors who were conversant with his emerging style. He had survived a lengthy and frenetic apprenticeship, with little public response to sustain him. He now began to write in a much more popular vein, not necessarily pandering to a broader audience, but certainly making his work much more accessible to them. His next three plays were produced by a more mainstream company, Toronto Free Theatre, and benefited from its more sophisticated stagecraft. By early 1978, three of Walker's plays had become successes in short order, and his achievements finally began to live up to his early promise.

In his post-*Ramona* plays, Walker has continued to use popular culture as a stylistic foundation, but has grown more articulate in its use. For example, his melodrama *Zastrozzi* (1977) has become something of a favourite among the critics (see, for example, Wasserman, "Towards" 178). In dealing with the power of evil, Walker exploits our own fascination and ambivalence towards evil by endowing the villain with many more intriguing qualities than the virtuous hero. *Rumours of Our Death* (1980) is a political parable written in the form of a punk-rock musical. It is undoubtedly the weakest of his post-*Ramona* plays, mainly due to the deliberate omission of distinctively human characters: for example, the King is a kind of automaton, two characters spend most of the play in a death-like trance, and all three female roles are given the same name. *Theatre of the Film Noir* (1981) is almost a rewrite of *Ramona and the White Slaves*, as perversity, mutilation and drugs once again permeate a shattered post-war society, this time in Paris after the liberation. Similarly, *Science and Madness* (1982) is highly reminiscent of *Beyond Mozambique*, again concerned with unnatural medical experiments in an exotic B-movie setting. In these last two plays, Walker is not so much tilling over old ground as he is bringing new dramaturgical skills to themes he had not fully exploited before. Although *Science and Madness* did not capture the public's imagination, *Theatre of the Film Noir* was a great success, and its Toronto run was followed by a national tour.

The foregoing review is not intended as an exhaustive criticism of Walker's dramatic output, but as an introduction to his other three published plays: *Gossip* (1977), *Filthy Rich* (1979), and *The Art of War* (1983). There are several reasons why these may be treated as a kind of trilogy. They each deal with a common theme, the problem of trying to be a good person in a corrupt society. They each have the same central character, a shabby journalist-turned-detective with the grandly inappropriate name of Tyrone Power. ("My mother's a romantic," he explains [76].) And finally, they are by far the most accessible of Walker's plays, containing more realistic elements and less violence and perversity that would offend a broad range of theatre-goers. It has been these more easily digestible works which have brought Walker national and international recognition. *Gossip* was produced in Vancouver, Chicago, New York and elsewhere. *Filthy Rich* was produced by regional theatres from sea to sea last season, and new productions are planned in England and Australia. And while *The Art of War* is too recent a play to have attracted other producers so far, the success of its companion pieces suggests that it too will be seen in other cities before long.

*Gossip* opens at a pretentious modern-art exhibit, with a toast "to minimal art!" (17). It is hard to say whether Walker is lampooning his own shift to more popular writing, or his own earlier pretentious plays; he may be just trying to make us laugh, for the matron who proposes the toast soon takes an undignified spill through a suspended rubber tire which is the centrepiece of the exhibit, the victim of a high-society murder. "Who killed Bitch Nelson?" snarls the hard-bitten investigative reporter Tyrone Power. "And who the hell cares?" (17).

Power is not the dogged champion of justice like the police inspectors of *Ramona* and *Film Noir*, nor does he cut a dashing romantic figure like Zastrozzi. He is middle-aged, balding, bespectacled, and wears an old poorly-fitting suit. His investigative interest is not stirred by apparently private vendettas among the privileged, but rather by violations of the public trust, political kickbacks, and legislative incompetence; and he balks at being assigned to a sensational story which he feels is irrelevant to the real problems of society:

> I'm a political journalist. I write about politics. I do not investigate the murders of celebrities. For that you need a police reporter or a gossip columnist. I am neither. I am a political journalist! (17-18)

But his publisher Baxter knows that the public is fascinated by this unsolved celebrity murder, while they have grown indifferent to political revelations. Gossip sells newspapers, and Baxter has to threaten to take Power's political column away to coerce him into digging some up. Although Power hates such "mindless prattle about people with expensive hair cuts," (19) Baxter has him over a barrel. To be able to write about what he thinks is important, he first has to write what the people want to read, perhaps echoing Walker's own shift to a more popular style. Power is given six weeks to solve a mystery that the police have failed to solve in six months.

Power sets about interviewing people who had been present at the art show murder: a homosexual director, a tough young actress, and the dead woman's sister, a misanthropic poet described as "a cross between Gertrude Stein and Jane Fonda" (28). He is also led to Bitch Nelson's lawyers, the Lewis brothers, who behave like comic buffoons but seem to have something to hide. At first, we see no reason why Power should be so indifferent to crime among the social elite: we see eccentricity everywhere, but no evil. As the scenes progress, however, we come to realize that there are no innocent people in this intrigue: there are only those who create and control the evil, and those who accede to it. The Lewis brothers are devious and perverted, and have staged their slapstick routine only to throw Power off the track. The young actress is their prostitute. Brigot Nelson ransacks Power's office, and threatens to kill both him and Baxter. The director Bellum is in cahoots with somebody, but there is no indication as to who is on whose side, or why. Only the romantic element seems untainted by all this corruption: Margaret, a young woman whom Power loves, seems to be merely adrift in moral confusion over her love affair with her politician brother. But we learn that even Margaret is involved in this sordid and complex intrigue, for she begins concealing evidence from Power. Her incestuous liaison turns out to be a symptom of profound mental illness, with suggestions of more severe ethical and sexual depravity. It seems that Power's jaundiced view of society, particularly of its upper echelons, is not so much pessimism as it is perceptivity.

In the final scene, Walker tries to tie up the loose ends of his complex plot without killing off most of the characters, as he does for instance in *Beyond Mozambique* and *Zastrozzi*. However, his resolutions of the second act are not so well crafted as his complications of the first. In a time-honoured device of murder mysteries, Power invites all the suspects to an elegant dinner. He has evidently been very busy during the intermission, for we learn that he has discovered or guessed the solutions to all the crimes in the play, including some that the audience doesn't even know about. In the rush of revelations, which may well be intended as a parody of the mystery genre, we learn that political corruption and social corruption are not the separate issues which Power thought they were; rather, they are two symptoms of the same disease, a decaying and cynical society. Confessions to political wrong-doings and cover-ups follow hard on the heels of other murders abruptly revealed and summarily solved. While the denouement may be thematically sound, it is not theatrically consistent; for example, the revelation that Bellum had been impersonating a murdered Lewis brother is inconsistent with the Lewis's private conversation in an earlier scene. Perhaps to conceal this dramatic flaw, Bellum is glibly poisoned near the beginning of the dinner, then just as glibly resurrected later when a witness is required. There is some ironic justification for Baxter's outrage when the other guests have gone and Power accuses him of the original murder: "Are you crazy? You can't blame it on me just because I'm the only one left" (71). The murder of Bitch Nelson is the only crime that Walker has left unsolved, and he has to pin it on *somebody*.

*Gossip* opens with Baxter complaining that Power is a nihilist obsessed with the end of the world: the most common words in his journalistic vocabulary are cataclysm, anathema, and Armageddon. As it closes, Power's world has indeed come to an end: his beloved Margaret has been committed, his friend Baxter has been arrested, even his dog has died. The room is a shambles, leaving Power to toast the empty table. Although the final scene is ragged, the ending is appropriate: the guilty, which is to say virtually everyone, are punished according to their deserts, and the nihilist Power has been the chief agent in reducing his world to nothing. Ironically, only Power and the misanthrope Brigot Nelson are able to maintain their humanistic beliefs in a cynical world. They may be lonely, and they may be dismayed by the perpetrators and tolerators of evil, but not enough to give up their liberal idealism.

This idealism may be an impractical set of beliefs, but it's better than being a lawyer or a politician with no moral code at all.

The sequel to *Gossip* is *Filthy Rich*, Walker's most polished play to date. In it, he uses the B-movie motif more thoroughly than he had since *Beyond Mozambique*, this time in a story reminiscent of old Humphrey Bogart movies, centred on a tough detective with a heart of gold. As the play opens, we find that Power has left the newspaper business and is living in a squalid office in a run-down part of the city. He is depressed and drinking heavily, working on his novel which Baxter had called the joke of the newspaper, supporting himself by "writing silly freelance articles on leisure for a silly weekend magazine" (79). As his writing projects indicate, Power has resigned from the real world as well as from Baxter's newspaper: when there is a knock on the door, he ignores it. He has replaced his dog with tropical fish, presumably because they require less emotional involvement. His fish serve as a model of disinterested behaviour: they seem to be observing, but they're really just passing the time, uninvolved and uncaring and therefore impervious to pain. "I want to be alone with my fish," says Power, and then "I wish I was a fish" (92-99). Although his pessimistic world view was vindicated by the events of *Gossip*, being right has not made him happy; on the contrary, it crushed the native optimism implicit in his humanitarian ideals. To protect himself from further disillusionment and despair, Power has quit the world:

> I'm a cynic. Get it? A cynic doesn't get involved with anything. It took me years to get this way and I have no intention of changing for anyone. I'm not happy. But I'm immune. (86)

To bring Power's disillusion into sharper relief, and to get him involved in the action, Walker introduces another venerable device: the sidekick. Jamie McLean is a delivery boy, a janitor, and a part-time student, precisely the functions of a good sidekick and certainly what Power needs. "I am a positive force", Jamie assures him, "I'm going to make you rise up from the living dead and be beautiful once more" (98). Power, who neither looks nor feels beautiful, wishes that his young self-appointed saviour would leave him alone with his fish: "Just think a few hours ago you were nothing but a smart-ass punk. There is a god. And he uses assholes for angels" (93).

Power's weary contempt for himself and the corrupt society in which he is mired is counterpoised with Jamie's romantic naïvéte and impulsive idealism, an idealism which hasn't been corroded with moral pollution like his own. To Power, all wealth is filthy, to be kept in garbage bags along with his trashy novel. While Jamie recognizes that money tends to corrupt ("Everyone can stoop, Power. The human spine is especially designed for it" [98]), he is young enough to believe that he can get rich without getting dirty. The other characters in the play, wealthy or worldwise, harbour no such illusions; but Jamie is a slum kid raised on old movies, perhaps like Walker himself, and he sees no reason why the good guys shouldn't win the battle and make a lot of money at the same time.

Power, of course, has no wish to get involved in any adventure, but the world won't leave him alone. First, a telegraph boy (Jamie) refuses to be shrugged off, then a beautiful heiress named Ann Scott walks in asking for help. Power's passing out doesn't stop the procession, as Ann's sister Susan slaps him into consciousness, and she is soon followed by an aggressive police inspector and a letter outlining the details of the case. It seems that Michael Harrison, a wealthy leading candidate for mayor, has gone missing, and is being hunted by influential rival factions. While the reigning mayor wishes to secure Harrison as his successor, Harrison's father, another wealthy power-broker, is trying to kill his son to prevent disclosures of criminal activity. Everyone in this intrigue assumes that Power is involved as a private investigator, a role which Power finally accepts when he learns that an old friend of his is also missing, a journalist named Fred Whittacker who had clung to his liberal ideals long after Power had given up in disgust. It is Jamie, the positive force, who literally yanks Power's head out of the fish tank, and goads him into playing a dangerous power game with unprincipled forces of cynicism. When Whittacker is murdered on Power's window ledge, carrying half a million dollars which could be profits from blackmail, the game is intensified. But while the Power of *Gossip* was outside the game, investigating events which had already occurred, the Power of *Filthy Rich is* a key player himself, with the action swirling around him. He doesn't have all the information that the other players think he has, but he bluffs and raises the stakes in the best Bogart style in order to find Harrison and to exonerate his murdered friend.

Punctuated with Walker's witty and explosive dialogue, *Filthy Rich* is a dandy detective yarn, a considerable improvement over *Gossip*. For instance, it has a much more economical structure, with only six characters and a single set, which contributes to the tautness of the suspense. While *Gossip* complicated political intrigues with personal vendettas, *Filthy Rich* maintains a single plot line, with twists rather than appendages. The offstage characters in *Filthy Rich* are important throughout the play, whereas in *Gossip* they were apt to be forgotten from time to time in the profusion of conspiracies: for example, Baxter had to remind Power of his failure to solve the original murder, a fact which the audience had probably forgotten as well. The other major improvement in *Filthy Rich* is in Walker's more patient exposition of the story, particularly in allowing Power to *find out* what is going on, rather than having him know it and merely present it as he does in the last scene of *Gossip*. The audience grapples with the mystery as Power does, accumulating facts as he does, being tricked or supported by other characters as he is. This greatly augments the audience's involvement with the central character, a crucial element in the mystery genre. We are as relieved as Power when an idealistic motive for Whittacker's shakedown scheme is revealed, and as surprised and fearful as Power when the gangster Duvall turns up. In *Filthy Rich* the audience participates more actively in the plot development, rather than passively being dealt a set of *faits accomplis*.

This improved dramatic structure allows the themes of the play to emerge more strongly than in *Gossip*. Once again, Power is an ethical man immersed in an unethical society. Even moral acts are corrupted by immoral means, as in Whittacker's attempt to prevent a rich man's election by (effectively) blackmailing him. Romantic acts of courage are ultimately self-destructive, as when Jamie is shot and apparently killed in the Bogart-like ploy of confronting an armed woman in the belief that she is morally incapable of pulling the trigger. That Jamie survives is due to his own canny subterfuge of replacing her bullets with blanks—a cynical safety play, if you like, in this game of cutthroats. The ultimate winner is the unseen Michael Harrison, a man willing to destroy his father in order to keep his own political skirts clean, a man who stays in hiding while the pawns play out a deadly game. In the end, punishment is not meted out on moral grounds, as in *Gossip*, but on the grounds of games-playing skill: Susan Scott goes to jail because she is clearly in this game over her head, while the gangster Duvall is out-finessed by Power, another deft strategist playing at his best. The losers may be morally reprehensible, but that's not why they lose.

But Duvall can gloat over his one consolation, the corruption of goodness by greed, when Power elects to keep the half-million dollars that Whittacker had died for: "Welcome to my world, Mr. Power. Money wins. And I love watching it win. Just love it" (129). Goaded by Duvall's smugness, Jamie's "death," and Detective Stackhouse's sheepish request that the whole matter be hushed up, in short the overwhelming conclusion that whatever game they play is controlled by the wealthy amoral Harrisons of this world, Power flings all Whittacker's money out of the window in a hysterical gesture of defiance against the next mayor. This action, in effect a clumsy attempt to bribe the electorate, is rendered ridiculous by society's innocent greed: all the money is scooped up in seconds by an unseen but presumably astonished populace below. As the play ends, Power and Jamie seem stunned by their rapid changes in fortune, from pristine poor to filthy rich and back again; they are left to contemplate life, groping for epigrams to make some sense of it all:

> **POWER.** You know what life is. Life is—
> **JAMIE.** Ah, who cares?
> **POWER.** I do.
> **JAMIE.** Well that's something at least.
> **POWER.** Yeah.
> **JAMIE.** Not much though.
> **POWER.** No. (*They look at each other.*)
> **JAMIE.** Not very goddamn much at all.
> **POWER.** No. (132)

If there is any sense of progression in the content of these three plays, it is in the progressive seediness of the fruits of liberal idealism. In *Gossip*, Power is an influential political columnist, taken off his regular assignment because, in Baxter's opinion, his superior intelligence would enable him to succeed where the police had failed. He wins the battle with relative ease, and presumably regains his position in the newspaper. In *Filthy Rich*, he is an alienated and deteriorating ex-journalist, who is dragged unwillingly into a political power-game, but plays it wonderfully well. His victory here is less clear-cut, however: some guilty people are punished, some are made mayor, and Power himself squanders all his money on a futile gesture, failing even to recoup his expenses. In a more recent play, *The Art of War*, Power returns as an obsessed and pathetic pauper, by his own admission "a freelance writer with diminishing talent" (141). In *Filthy Rich* he was a reclaimed drunk, heroically fighting the forces of evil; in *The Art of War* he's just a drunk, retreating to his bottle whenever he becomes too overwhelmed by the futility of his struggle. "I'm depressed", he keeps saying, as well he may be given his own impotence in fighting pragmatism with self-righteousness.

*The Art of War* takes Power and Jamie away from the urban setting with which they are so familiar, to spy on Hackman, a political strongman whom Power suspects of unspecified illegalities in supplying arms to Third World countries. They camp on a cliff overlooking Hackman's Nova Scotia estate, an environment in which Power's incompetence is quickly evident: "Throw my tent", he tells Jamie, when he means "pitch" it (141). This Power is not the crusty but lovable dropout we saw in *Filthy Rich*; he is a man obsessed, a moral voyeur looking for evil through binoculars. In *Filthy Rich* the evil sought him out and surrounded him, eventually forcing him to respond and take action; here, the evil is a distant monster, on a remote rural estate with connections in Latin America. Power is looking for trouble, as was the journalist Reinhardt who was murdered in the prologue while rifling Hackman s private papers. Power terms Hackman a maniac, but it is his own behaviour which appears unbalanced to the more objective Jamie: "Well you can look at us, Power. I'd say our behaviour is pretty strange. Sitting on top of a cliff a thousand miles from home at five o'clock in the morning" (138). Unlike in the previous two plays, there is no hard evidence of a crime having been committed, nor any palpable motivation for Power's investigation, no newspaper assignment or damsels in distress or hope of a reward: "We're not private detectives. I'm just a concerned citizen. And you're a punk who follows me around" (139). Jamie accurately describes Power as a disillusioned paranoid drunk, and accuses him of hunting for right-wing conspiracies under his bed:

> You're all the same. That generation of yours. Scandals in every corner. Corruption on every level. I'm going home [...] you're a cause in search of an issue. Life is precious, Power. And I don't want to waste it trying to reconstruct your social conscience. (140)

In *The Art of War* Walker has removed the romantic B-movie lens which gave their shenanigans such a roseate glow in *Filthy Rich*. They have come down to reality with a bump, although they disagree as to what reality is. To Power, it is the evil beneath a glossy surface; to Jamie, it's not having enough money to rent a car.

The audience is not invited to identify with Power in *The Art of War* as they were in the previous two plays. His quips are more laboured, as he is sapped of humour by his obsession with Hackman. When he and Heather, a young local journalist, gain an interview with Hackman, Power's coarseness makes a poor contrast with Hackman's urbane good manners; Jamie later reports what the audience has already observed: "I was eavesdropping. I overheard your entire conversation. He sounded perfectly rational. You sounded perfectly obnoxious" (151). As in *Zastrozzi*, the villain has many admirable qualities which the hero lacks. For instance, Hackman loves art, although perhaps for the wrong reasons; he is amused by his false political identity as an advisor to the Minister of Culture, and he casts art in his own image as "the leisurely reflection of an elite society" (162). Power hates art as he hates discrimination, as "'the leisurely reflection of a dying society'" (159). Typically, Jamie articulates a common-sense compromise position, suggesting that both men have lost touch with the common man, and perhaps with objective reality:

> They say this country has no real working-class art. And I think that's because it's always presented by a bunch of middle-class academics who patronize the shit out of the working-class with a lot of romantic bullshit. (165)

The romantic bullshit of *Filthy Rich* is gone, particularly in the character of Power; in this unromanticized war, the combatants are undignified and inelegant.

For Hackman is not the engaging figure that Zastrozzi is, nor does he have Power's ingratiating ineptitude; moreover, he is callous and off-hand about his cruelty, manipulating and killing people without relish and without regret. Beneath his cool exterior, he hates Power as much as Power hates him: "He's the enemy. The humanist. The egalitarian. The constant appeaser. He wants to turn the world into Jello" (166). Intolerance is ugly, and both Hackman and Power are disfigured by it. Therefore, since Walker cannot depend on strong antithetical central characters to sustain the audience's interest, he instead divides the cast into two almost geometrically balanced teams. The teams are the liberals and the fascists, headed by Power and Hackman (whose names are beginning to carry suggestions of coercion and mutilation). Each team captain has a henchman, in Jamie and the ex-commando Brown. Each also has a female cohort, in Heather and Karla Mendez, the daughters of a newspaper publisher and a fascist revolutionary respectively. The personal war between Power and Hackman becomes a symmetrical chess game, as they pull a gun on each other, take each other's female pawn as hostage, and comfort their physically battered knights in preparation for the climactic final scene.

It is physical toughness which wins the skirmish for the bad guys. The intrinsic weakness of the liberal position is that they are honour-bound to (instinctively) play by humanitarian rules which the other side despises. Verbal abuse is the strong suit of the liberals, but it is ineffective against physical abuse. "That really pisses me off," rants Heather, who is simply ignored (146). "Go fuck yourself," says Jamie, who is summarily knocked unconscious (166). Brown observes that the battle is not an even one, and Hackman concurs: "It's a pathetic little war. But it's the only one we've got!" (167). In the end, Karla proves to be tougher than Heather by escaping without being rescued, and only a lucky shot by the incompetent marksman Jamie prevents a thorough rout for the forces of reaction. Karla is able to easily disarm Power because shooting an unarmed person is against his moral code; she on the other hand has no such compunction, and her parting shot is ballistic rather than verbal. Hackman points out the weakness inherent in Power's humanitarian beliefs: "No chance, Power. You had no chance. She hates you. She'd risk everything to beat you. You have to risk taking action!" (182). Hackman leaves the bleeding and grovelling Power on the beach, smug in his present and ultimate victory: "Please. No need to stand on my account. Besides, I want to remember you just as you are" (183). Power is frustrated, helpless, and in great pain when Jamie finds him:

> She shot me. She got loose because you didn't tie her up properly and she came down here and shot me. Why can't you do anything properly. Why can't *we* do anything properly. It's so goddamn depressing. (183)

The liberal team has stormed and captured the beach, but the fascists look down on them unassailably from the cliff, waving sardonically as the play ends. "I'm tired of losing," moans Power, "it's so ... depressing" (184).

While *The Art of War* continues to exploit Walker's skill in cinematic techniques, it would be inaccurate to extend Johnson's argument that the B-movie is "characteristic of all his subsequent work" (93). *Zastrozzi* does not fit comfortably into this mold, nor do several of his recent plays. Although *Filthy Rich* is unmistakably a Bogart-style B-movie, with its neon signs, tough-guy dialogue, and omnipresent wail of a street musician's saxophone, *Gossip* has very little in common with this genre, and *The Art of War* even less. In this last play, for example, Walker has deliberately de-emphasized the central character by giving him a strong antagonist and allowing teams of characters to carry the action. He has also de-romanticized Power himself, allowing him to drink heavily with little provocation, to indulge in self-pity, to repeat himself tediously, and to lose the kind of climactic showdown he won so splendidly in *Gossip* and *Filthy Rich*. While his drinking was an understandable anaesthetic for loneliness in the earlier plays, existential nausea here is just an alcoholic's excuse: "You drink for the pain in the universe and the soul of mankind," observes Jamie. "You're not a common drunk. You're a common pretentious drunk" (151).

With neither Hackman not Power worthy of the audience's sympathy, Jamie emerges as the play's most attractive character. He tackles the stronger forces of evil in the certain knowledge that he will be beaten up for his presumption. While both Power and Hackman resort to devious and violent strategems, Jamie believes that protecting his friends is more important than winning the game. While Power is willing to leave Heather in the hands of a lethal enemy in order to capture an opposing piece, Jamie refuses to leave his wounded friend on the beach in order to pursue the bad guys. Amid the flurry of hostage-taking, Jamie is cool and insightful enough to restate the situation in objective terms, clarifying the issues for both himself and the audience:

> War. Yes. I'm seeing it all now [...] This is a battle between two men. One of them, Power, wants the world to work properly with justice and equality and all those things. The other one, Hackman, just wants the world to work. Period. I figured all that out a while ago but I couldn't figure out my part in it all. But I learned. Experience taught me. I'm a pacifist. (181)

Jamie is beginning to understand this bizarre game, and he has no wish to play. Through him, the audience is made aware that non-involvement in political issues need not be a sign of cowardice; when both sides have lost their original positive differences in a maelstrom of rhetoric and revenge, Jamie's may be the only rational position.

Although Walker's later plays no longer contain any self-conscious literary imitation of European models, there remain a number of deeply-embedded characteristics reminiscent of the plays of Bertolt Brecht. The progression of self-contained scenes, the exotic locations, musical accompaniments and songs, and the characters' own commentary on the action are all features associated with Brecht's theatre. Other techniques of alienation are also used to prevent the audience from feeling too much empathy with the characters or from getting too involved in the action; for instance, Walker's frequently preposterous situations and incongruous epigrammatic dialogue forestall an extended suspension of disbelief. In addition, the characters' periodic verbal reminders of just who stands for what ideologically encourages the audience to critically examine the validity of what these people believe in, or what they say they believe in, if they believe in anything at all. Walker pays tribute to Brecht's influence in *The Art of War*, whose title is apparently taken from a passage in *The Messingkauf Dialogues*: "The art of acting needs to be treated simply as an elementary human utterance which contains its own purpose. That's where it differs from the art of war, whose purpose is external to itself" (98). The Brechtian contrast between rational and emotional appeals is also particularly strong in *The Art of War*, in the way we sympathize with the liberal humanitarian team despite the fact that they behave so stupidly.

Walker's choice of settings and themes may do something to dispel the oft-repeated notion that Canadian drama must reflect local and regional concerns. Although the exotic settings of many of his plays do not draw on any common experience within his audience, they at least put the audience on common ground, purposely using the popular misconceptions of jungle primitivism or post-war nausea as a kind of film-induced pop mythology. In his Tyrone Power "trilogy," Walker instead uses a generalized North American urban setting which is also common ground for a Canadian audience, either through their own urban lives or through the dominant urban imagery of television and film. In these three plays of modern liberal angst, he is also exploring themes which are of personal concern to a broad segment of society. Walker is writing about the loss of political innocence experienced by his contemporaries, the children of the baby boom, at the same time as their loss of youth. In the 1960s, this generation believed that they were able to change the values of society by virtue of their own liberal ideals, a rather naive faith sustained by their youth and their disproportionately large numbers. As the decade ended, this faith was shattered by violence, the certain knowledge gained on the grounds of Kent State University that the forces of reaction would shoot to kill. In the 1970s this generation backed away from their social causes and turned inward, establishing an alternative lifestyle outside the system or a career within it, turning from the Age of Aquarius to the Me Decade. These stages are recapitulated in Power's circumstances in *Gossip* and *Filthy Rich*; he is an equally sympathetic character as a career truth-seeker of the '60s or as an embittered dropout of the '70s. But when Power takes up the old crusading postures again in *The Art of War*, he looks ridiculous. More balance and more self-awareness are needed if idealism is to make a comeback, qualities only displayed in Jamie. Despite his unimposing stature, Jamie has great courage, including the courage to refuse to play a destructive game. His is the spark of a new idealism for which the congealing liberals in the audience have been waiting and hoping. For Jamie is young and street-smart, and is not likely to make the same mistakes.

There is certainly no "school" of Canadian playwriting into which Walker may be conveniently slotted. This is partly because his work is so recent and his style is so distinctive, but also because this style continues to change. Despite his status as one of Canada's most-produced playwrights, Walker still seems to be a playwright-in-progress. Since re-affirming his commitment to theatre about the time of *Ramona and the White Slaves*, Walker has moved into a decidedly more popular theatrical vein, as several critics have noted:

> The man who appears to be among Canada's most abstruse and esoteric playwrights has, in fact, a thorough grasp of populist techniques, and can use the forms of popular theatre as both popular vehicle and as a means of sharing with a broader audience a more demanding dramatic view. [He addresses] a popular, middle-class audience within the conventions it knows best, and in the process, he gives them some penetrating analysis of themselves. (Johnson 101)

This reaching out to a larger audience is not to be confused with pandering to the lowest common denominator, *à la* [Allan Stratton's] *Nurse Jane Goes to Hawaii.* In Walker's more accessible plays, he is not welching on his promise, but rather fulfilling it. He is developing forms which entertain his audiences and themes which intrigue them. Walker has not attracted very much serious criticism to date, perhaps because his earlier plays did not warrant it, or perhaps because his delight in the forms of popular culture conceal his more serious intentions. His style is still undergoing rapid and positive evolution, and its ultimate destination is not clear, but those who watch Canadian theatre had better watch George F. Walker.

(1984)

## Notes

[1] For biographical details, see "Biographical"; Wasserman, "Making" 101; Wallace and Zimmerman.

[2] Dates given are those of first performances rather than of publication.

## Works Cited

"Biographical Checklist: George F. Walker." *Canadian Theatre Review* 25 (Winter 1980): 39-41.

Brecht, Bertolt. *The Messingkauf Dialogues.* Trans. John Willett. London: Methuen, 1965.

Fraser, John. "Walker Turns to Murder with Comedy." *The Globe and Mail* 19 April 1977: 16.

Gass, Ken. Introduction. *Three Plays: Bagdad Saloon, Beyond Mozambique, Ramona and the White Slaves.* By George F. Walker. Toronto: Coach House, 1978. 9-15.

Johnson, Chris. "George F. Walker: B-Movies Beyond the Absurd." *Canadian Literature* (1980): 87-103.

Walker, George F. *The Art of War. The Power Plays* 133-84.

———. *Filthy Rich. The Power Plays* 73-132.

———. *Gossip. The Power Plays* 15-72.

———. *The Power Plays.* Toronto: Coach House, 1984.

———. *Three Plays: Bagdad Saloon, Beyond Mozambique, Ramona and the White Slaves.* Toronto: Coach House, 1978.

Wallace, Robert, and Cindy Zimmerman. *The Work: Conversations with English-Canadian Playwrights.* Toronto: Coach House, 1982.

Wasserman, Jerry. "Making Things Clear: The *Film Noir* Plays of George F. Walker." *Canadian Drama/L'Art dramatique canadien* 8 (1982): 99-101.

———. "Towards the Definitive Anthology." *Canadian Theatre Review* 34 (Spring 1982): 172-79.

## Looking for the Light: A Conversation with George F. Walker

by Robert Wallace

**Wallace:** It's been approximately six years since we talked about your work. Has it changed during those years?

**Walker:** Well, I've changed, so I suppose it must have—in obvious as well as subtle ways. I think the voice is still the same but, thematically, the work has diversified and gone in different ways. Sometimes I'm aware of the changes but mostly I'm made aware of them by people who are alarmed by them. So much categorization and labelling takes place in the theatre, especially if you have a body of work. People come with expectations and if you don't fulfill them, then they think you've made a mistake. In fact, you're just naturally, organically, moving in another direction, just trying to do different things. The stories become different, your concerns become different. For me it was a matter of letting more light into my plays; just naturally, I felt I had to do that, see what sort of hope—that's not a good word; "possibility" might be better—I could find. More than anything, that's the major change I think: I'm getting more possibility, more future, into the work. The early plays don't have much hope for the future; their essential concern is "what is the world?"—what is the nature of the chaos there? Now it's more a question of how to deal with it, how to fight through it. And, if anything, it's a stronger question.

**Wallace:** When we talked about your work in 1981, you had just finished writing *Theatre of the Film Noir*. After that came *The Art of War*, which finished the Power trilogy. Then you seemed to shift into a new subject area related more to your own biography, specifically to your life in Toronto. When you look back at your early plays, those that are published as *Three Plays*, how do you feel about them now?

**Walker:** Well, it depends. Sometimes they seem very far away; but occasionally—and, again, I think it's because the voice is the same—they're very familiar. I think it's partly because the sense of humour remains the same throughout the work. I just think of them as a younger me. I recognize the energy in them, and I can't—don't—try to reproduce it: I don't have it anymore. I hope I have something else. I recognize the anger in them too; or maybe not anger so much as hunger, a hunger to find something. I don't feel located from them, but I don't feel precious about them either. Just last year I heard about a very interesting production of *Ramona and the White Slaves* in Vancouver by a young director who had directed my plays in school and wanted to take a shot at *Ramona* in a professional setting. I would have loved to have seen it; just hearing about it, and reading some of the reviews, made me really excited because they seemed to get it. There was one luscious review that talked about the hypnotic and hallucinogenic quality of the material in which the reviewer said "I don't know what it's about, but it's infecting;" and then he took a stab at some of the themes and he was dead on. That means something—to hear about a young director coming together with your young work.

**Wallace:** When you talked about *Ramona* in 1981 you said you'd like to have a crack at reworking it, because you felt you were on to a subliminal way of writing that was important. You also felt that you were working in somewhat the same manner on *Theatre of the Film Noir.*

**Walker:** That method pops up every once in a while, but never in one whole play like it did in *Ramona*, because *Ramona* was designed to respond to the rhythms of dreams. But as I become more confident, and as I deal with a larger audience, I let more of myself into the work, and then that method just becomes natural, I think. Now I trust that if I write something, it's me, no matter where it comes from. But I'm also responding more to where the play is going to be done now. For example, I knew that *Nothing Sacred* was going into Toronto's Bluma Appel Theatre if it was going anywhere. The first time I worked in that space was with *Better Living* which was written without such a big theatre in mind. I learned a lot from seeing that play occur in a theatre for which it wasn't planned. You have to keep those things in mind, I think.

**Wallace:** Although you had directed your own work before—I'm thinking specifically of the second production of *Beyond Mozambique* in Toronto—it was with *Theatre of the Film Noir* that you really announced yourself as a director of your own work, picking up Dora awards for best director and playwright that year. Since then, you've frequently directed your own plays, although you still allow other directors to do them on occasion. Why is this?

**Walker:** Well, I tend to like the spirit my closeness to the material allows the actors to achieve. In fact, I'm not as protective about my work as a lot of directors are; I encourage actors to "free fall," telling them that the material will hold them. You know, as long as an actor puts his soul into a character it doesn't really matter to me how he says a line; what's important is that he believes it. I enjoyed directing for quite a while. But then I got the feeling that I wasn't trusting other people to direct and, you know, the essential truth of theatre is trust and collaboration. So, in the last couple of years, I've backed away from directing and said, "I must find collaborators." Besides, it would be pretty awful if you had to go everywhere to direct your own work. You might even lose trust in actors, and then you'd have no right to be in a theatre. Originally, I started directing because I wanted to work with actors and make something—to enjoy theatre in the way that actors can. Playwrights often seem detached from the process of making theatre, as if they're just there to protect their own product. I think that my directing came mostly from trying to get closer to the fun of theatre, to the creativity of it. Before that, it was like I wrote a play on my own and then went into the theatre essentially as a translator, a protector. That didn't seem to me a very creative thing to do.

**Wallace:** It's fascinating to hear you say this because your attitude brings up contemporary arguments about the authority of the playwright, his or her "ownership" of the text. If I understand you, you're indicating your belief that theatre is much more than just the text, that it is, in fact, what happens between actors and audience in a particular space and time. And you're also suggesting that you are as much interested in being a part of that event of movement, light, and sound as you are in writing the text. Do you have any thoughts about the current questions surrounding an author's rights over the interpretation of his text—*when* the play happens, and how?

**Walker:** I guess it can happen both on the page and on the stage with the actors; and one version can be an enhancement of the other, or can offer a totally different prismatic effect that you didn't expect. I don't think there are any rules about this; but I believe you have to intuitively trust the text, yet you must write for theatre, allowing that space into the work. If you do, the voice of the work should remain intact. Sometimes an actor will ask me, "Is the character sad or happy at this particular moment?" Well, I say, if you can convince me of either, I'll buy either, because I think it's open to interpretation. Which is also the way I write. Is that line funny? Well, we'll discover that, won't we? And we might discover that while it's funny one night, it's startling another night, and just nothing some other night—that that laugh that was there has moved two pages on in the text. It's both the nature of theatre, and the way of my work. I don't structure the plays comically with that "set up, set up, punch" design. It's all up for grabs. I leave the actors room. I believe that I put the characters in the play and that they are who they are, and that five or six different actors can do them and they'll still be who they are.

**Wallace:** So you're open to discovering what the actors discover. Even when you think that you've written a character or a line in a particular way, and then find it presented quite differently in performance.

**Walker:** Yes, but I still can think that I've written that character a particular way. What can happen is that I can put the actor's version together with the one I had, because I've left the space for that. Finally, I believe that you can take everything away from theatre except the actor and the audience; you can even take away the text. I think that the actor is the theatre, and he is your text. If you don't trust actors, and if you can't get them to trust you, you're out of luck. I've been very fortunate to work with actors who believe in the material and who also have come to understand that the best way to do the material is to free fall, is to trust that things can occur without having to set them up to occur, that the character you thought you had at the beginning might be totally changed by brushing against other characters in the play, that new things can occur that none of us imagined before we began rehearsal: that there is a kind of a soul to the work that always remains intact.

**Wallace:** Could we talk a bit about a specific character, then,—Tyrone M. Power, the central character of the Power plays. Are you finished with Power?

**Walker:** I don't know. I mean, at the moment I am. At the end of *The Art of War* which saw him wounded, dispirited and defeated, I thought I should leave him there and let him die; but I might bring him back. I still haven't decided. I did have one more play in mind.

**Wallace:** For me, Power suffers a process of persistent demoralization: with each play, he seems to lose more ground, as well as his friends, dog, fish, and his vocation. But he does find a sense of his identity which, in *The Art of War*, is partially fuelled by his obsession to stop Hackman.

**Walker:** Power's a guy with the potential to take on the world; but the more he tries, the smaller and tighter his focus gets; and the more cranky and miserable and indignant he gets, the more ineffective he becomes. His obsession comes out of some kind of moral clarity, but something happens to him that renders him pathetic and useless, impractical and frighteningly ineffective. I felt that Power was taking a natural journey in those plays. In *The Art of War* he is presented with a dilemma that he cannot solve: he comes face to face with his enemy—the fascist mind that he most despises; yet while his enemy is ready to kill him, Power is not willing to kill him; so he turns into a puddle on the floor. It's the old liberal predicament. I couldn't resolve it for him, but I see now that the future lies not so much with Power as with Jamie, who provides a kind of practical answer in the play, safely away from ideology. For Jamie, if we're going to take on these guys, we're gonna do it to win, or at least to survive; we're not just gonna go in there with our indignation and our words. So if there's a fourth Power play, I think it will be about Jamie who will have something to teach Power about how to fight his enemies in this world. The only thing I saw about the fourth play was that it would be a continuation of *The Art of War*. It would allow for Power's revenge, but it would have to start with Power even farther down, sort of sitting in a wheelchair reading Thoreau, trying to reaffirm those liberal notions at the most pathetic level that I could find. Jamie would be plotting some kind of revenge. By this point, Power would have convinced Jamie that there is something more in life than money, that there are notions of justice and stuff …

**Wallace:** And Jamie would have given Power a way to live, perhaps. By the end of *The Art of War*, the two characters certainly seem necessary to each other.

**Walker:** Oh yes, I felt that as soon as I put them together.

**Wallace:** Like Zastrozzi and Verezzi in *Zastrozzi*; or, to jump ahead five years to *Nothing Sacred*, like Bazarov and Arkady? Actually, Bazarov reminds me of Power in that the more he asserts his nihilism, the more he ends up telling everybody he loves them; the more that he sets out to destroy the existing order, the more he effects reconciliation amongst the people he meets. After all, his death at the end of the play—the death of a nihilist—would hardly elicit the sympathy it does if he hadn't been able to affect other people with love, even if it was against his wishes.

**Walker:** I think that's the difficult nature of Bazarov and his journey. At the top of the play, clearly he is unable to talk to the peasant who he saves from a beating, telling Arkady to deal with his wounds; he can't even say "you're welcome" to him, the notion being that he can't look the peasants in the eye until they get off their knees. During the play he somehow comes to understand that he has to do that, and that the roots of his nihilism are a profound concern. Unless you reconcile the roots of nihilism with the ways in which your actions affect people, you really are a person out of your time, perhaps out of your planet. If you forget that your work, and all your indignation and your anger, comes from the way people are being treated—the so-called victims—then you can't talk to the victims, and your feeling for them is useless. I watched Bazarov make that journey, took it with him; and I tried to lay in that understanding so that he would undergo more than a mental exercise.

**Wallace:** The journey that Bazarov undergoes in *Nothing Sacred* seems very similar to the overall journey charted by your plays. If you look at your characters all the way from Ahrun in *Bagdad Saloon*, who is desperate to find or create some sense of self in what is basically a moral and spiritual desert, to those in the East End plays, many of whom are victimized by their marginalized social status, they describe a sort of arc which moves from nothingness—which you might want to talk about as nihilism—to a type of social commitment, even action, in the face of social problems.

**Walker:** I think that's very accurate. You begin with anger and energy; but then you face things—the details of life—and you meet the emptiness that you're afraid of. I think that's true in my work, and it's probably true in my life. It's funny that I'm writing about Bazarov at this time because I read *Fathers and Sons* when I was 17 years old, and I related so strongly to that character then. That I should get around to writing about him when I'm 40, and still relate to him so strongly, is odd because I'm no longer just a son; I'm a father, too, and I have to come to grips with that, to understand that as well.

**Wallace:** Could we talk about the East End plays, because we haven't covered them before. *Criminals in Love*, *Better Living*, and *Beautiful City*. Are they a trilogy?

**Walker:** I guess they could become one in some ways. I mean, they're all about the East End of Toronto, and two of them are definitely connected character-wise; and the third, *Beautiful City*, is connected in spirit as well. I guess you could call them a trilogy; they're close enough.

**Wallace:** Perhaps we could focus on *Criminals in Love*, if only because it's the best known of the three. I particularly like the character of Junior Dawson who works for me as an initiate in the play. I mean, he's being taught about life, initiated into practicalities with some very cruel experiences. At the end of the play, there seems to be very little future for Junior inasmuch as he will probably end up in prison like his father. Yet you give him a moment's respite in Gail's arms, so that we can truly remember him as a "criminal in love." But because he is doomed, his love seems all the more poignant, if not tragic. Is my reading of the ending more negative than yours?

**Walker:** I think your reading doesn't include what might be possible, that the love which the two characters feel for each other might somehow get them through. Their love is so strong and clean and clear-headed, especially hers, that it might be able to meet the challenge. As long as she keeps her head and he keeps his heart, they have a fighting chance. I thought the ending was pretty desperate but that there was some kind of hope or, if not hope (I really don't like that word), then possibility for the future. I guess that's when I began to let possibility enter into the endings of my work.

**Wallace:** It's quite a change from *Mozambique*'s power of evil growing in the jungle or even Power's disillusionment and fatigue, perhaps impotence, at the end of *The Art of War*. With the East End plays you seem to be suggesting salvation through love, or the possibility of it. This is really clear in the ending of *Beautiful City* where there's a union of two people who have been very skeptical about one another throughout the play. It's almost as if, after the Power plays, you begin to suggest that while the future might be limited by social constraints, it's still possible. And that the future lies in love.

**Walker:** I think it really is a matter of searching for possibilities, of looking for the light; wherever I can, I let the light come through. You know, I was accused by some people of creating a sentimental ending for *Beautiful City*. I think the ending *was* full of sentiment, but that it grew organically out of the play; I believed that ending had to happen. I never said the characters were going to be happy, either; I said they might get married, that they *wanted* to be happy, how bout that? But you're right, that's a big difference: the characters really want to be happy. I'm tired of being wretched and self-consumed. I wanted to let the characters find each other. You know, writing really is funny like that; at a certain point, you begin to ask yourself, "Have I been preventing people from finding each other all this time? Have I been what's in the way?" So I just started to get out of the way sometimes and let the possibilities happen. There's still some pretty nasty stuff going on in this world: I'm not trying to hide away from it. But I believed in the ending: I wrote that play hot, and it happened.

**Wallace:** For me, the East End plays also are more political than the work that precedes them. The moral emptiness that led to aesthetic exploration in the early plays changed in the Power plays to a concern with moral corruption and Power's despair. In the East End plays, moral corruption becomes social oppression, the thumbs of money and position pinning down those who are marginally positioned in our so-called "beautiful cities" like Toronto. By the time we get to *Nothing Sacred*, the various types of people that you've been writing about throughout your work are brought together—the nihilists, the underclass, the upperclass—yet none of them is valorized, none is privileged over the other because each is made a student of the other. This is one of the reasons why the play is so satisfying to me.

**Walker:** Again, it's probably the end of a cycle or the beginning of another one. Like *Zastrozzi*, it's a watershed play. I believe that the East End plays allowed me to get closer to the bone. I started them because I thought I was avoiding stuff in the writing—where I was brought up, notions of class … I wanted to address these things with my own voice. I have a friend, an Australian writer, who wrote me a letter after he read *Criminals*; he said he liked it so much because it talked about bad luck; I believe that after all the theories have been written, there's still the hanging shadow. That's what Junior's going on about with his "why won't anyone listen to me, I just don't deserve this kind of stuff." Like he says, "I really haven't brought this on myself at all, I've tried, I really have tried."

**Wallace:** I know you read a lot; do you read with an attempt to achieve or articulate an ideology? Might the changes in your plays that reflect a growing political awareness or social consciousness have anything to do with a political or ideological position that you are pursuing?

**Walker:** No, I don't think so. My ideological position has always been one of not understanding ideology, of just trying to come to grips with what I think are the moral injustices of the world. I generally distrust ideology as a limited road to a limited truth. I just try to get close to my characters and their situations, and let my concern for them be open.

**Wallace:** But you create their situations: they don't exist separately from you, even though you like to talk about them as if they have lives of their own. I mean, it's you who puts them into a social context where they are, say, underprivileged; you put Junior into a family in which the father is a petty thief.

**Walker:** Right, I'm loading the deck or, more, I'm loading the gun. I remember at a performance of *Criminals*, Jack Layton, an NDP councillor for the City of Toronto who had come to see the play, got up and said how much he enjoyed the show, although he didn't know what its politics were. I said to myself, well, of course, cause he's trying to slot the play into his socialist ideology and I'm just writing about the politics of life. I suppose you could probably find a kind of socialist critique in the play, but it wouldn't cohere finally because, at some point, like I say, the play starts to talk about bad luck, which is more than being oppressed; this is *bad luck*, the hanging shadow, and I guess I'm saying, "stay alert, cause there's no ideology's gonna get you through this." These are the problems—here, here, and here—and we'll solve them any damn way we can with any resources we can come up with, including trickery or love. You always get someone trying to fit the plays into their ideology, and when they can't, they think there's something wrong with the politics of the play or even that it's not political. I think all three plays are very political in different ways. *Better Living*, for example, is political about the family; it's about patriarchy, and that's political. I mean that's the essential question of life on this planet: who's gonna run these things and must it always be that kind of pressurized male soul?

**Wallace:** Nora, the mother in *Better Living*, is an amazing character. One of the things I find really interesting about what she's doing in the play, theatrically, psychologically, and, I guess, politically by implication—undermining the kitchen: she's digging a pit or a bomb shelter or some sort of post-modern variation of the old root cellar underneath the kitchen, continually removing dirt and hauling in planks.

**Walker:** Nora, in fact, is the first East End positive character I wrote because, chronologically, I wrote *Better Living* before *Criminals in Love*, even though it was produced after. Nora is my first clear response to what we've talked about as the change in my writing, the focusing on my past, what I'd been avoiding. All Nora is doing, really, is taking everything she possibly can and trying to make it better. She has no space in the house, so she tries to create space; this is typical of her response to any problem that comes up in the family; she turns it into something good or, at least, she tries to. She doesn't give up even when she gets a madman for a husband: she tries to turn him into something better. She is the first of what we've talked about as a "possibility" character. Because it was important for me to test this type of character, I put her under a lot of pressure, to test the possibility, to see how far she would go. What was important was that she held up. The worse things got, the better she got in some way; she took all that stuff and translated it into "betterism," as I call it. Sometimes that meant not exactly hearing the way the other characters speak, or not looking as if she knew what she was doing; but this was only part of her process of turning things into something better.

**Wallace:** She's got all those daughters to deal with too, as well as that husband. In retrospect, this seems to have been your play for women; I don't mean a play for women in the audience, but one that allows you to introduce a variety of women who represent a spectrum of social positions.

**Walker:** Again, that was a turning point for me, another watershed play. As I said, one of the things I'd avoided dealing with in the work was where I'd been brought up; another was the fact that my life has been composed primarily of women. I have three sisters, my first wife had three sisters, my current wife has a sister, and we have two daughters; I've always had women in my life. But *Better Living* wasn't just an ode to them, it was me saying okay, here they are. Up until that point when I was writing about women I always tried not to pretend that I was writing about them with any kind of psychological authority; in my early plays I tried to make women socially and psychologically aware of how men looked at them; I always tried to give them that ability. From that point on I've tried to make them rich and deep, have tried to deal with the psychology of the character seriously.

**Wallace:** Did the shift to the new subject matter and your more personal relationship to the material result in any deliberate changes in style? Did you find yourself wanting to write a different type of character differently?

**Walker:** No. And I think part of the reason that I had avoided this material earlier was that I was afraid that it would affect the voice. But when I shifted I felt that the voice was intact, and that it would go to this new work and that whatever happened to it would just be natural. When I started *Better Living*, it was just a great rush for me; I felt I had been released. This all ties back to *Sacktown Rag*, I guess, the first time I tried to deal with this material, which wasn't very successful.

**Wallace:** It's interesting to me that when you began to write you chose not to deal with your own background and, perhaps as a result, chose a style that eschewed naturalism. In retrospect, it seems fortunate that you found your voice in theatricality, because when you finally began to address biographical details, you didn't have to resort to naturalism. It's very important for me to go on record as saying that I don't believe any of your work is naturalistic; in that sense, the work following the *film noir* plays does not represent so much a stylistic change as a modification. Would you agree?

**Walker:** Yes, yes, exactly true. And if I hadn't felt that was possible, I probably would have put them off for another five or ten years. They were ready to be written and I felt the voice opening up.

**Wallace:** It does seem to me, however—and I'm not trying to trick you here—that there are two types of characters and, as a result, two types of scenes in your newer work: for example, the scene between Junior and his father that begins the second act of *Criminals in Love* achieves a manic, grotesque theatricality, as does the scene where William visits the father to plead on Junior's behalf; yet, in the same play, the scenes between Junior and Gail are much more subtle, approaching a quality of naturalism. In *Nothing Sacred* I also picked up the same dichotomy, for you give us a type of character who is played like a grotesque or a buffoon—Piotr, for example—and other characters, like Akardy or Fenichka, who function in a more naturalistic mode. Would you agree that there are these two types of characters in your newer plays?

**Walker:** Yeah, and I think they're riding the edges of each other, and they're meeting more carefully now. I think the voice, my writing voice, is with them both, trusting the shifts in tone, trusting those extremes more, trusting that these two types can be together, like different colours. In effect, I'm saying that's what the world is like, and I'm opening up the panel more to see more of the world.

**Wallace:** In effect, then, you're saying that the world has its Winevas who, as in *Criminals in Love*, we may or may not perceive as mad, and, at the same time, it has its Juniors who are ostensibly ordinary, but who, in fact, can be considered extraordinary. I'm stressing this point because it counters the critical objection that some of your recent work is "uneven," is foundering somewhere between the naturalistic and the grotesque.

**Walker:** If people are having trouble, it's probably because they are referring back to earlier models like *Theatre of the Film Noir* or *Zastrozzi* which were more stylistically consistent. I don't think my new plays are any less successful; in fact, for me they're much more successful because they're trying to bring more things together, they're trusting the stuff we talked about in '81—like the fusion of the comic and the serious—not just stylistic differences but tonal differences as well, just letting them ride. As I said, if you maintain one model for my work, the new stuff is gonna look wrong. But I don't think it's uneven, I think it's in process. Of course it's flawed. Flaws are essential to its strength.

**Wallace:** I'm glad to hear you say these things because when I saw *Beautiful City* I worried that there might be more than a coincidental connection between you and Paul Gallagher, the central character of that play—that his crisis about the meaning and utility of his work as an architect might also be your crisis as a playwright. Specifically, I remember that his speech in the second act, in which he talks about the people who inhabit the buildings he has designed, made me think of you: I wondered if you were questioning or criticizing the people who "inhabit" the theatres in which your plays are presented—both the audience you attract and the characters you create. Because of the connections I was making—and I realize they were completely subjective—I found this play the most personal of all your work, and perhaps the most moving. Am I off-track here?

**Walker:** No, I think Paul is me, but I'm not sure at what stage. You're not the only one to have mentioned that connection, or that specific speech. Obviously I was aware of its significance as soon as I wrote it. It had a lot to do with feeling trapped in a career choice that I don't even remember making. You know, when you turn 40, you're inclined to ask, "Am I gonna be doing this the rest of my life?" And, "what have I done; have I accomplished anything; and will I accomplish anything, and what about all this stuff—Who's it for, who is it for?" I think the questions had a lot to do with turning 40 but also with Toronto, not just theatre in Toronto, but Toronto in Toronto—you know, growing up in a city that, well, you didn't even have to love because it was just home, just a place, and then seeing what was going on here, how it was becoming scary and sad and alienating. I was questioning Toronto, as well. Anyway, whatever it was, it ended with the writing of the play.

**Wallace:** I felt that it would have to end, that you would come out of it with something new, or you wouldn't come out of it at all. It was therefore very important for me to see *Nothing Sacred*; after *Beautiful City* I wondered if you were adapting Turgenev as a way of filling time before you found a new direction—adapting someone else's work because you had nothing new to say or explore on your own. It was wonderful to find that *Nothing Sacred* is not so much an adaptation as a transposition. It really is much more your play than Turgenev's novel.

**Walker:** Another watershed.

(1988)

## Walker's Women in the East End Plays: *Love and Anger*

by Mary Pat Mombourquette

*Love and Anger* is deceptive; like *Criminals in Love* and *Beautiful City*, it seems to tell one man's story. At the beginning of *Love and Anger* Maxwell appears to pick up where Paul in *Beautiful City* left off; like Paul, Maxwell wants the ultimate form of love, self-recognition, but unlike Paul, he does not look for satisfaction from a woman. Maxwell looks to society for self-recognition and therein comes the anger. Maxwell's desire for love is transformed into anger by a society that deems beings worthy of recognition only in relation to its dominant ideology. Because Paul is young, white, middle-class and male, he may perhaps find a place for himself within the society of the "beautiful city." *Love and Anger*, however, exposes the problems of others—the infirm, the black, the poor, the insane—as they try to find their place in society.

When Walker brings these others on stage the play shifts direction from being just one man's story to encompass a multiplicity not apparent in the East End plays. The other characters in *Love and Anger*—Sarah, Eleanor, Gail, Conner, and Harris—are distinct personalities with the ability to make a connection to Maxwell, as well as to the spectator. Unlike Walker's characterization of Junior and Paul, the character Maxwell does not want someone to stand in for the pre-Oedipal Mother who will recreate for him the prelinguistic universe of wholeness. As Walker portrays him, Maxwell is looking to create a new society, albeit based on this fantasy. "I want to undermine the entire institutional bias of our culture," (14) Maxwell tells Gail. However, in *Love and Anger* Walker not only explores the manner in which Maxwell tries to subvert society but he sets up a conflicting pole in Sarah and exposes her method of dealing with the crisis she faces as she tries to establish a place for herself within the social system.

*Love and Anger* is set in a "damp grimy office in the basement of an old building" (12), which establishes the world the characters inhabit as the world of the downcast. Within the confines of this playing space Maxwell, a formerly successful lawyer who has now found the error of his ways, tries to recreate a social system that takes into consideration people not considered to be of much consequence in a patriarchal society. Maxwell is aided in this quest by his loyal but unsympathetic secretary (Eleanor), her mentally-ill sister (Sarah), and a young black client who wants her husband released from prison (Gail). Together, yet in their own individual ways, they fight the forces of evil in the form of Babe Conner, a newspaper publisher, and his lawyer Sean Harris.

Maxwell goes about undermining society, which caters to Conner and Harris and their ilk, by subverting the institutional bias on which that society is based, the system of exchange. As he informs Gail, "More and more I've come to believe you have to take money away from these people and their system in order to be truly satisfied. I mean it's the thing they and their system value most" (14-15). Maxwell, a "former greedy prick" (70-71), has knowledge of the patriarchal society where one can only fight power with equal power. His past privileged position within that society has established his thought process whereby he believes he must create a power base, because without one his cause is lost. Maxwell's plan to "deke the legal establishment right out of its pants" (14) has nothing to do with justice; it has to do with establishing dominance. His plan of the moment involves: "blackmailing a judge with some invented indiscretion. Getting him to grant an appeal to save his own reputation. Perhaps even getting him to recommend a financial compensation for wrongful imprisonment" (14).

In *Love and Anger* Walker illustrates that within society, power is the highest good and law is the embodiment of power relations in society, relations created by economics. In other words, money is power and power is money, and the law will do its best to uphold the powerful. Harris and Maxwell acknowledge this point:

> **HARRIS.** If we bankrupt the country all the rest is more or less meaningless. Even with your new philosophy, whatever it is, surely you must still understand that the economy is everything.
> **MAXWELL.** The economy as it stands. And you and your kind define it. (27)

Maxwell explains this system to Gail: "You'll get no true satisfaction from the law. You're marginal. Your cause is marginal. Outside the corridor, so to speak" (13). The "corridor" Maxwell speaks of is the corridor of power and as power is an euphemism for money Gail is placed outside its realm. Within society Gail's economic value is minimal; thus she is termed "marginal" (13).

The law is connected to Gail's marginality because within its boundaries Gail is rendered powerless. Maxwell talks about the law as being "vulgar. Just like religion. Vulgar things both of them. Institutions corrupted by their own self-importance. I'm immune to their seductive power"(13). The "seductive power" of the law, and likewise religion, is that it has the ability to absolve us from our guilt. Both religion and law gain their authority from a transcendental power, God. This authority is used to undermine the state of being where instincts reign absolute and replaces it with values and morals that exist to establish society and its elite class at the expense of marginal beings.

In Walker's earlier East End plays, he illustrates how an individual's initial desires are compromised by society to benefit that society. In *Beautiful City* Paul's desires create a being fraught with guilt. It is only after these desires are repressed and replaced by socially acceptable desires that he can be free to exist in society, absolved from any guilt. In *Love and Anger* Maxwell acknowledges that the laws of society are created to make man in an image society deems acceptable: "I was talking about the law. Trying to let you know that even though I'm constrained by it, I'm not impressed by it. The law is vulgar in its rigidity. Insensitive to the nuance of human existence. Derived and constructed from knowledge within a narrow historical corridor. In short, it's in love with itself" (13). Maxwell's description of the law recalls Marx's account of the need for creative flexibility to enable social progress:

> [W]hat [is wealth] if not the absolute elaboration of [man's] creative dispositions, without any preconditions other than antecedent historical evolution which makes the totality of this evolution—i.e. the evolution of all human powers as such, unmeasured by any *previously established* yardstick—an end in itself? What is this, if not a situation where man does not reproduce himself in any determined form, but produces his totality? Where he does not seek to remain something formed by the past, but is in the absolute movement of becoming? (*Pre-Capitalist* 84-85)

Marx's views on progress—that it is creative, not bound by the past except for past evolution—are suggested in Walker's characterization of Maxwell. Maxwell is portrayed in *Love and Anger* as in "the absolute movement of becoming" or as he states it, "we are about to become history in the making" (15). This is reminiscent of Mary's line in *Beautiful City*, "we don't care to make history" (246), which in that play brings Paul's image to mind. The similarity between Paul and Maxwell—in their commitment to producing their "totality" (where social identity and personal identity are bonded) and not "to remain something formed by the past"—is further embellished when Maxwell talks to Eleanor about life before his stroke:

> **MAXWELL.** [...] I was a lawyer. I defended the obviously guilty. And the obviously not guilty. You typed. You answered the phone. You prepared affidavits. Where did it get us. Where did it get the world. What did we accomplish.
>
> **ELEANOR.** It was a job. We did our jobs.
>
> **MAXWELL.** It was death. Death was surrounding us like a demon inevitability. I suffered a stroke. It was something I could have done without, but I decided to turn it to my advantage. My brain is new. (17)

Maxwell and Paul both find themselves in a position where life is seeping out of their bodies because of the social constraints placed on them. The function of work, as illustrated by Walker in both these plays, is to kill the dreams and aspirations of the being by keeping him or her busy with trying to attain the dreams society deems acceptable.

Like law and religion, work is a controlling device used by the elite class which affects the submission of the socially disempowered. As Maxwell explains it to Harris, "work is part of a systematic oppressive machine which conspires to deprive people of the options and the knowledge which are their fundamental rights" (25), or put more simply by Tom in *Better Living*, "[Y]ou make work.[...] to keep people busy so they don't think" (176). For both Paul and Maxwell their work is initially successful in keeping them isolated from their selves but as the death of their psychic being becomes represented by the dying of their physical being they both begin to look inwards to find some solution to their problems. The difference between the characters is in the seriousness of their physical illnesses which are metaphorical representations of their guilt.

Whereas Paul is described by Gina Mae as "sliding into hell" (255) with "a lot of money, good connections, [and] a strong support system" (255) still intact, Maxwell is described by Conner as "in the bowels of hell without any resources" (50). Paul is sliding but he has not lost everything and he still maintains the dream of salvation in the form of Gina Mae. Therefore he still harbours some hope for the social order. Maxwell, however, has hit rock bottom. And Maxwell now maintains, "I no longer recognize this society or its governing body. I am a citizen of the new era. I call this the age of getting even" (22). Paul's existence is based on guilt; Maxwell, on the other hand, has gone beyond guilt: he has "repented" (70). As Maxwell explains it: "You just say to yourself 'I repent.' You send a message out to the world that you're sorry for what you've been. Any kind of message" (70). Repentance by definition is "sorrow, regret or contrition for past action or conduct." In Maxwell's case repentance carries with it a sense of past and of history. For Maxwell repentance implies a sense of returning to the point of departure after completing a full cycle, which he admits when he tells Harris, "I'm back! I'm reborn. I'm like a little kid—still half-formed. But I'm growing" (26).

Maxwell repents to effect inner healing. It comes out of his guilt, his feeling of being unworthy. Walker brings this situation back into the Oedipal configuration. Paradigmatic of the child who recognizes the mother's desire for the father, a desire which excludes the child and thereby establishes his or her lack, Maxwell recognizes his wife's desire for some other and thereby his lack is established. Maxwell describes his former self: "The man I used to be didn't deserve a good marriage. Even to a jerk like Sandra" (31). Maxwell's self-contempt over the "distracted" (32) state his life had become is admitted to Harris: "Did I ever tell you how much it hurt me when I found out about you and Sandra. [...] It killed me a bit. It darkened my life. Made me feel like one of God's lowest creatures" (32). By defining himself as "one of God's lowest creatures," Maxwell establishes his position in relation to The Father. God, the transcendent being, is used to perpetuate the myth of a higher good than the individual, to establish human lack. The myth that there is something more than the human is in fact a way of harnessing the individual's being to serve society and its goals. It assumes control and creates structure within the flux of nature. It carries with it society's promise of permanence, structure, and immortality which does battle with nature's passage of time, experience and life (see French 92-93).

Maxwell does not accept the traditional patriarchal deity that establishes his lack. The Father belongs to "the man I [Maxwell] used to be" (31). When Eleanor asks for God's help, Maxwell answers with ironic playfulness, "Sure. If *she* has the time" (42, emphasis added). Finding only lack within the realm of the Father, Maxwell looks to the Mother. Maxwell's God is "the avenger" (71) who he claims is "Me! Me! The demi-god" (70). Because of Maxwell's desire to overcome lack, he creates a deity more in line with the remembered plenitude of the Mother. When Gail feels "like praying or something" (71) Maxwell tells her, "Good idea. Everyone look inside your head. Locate your individual God. Have a few words" (71). Maxwell's God is the being within himself, the being who has been controlled, censored, and repressed by society. He describes his experience of meeting this God: "You see a few months ago I had occasion to stare into the benign eye of God. And as God shrugged and gestured sadly for me to come rest in purgatory for eternity unless I got my priorities straight, I made myself some promises" (22). Maxwell's God calls him to action for the sake of his self, not a society.

Another point of view is illustrated by Walker through Babe Conner, the owner of a newspaper that Maxwell calls "a fascist rag" (21). When Maxwell, Gail, and Sarah are locating their "individual God" (71) before they start Conner's trial, Conner ironically calls out the expletive, "Jesus Christ!" (71). Using "Jesus Christ" as an expression of frustration, Conner illustrates how pervasively Christian ideology is embedded in our culture. As Sarah says, for Conner Jesus Christ is a "typical choice" (71). Conner calls on his God, the patriarchal deity, for help. His God is connected with laws which invoke outside authority to justify his action. Conner's God validates his actions because he casts God in his own image:

> Are you hearing all this God. This is the thanks I get for being a good citizen? Making my contribution? Providing over three hundred jobs? This is my reward? Putting my fate in the hands of these lunatics? Oh man I'm confused by this. I'm right on the edge here. (*He drops to his knees, closes his eyes, begins to pray.*) Oh Lord. Give me your wisdom here. Pass it along, Lord. Help me defeat my enemies. Help me find my way back into the light. Help me stay prosperous and productive. Dear Jesus. Help me crush these assholes. Help me to— (78)

To Conner's way of thinking he has the God-given right to be in control; he and the Father are on the same side. In Conner's words, his "contributions to this city are legendary" (80). He supports "the opera," "the United Appeal" (80) and many other charitable organizations in the city including "the building of sports facilities in this city" (80) because "sports are very important. They keep people healthy" (80). But sports do more then keep them healthy; sports are quickly coming to the forefront, as the power of religion recedes, to take its place as an opiate of the masses.

Sports are a diversion which take the mind away from the central concerns of living and focus primarily towards the aspects of competition. Sports are based on an ideology of difference, which helps establish the linearity of the patriarchal realm. They are predicated on the basis of winners and losers, which sets up a hierarchical structure. Like society the linearity of sports is achieved by rules which promise tangible rewards to the best and fittest. This thinking has invaded every aspect of the social being's life; excelling in sports can be seen as a parallel to succeeding in society.

Walker makes this connection through Harris and Conner: "People who want to be healthy. People who aren't afraid to meet life head on" (80) are "people who want to be successful [...] on the right terms" (80). Harris calls these people "the foundation of our society" (80) because they are the best, at least by the game's standards. They agree to "the terms of a true consensus" (80) which is based on making the city "a place for winners" (81), keeping "the momentum going" and letting "the slower people pick up the jet stream" (81). Conner sums up the situation, "Fuck the people living on the fucking street. [...] We've got to get richer. The only alternative is to get poorer" (80-81). In effect, the game is rigged.

The "consensus" Harris and Conner talk about is based solely on their rules, devised from their frame of reference. The street people have no place in Conner's city of "winners" (81); therefore they are not considered. Money is thought of from Conner's and Harris's perspective—"richer" or "poorer"—not from some other's perspective, where it may mean survival or death. The weak and infirm, the marginal, are not a party to the contract; they dictate no clauses. Conner, Harris and their ilk, what Maxwell calls "the secret societies" (29), have written the terms for the contract between society and the individual based on who they are—white, middle-class, male, and healthy. In Maxwell's words, this contract is "derived and constructed from knowledge within a narrow historical corridor" (13).

Walker reinforces these sentiments through Sarah's monologue about "big, beefy, white guys" (33) who "form a club" (34) and who

> hate little people. And little cars. But mostly they hate black people, and brown people and yellow people. So they surround a town and they take it over and they become the power. They're indestructible. They're armour plated. They're full of hate. And now they've got a headquarters. A centre of operations. First thing they do is kill everyone who isn't beefy or white. Kill all the skinny people. And the two black people in town. And the old guy who owns the Chinese restaurant. Kill them openly. Kill them without fear. Because they're in control. They're free to be themselves. (34)

The "big beefy white guys" make up the "secret societies" (29), the elite who in effect have the power to determine what standards to use in society's value system. These standards are based on the reality of society where power reigns supreme. Power is predicated by the dominance of an elite class over a submissive class that recognizes the other's power. Recognition of the dominance of an elite class is accomplished through the acceptance of the dominant class's ideology by the submissive class (see French 507-09). In Sarah's monologue she suggests that eradication of the submissive class is the "big beefy white guys"' method of choice in attaining domination.

As presented by Walker these choices are only an option of the elite class. When Gail talks about being black she says, "It's not like we have a choice. I mean does it take courage to be what you are when there's no way you could be anything else" (35-36). Gail's absence of choices, which in social terms translates into a lack of power, disallows her a place on society's playing field. Without power Gail presents neither a threat nor a promise to society, which therefore holds no place for her; she remains on the margins of the social world.

Yet Gail's very marginality gives her access to a reality denied within society. The opiates available within society are denied her so that life's complexity has not been lost amid the hype and propaganda that goes hand in hand with social life. Maxwell and Sarah illuminate the difference between relationships in this realm as compared with social relationships which are based on dominance and submission:

> **MAXWELL.** I saw him. He saw me. We recognized each other immediately. We talked. He told me his story. I told him mine. His was truly painful. But mine was much longer … Well, more complex. Somewhere between his pain and my complexity we reached a common ground.
>
> **SARAH.** The commonality of complex pain. That makes sense. It's the thing that ties us all together. All living things. Regardless of race or religion. (36)

As Maxwell says, within society it is possible, even preferable, to "rob the situation of complexity and then clarify an essentially fraudulent simplicity" (14). Within this new society that Maxwell tries to create with the help of Gail, Sarah, and Eleanor relationships are based on "a serendipitous union of intention" (14). Rather than a society based on definition by opposition, Maxwell tries to create a society based on definition by similarity.

Out of Maxwell's anger at a society that will recognize only those who reinforce and perpetuate the dominant ideology of society comes love. This love is not a selfless love based on attaining some connection with a transcendent other but a love based on mutual recognition through "the commonality of complex pain" (36). It is a love which involves illuminating the core of the being rather than distorting it. This love's point of origin is within the self as opposed to society's promise of love, which must come from the site of the other. Bonnie Kreps comes close to describing what Walker implies: "For me, it means becoming aware of an ongoing developing process of knowing who one is. Not in any intellectual kind of way, but in recognizing a pattern of learning and living, which seems always to have been there" (157). This love requires that each individual find his or her own specific place in the universe and in so doing acknowledge the right of others to a place. This is in contrast to Walker's *The East End Plays*, where the women—Nora, Gail, and Gina Mae—are elevated to a place where their absence or inaccessibility represents male lack. In Roland Barthes's *A Lover's Discourse* he articulates the difference between these two positions. The former position is based on loving and takes into consideration the other's subjectivity (42). This is illustrated by Maxwell, who acknowledges Sarah as a being in her own right: "She is what she is. She'll do what she has to do" (42). The latter position is based on being-in-love and here the other is denied subjectivity. As Barthes describes this position it replicates the dyadic moment, where the beloved is positioned as the site of plenitude: "The being I am waiting for is not real. Like the mother's breast for the infant, 'I create and re-create it over and over, starting from my capacity to love, starting from my need for it': the other comes here where I am waiting, here where I have already created him/her" (39).

However, in *Love and Anger* one woman has the attributes of the good mother as depicted in Walker's earlier plays. This woman is Eleanor, for whom there is no imaginary world beyond the stage. Eleanor is the selfless, all-giving picture of femininity whose existence is based on service to some other. Sarah comments on this when Harris wants to make Eleanor the judge in Conner's trial: "Standing there the way you do. Standing there all rational. And deferential. Looking perfect for the position. Just waiting for the chance to serve" (78). Eleanor is always available, just "waiting for the chance to serve" because she never leaves the playing space. The script gives no indication that there is anything outside of the playing space that has any effect on Eleanor's life. She is portrayed as the woman who will love and nurture Maxwell steadily and unconditionally without effort on his part, which is reminiscent of the mother/child dyad. But she is not recognized by Maxwell as such until the end of the play, when he is near death:

> **MAXWELL.** Eleanor, you look like my mother.
> [. . .]
> **ELEANOR.** You never told me that.
> **MAXWELL.** You never looked like her before.... Until just ... this moment. (84)

Throughout the play Eleanor does what is expected of her. She is steadfast, as shown by her loyalty towards Maxwell, which extends to working for him without pay. She is nurturing as shown by her care of Sarah. But Sarah, like Maxwell, does not recognize Eleanor's place as the mother: "I'm not your child, Eleanor. Be careful you don't talk to me like your child. There is no gain in that for either of us" (39).

Although Eleanor's maternal claims are denied by Maxwell and Sarah they are still central and inviolate and Maxwell admits, "She's actually the heart and soul of my operation" (16). Eleanor is the personification of the promise of completion made by society. She is aligned with the social; she believes she has a "choice" (38). Her choice is, as Maxwell describes it, "to find something to remove the grime in this place" (25). Eleanor exists to give comfort, an existence which is mapped out for her in the social world. And although Eleanor chooses to serve Maxwell, Sarah, and Gail, she does not commit herself to their desire for a new society. When Conner calls Maxwell, Sarah, and Gail "pathetic!" (79) Eleanor defends them: "No they're not! They're just struggling. Struggling to replace a ... a ... system that has let them down for some reason. Be nice to them! They're only looking for a little justice" (79). When Eleanor defends Maxwell, Gail, and Sarah, she dissociates herself from them. As Maxwell says, Eleanor still has "a reservoir of faith in the veneer of civilization" (58). She buys into the ideology of the phallocentric society that is based on dominance and becomes culpable of her own submission.

On the other hand, Gail refuses to be defined by society as powerless. As she watches Conner and Harris walk away from the trial with no guarantee that they will take responsibility for their actions, Gail says, "There's something I'd like to add to the argument" (82). Gail illustrates Claire Johnston's thesis that women react against and transgress the male discourse which entraps them, not by sweeping aside the existing social order of aggression and establishing a new order but by asserting their own power in the face of the masculine realm of power (39). Gail's power is not based on the linear logic of language; it is based on a reality unrepresentable in language. Gail cuts through the phallocentric mediated method of aggression and shows Conner and Harris a pure expression of power and dominance: "This. It's real" (82). As Gail explains it:

> And this is it. The gun. See it? If you cross me or my husband again, I'll use it. If you make me mad again I'll find you and put it against your head and pull the trigger. Maybe because I think you're wrong about all the things you talked about. Maybe for ... some other reasons. We'll never know for sure why I use it. I'll never know because I'll be too busy getting on with my life to ask myself questions like that. And you'll never know because you'll be dead.... (83)

Gail has "learned to be prepared" (82), to find her "protection" (82) in her instinct for survival. This was the clause not written into the contract between the individual and society. Harris and Conner deal in the abstract "richer" and "poorer" (81); Gail deals in the fundamental, "my life" and "you'll be dead" (83). Since language represents experience from the dominant class's point of view, a class from which Gail is excluded, she admits, "We'll never know for sure why I use it" (83). Gail's speech suggests an inability of language to survive such an extreme dislocation.

Walker echoes this supposition through Maxwell. When Gail asks him whether he's "planning a strategy or something" (23), he answers:

> No time for that. Strategies require thinking. Thinking just removes you from the only necessary thing. Feeling it. You know, the anger, the burning, the deep honest anxiety. Look, would you feel better if I told you to go home and leave it to me.... I could do that, but I wouldn't agree to it if I were you. I haven't got a clue how to get your husband out of prison. Legally, strategically—any other way. (23)

Although Maxwell decides to oppose patriarchal values and create a new system, he can find no clear direction because the systems within which he must work to effect change are invariably hierarchical, designed and retained to transmit power. And because power reigns supreme in society no alternate system is successful (see French 489-95). Because Maxwell works within social systems, like language, he confronts a closed and vicious circle.

This circle is perpetrated by the fact that the self can only be attained in its relation to an other, a relationship based on power and dominance in society. The women in *Love and Anger* also recognize this fact. As Sarah says of Maxwell: "I need him Eleanor. I need him back. He created an environment that was good for me. He made a connection in my head. His anger connected to my anger. It blotted out the voices" (85). But for the women, because they are not part of the dominant social order, their relationships are based on something other than the immutable hierarchy of power; their relationships are based on the mutable network of pleasure, of human well-being (see French 498). The women form relationships that are not based on dominance but on attraction. Gail and Sarah form such a relationship in the final scene of the play, after Sarah expresses her need for Maxwell:

> **GAIL.** I can do that. I can do that for you.
> [...]
> **SARAH.** So ... well ... what can I do for you.
> **GAIL.** You're great. It's just great to be around you. We'll just be friends. It'll be exciting for me. You're the most amazing person I've ever met.
> [...]
> **SARAH.** We're going to be friends. [...] You're not saying all this just because we're the same colour, are you. (85)

Sarah's definition of herself as "the same colour" as Gail, black, has no foundation in external reality because she is visibly white. Yet in Sarah's reality she is "black" (34) because her concept of black does not necessarily translate into society's concept of black. As Eleanor says, "Well maybe she wants us to think she's black. Or maybe she just wants us to think she thinks she's black. It's hard to say.... Or yes maybe in her mind, truly she's black" (35). Eleanor goes on to allude to the possibility that Sarah says she's black "to manifest her courage" (35).

Whatever Sarah means when she says she is black is not easily accessible through the codes and ideologies of the present social system. Sarah retains the ability of manipulating language to suit her state of being rather than society's method of manipulating the state of being to suit language. Sarah's representation of herself has a direct link with the Mother's order. It is a disruptive force because it is incompatible with the order of the Father. Sarah's being is always in a mode of performance. She acts herself out with the self-reflective knowledge that the self is an unstable entity, unrecognizable to itself. And because society is based on immutability, Sarah is defined as "incurably insane" (38).

Sarah has a freedom not experienced by the others on stage (with the exception of Gail at the play's end). She changes her identity as she changes her mental disorders: "I had myself re-diagnosed. Obsessive-compulsive. I told them I just wanted to wash my hands all the time. What harm can that do" (36). Sarah manipulates her external reality through language, changing the rules the patriarchal society plays by. She will not be confined and defined by the language of some other; she demands continual reprogramming of the other to keep up with the manifestations of her being.

Although Sarah identifies herself in language, she denies the permanence that society associates with identity and language. According to the moment Sarah may appear as "insane" (38), "black" (34), "courageous" (35), "scared" (44), "a dreamer" (44) or "a lawyer" (45). There is no common language among the personae Sarah manifests. She exists within a discreet moment, which establishes the foreclosure of history. She exposes a fractured being and the other characters around her must relate to whichever identity Sarah chooses to create at this moment. Her language is stripped of referentiality and therefore of its permanence. She denies history and in so doing denies the power of the patriarchal society. Sarah does not enter into communication with any thought of creating a permanent identity. As she says, "I used to be from some other place. I'm from here now" (46). Sarah uses language to convince other characters and the spectators of what she is at the moment, not what she has been or what she will be. Sarah's language is based on pure exchange value; she does not try to capture some immutable, true self through language. There is nothing beyond what she is saying at the moment of her speech.

Sarah subverts patriarchal society's brutal struggle for power by a power of her own, which is invested in the maternal and not tied to some past experience or future dream. Sarah is alive in her immediacy; she demands authentication for the moment of being which may change at any given moment. She tells Conner and Harris this during the trial: "I was just expressing my true feelings. I think it best if the court is honest about these things. It doesn't mean I can't be turned around or anything. You guys have forgotten almost all the important things about life haven't you" (77). Sarah's power is based on her flexibility, which undermines Conner's and Harris's false sense of stability. Because Harris and Conner are caught up in the end product of winning the game, they view their existence in linear terms, ignoring the possibility of capricious nature. Sarah's existence is not overlaid with the linear structure of society; hers is one of imagination, spontaneity, opportunism, and joy; it takes into account the fickle quality of nature.

These qualities of Sarah's are illustrated by Walker when she encounters Conner and Harris for the first time. When they enter Maxwell's office and meet Sarah, she is at first scared of their "*black and white formal wear*" (43) and says, "Holy shit! You look like a couple of vampires! ... You can't walk around with those things on. Don't you realize the images those things conjure up. [...] You look like machines. Nazi vampire machines. I'm getting scared. Look guys I really mean it. ... loosen your ties!! (43-44). Sarah is successful in getting both men to loosen their ties and in so doing establishes her power over the rigid uniformity of Harris's and Conner's domain. Formal wear can symbolize wealth and power but only if some other authenticates it as such. Sarah, by denying that authentication and granting it one of her own, sets herself up as the site of the other. This is carried further when Conner asks Sarah to identify herself:

> **CONNER.** Hey you! what are you doing here. Are you a client.
> [...]

**SARAH.** Client? What made you ask that. Why didn't you ask if I was a lawyer. Does it look like I couldn't be a lawyer ... for some reason.
**CONNER.** Are you a lawyer.
**SARAH.** Yes. (44)

Sarah creates her own image and, by Walker's stage directions—(*And now SARAH is a lawyer. A pretty good one.*) (45)—it is an image that needs no authentication from Conner or Harris. Sarah's conversation with Conner and Harris has to do with who she is at the moment of doing. She is not involved in a linear evolution of an identity that requires some other to reflect back a picture of herself because, by the time that picture is reflected back she may have changed. Conner wants to label Sarah, either as a client or a lawyer, but something outside herself so he will be able to deal with her in social terms. Sarah accepts the label of "lawyer" (44) for the time being but, because it is not an inherent quality of her being, she reserves the right to throw it off at any moment. Harris and Conner though have established themselves in the realm of the social and in so doing have cast off the freedom to change without authentication from some other. With this conversation Walker explores society's method for confining the individual through language. And he gives an alternate picture, through Sarah, of a method for subverting that dominance. Conner uses words as a violent tool of domination but Sarah refuses to be dominated and by altering the meaning of his words, by denying Conner an identity as the figure of authority, she undermines the social hierarchy.

However, within the social arena Conner is given the identity of a figure of influence. Conner's newspaper is a tool he uses to dominate and manipulate the public. Maxwell calls it "a fascist rag. It panders to everything weak and uncertain and uninformed in the human race. It has the rights given to it by a society which is essentially indifferent to the weak, uncertain and uninformed" (21-22). And Maxwell goes further to detail the violence that underlies Conner's manipulation: "Your particular place in the historical corridor allows you to modify your behaviour for appearances, but you are still a Nazi. If you were put in a position of power in any society desperate for a violent purging you'd buy yourself a uniform—and you'd be a Nazi!" (22). Conner is part of a society that uses domestication to keep individuals in line. He attains his power by educating the public in society's morality. The people Conner's newspaper addresses, "the weak, uncertain and uninformed" (22) internalize the morality of the institution and therefore support it without coercion. Because society's stability hangs on the widespread acceptance of the dominant class's ideology, its importance cannot be overestimated (see French 508). Sarah undermines the ideology of Conner's class and shakes up the stability of a society which does not take her into consideration. She refuses to acknowledge Conner as a figure of authority and further she refuses to admit the existence of "the people" (73).

Maxwell defines "the people" as "victims" of "societal crimes" (73). Harris defines "the people" as "an amorphous mass outside" (73). For Sarah "[i]t's just a word. People. I can relate to what he [Maxwell] means. Don't worry. This court isn't too crazy about 'the people' anyway. He doesn't get any advantage saying shit like that around me" (73). What Sarah makes clear in her performance is that the "victims," "the amorphous mass," (73) have the power to undermine the perpetrators of social crimes and by denying their power they become complicit in the act of aggression against the individual.

Sarah does not acknowledge the duality of victim/aggressor, just as earlier she did not acknowledge the duality of black/white. Maxwell tries to create a new society but he works within the confines of the current society, buying into its ideology, which is based on definition by opposition. Also, by working towards an end goal Maxwell emulates the linearity of patriarchal thinking. On the other hand, Sarah, by ignoring future goals, which would lock her into a linear path of being, and by being open to the transient qualities of nature, offers a real alternative to a patriarchal society based on aggression.

Like Walker's earlier East End plays, *Love and Anger* is about the individual's conditions of survival. Yet generally the characters in those plays are fed, clothed, and have shelter. The conditions Walker addresses are desire and desirability as represented through language in society. He creates a paradigmatic space on stage and the audience watches as Walker displays his control of their desire. Walker's position as playwright allows him to control an image that refers to events no longer present. In this way he stresses the tenuous alliance between the spectators' knowledge of the illusion and their belief in its reality. In effect, Walker invites the audience to play in the gap that he unveils.

In *Better Living* the gap Walker unveils illustrates Tom trying to create a new society but in so doing destroying a real alternative to the threatening social order he tries to escape. In *Criminals in Love* this gap is depicted as space between chaos and socially constructed order. In *Beautiful City* Walker examines the gap between an authentic identity and a social persona. And in *Love and Anger* the gap unveiled is between the flux of nature and the linear construction of society. Confined within a narrative Walker must write around this gap, but by this effort he manages to focus the spectator's attention on what is not articulated, what cannot be articulated.

(1990)

## Works Cited

Barthes, Roland. *A Lover's Discourse.* Trans. Richard Howard. New York: Hill, 1978.

French, Marilyn. *Beyond Power: On Women, Men, and Morals.* New York: Summit, 1985.

Johnston, Claire. "Dorothy Arzner: Critical Strategies." *Feminism and Film Theory.* Ed. Constance Penley. New York: Routledge, 1988. 36-45.

Kreps, Bonnie. *Subversive Thoughts, Authentic Passions: Finding Love Without Losing Yourself.* Toronto: McClelland, 1990.

Marx, Karl. *Pre-Capitalist Economic Formations.* Trans. Jack Cohen. Ed. E. J. Hobsbawm. London: Lawrence, 1964.

Walker, George F. *The East End Plays.* Toronto: Playwrights Canada, 1988.

———. *Love and Anger.* Toronto: Coach House, 1990.

## Slashing the Pleasantly Vague: George F. Walker and the Word

by Stephen Haff

> Get to know your limitations. Then remember that as you go through life there are only two things worth knowing. The first is too complex for you to understand. The second is that life is a series of totally arbitrary and often meaningless events and the only way to make sense of life is to forget that you know that. In other words, occupy yourselves. (*Zastrozzi* 54-55)

Canadian playwright George F. Walker (b. 1947) has called his mind, like many of his generation, "sort of a media garbage bag sometimes" (Fraser). Rather than taking out the trash, he has spent much of his career making something from it, fashioning a unique dramatic voice from the detritus of American pop-culture. The affinities between Walker's writing and the "acrobatic" dialogue of Stoppard, the pared-down speech of Beckett, and the American pop idiom of Shepard have been rightly noted before. Walker's characters are sharply defined by their language, but not, for example, by the delicate accuracy with which their rhythms and levels of speech are rendered, as, for example, are Tennessee Williams's characters for whom language becomes a personal poetry, an individualizing music. Walker's characters all speak with one precise, controlled language which is no less articulate or peculiarizing for its uniformity. They avail themselves of a common implement and exert the primitive power of naming in a heightened, but very true, attempt to stabilize arbitrariness with rigorous rules. In Walker's theatre, the word is used as if it had physical power. *Zastrozzi* (1977) [1] makes the purest use of this disciplined, direct and energized language. *Love and Anger* (1989), whose structure and characterization furnish convenient points of comparison with *Zastrozzi*, simultaneously employs and steps beyond the bounds of Walker's earlier, absolutist dramaturgy.

Walker's first play, *Prince of Naples* (1971), an "absurdist" dialogue modelled after Ionesco, and its successor, the Beckett-like *Ambush at Tether's End* (1971), demonstrated Walker's skill as a dramatist, but his insights were so deeply couched in the idiom of those European models as to relegate the plays to obscurity. Walker's own distinctive dramatic voice emerged when he turned to pop-culture, particularly the styles, structures, and icons of B-movies and *film noir* as sources. What developed was a dramaturgy marked by a series of short scenes which were "cut" filmically by blackouts, ending in a state of unresolve; archetypal characters based on the stock figures of various films; and terse, axiomatic speech. As Chris Johnson points out, Walker's use of his sources was not mere camp or "slavish imitation" ("B-Movies" 91), but a darkly comic, ironic turning of substance against form. In this regard, Johnson places Walker's efforts in distinguished company: "Beckett and Ionesco draw from music hall and film comedy; Pirandello, Chekhov, and Ibsen drew from melodrama; and, of course, Molière made use of the characters and conventions of Commedia dell'Arte" ("B-Movies" 94). Walker is not, as his American contemporary Sam Shepard sometimes tends to be, over-awed by the pop iconography he draws on. He uses film for cultural reference-points, but his work bursts out of its frame to comment on both the frame itself and the world that nurtures it. The size and theatricality of his work don't swallow, but heighten, political awareness. As Walker said to Robert Wallace of *Beyond Mozambique* (1974), which is set in an archetypal Hollywood jungle, he shows what he thinks "those jungle movies were really all about," the racist, erotic and violent horror they only hint at and exploit for entertainment value (Wallace and Zimmerman 218).

Walker's early plays gain their nightmarish quality from a scientific, objectifying approach, a following of implications to their logical extreme in order to expose "truths." He dramatizes obsessions which lie behind familiar types, and presents them also as obsessions responsible for some of the most horrifying violence of our century. *Beyond Mozambique*'s mad scientist, Rocco, declares that "there's something about committing crimes against humanity that puts you in touch with the purpose of the universe" (126). For the "advancement of medical science," Rocco condones murder (91). Thus, Walker has revealed what he sees behind the familiar mad scientist archetype, and has also commented on a similar presence in the world of the audience. Johnson calls this presence the "historical nightmare" represented by concentration-camp experiments ("B-Movies" 95), but it can also be seen in more general terms as the horror of the logical extreme of the need for the scientific method to objectify the world. Walker exaggerates and extends the type to reveal what he sees as the truth behind it and so to confront us with an absolute. The audience may laugh at the parody, but the laughter is designed to make people question the assumptions behind the source, and their own reactions to it.

*Zastrozzi* represents a peak of Walker's early stagecraft, the honing of the voice for which he was searching. Set in 1890s Europe, "Probably Italy" ([9]), it is organized around three poles: Zastrozzi, the self-proclaimed "force of darkness" and "master criminal of all Europe" (12); Verezzi the *artiste*, the self-proclaimed "Messiah" (47); and Victor, Verezzi's tutor and self-proclaimed "ordinary man" (66). The title character hunts Verezzi, professedly to avenge the murder of his mother, but really because he wants to prove that everyone, even artists, must be made "answerable" (66). Zastrozzi is joined by Matilda, "the most accomplished seductress in Europe" (20), and by Bernardo, the henchman who, in his own words "follows [Zastrozzi] around like a dog" (58). Victor stands apart as the one who tries to cut through with persistent and improvised reason what he sees as the insanity of his master and the wrongness of Zastrozzi's logic. Finally Julia, the virgin, arrives, as she describes herself, "a product of healthy civilization thrown into a jungle of the deranged" (60).

The building block of Walker's dramatic language is the concise, epigrammatic line. Zastrozzi declares, "mankind is weak. The world is ugly. The only way to save them from each other is to destroy them both" (12). There is a self-conscious cleverness through a precision in the line that makes it stand apart from the action of the play. It is the twisting of a platitude, the extension of a B-movie line. Walker borrows the grand, sweeping statement of the B-movie/melodrama and pushes it a step further, so that it turns and comments on the source. This sets up reverberations which can be heard by an audience familiar with the form, jarring them into an awareness that this is not merely imitative, but re-evaluative language. Walker exposes larger truths behind Zastrozzi's frequently articulated intellectual/moral ideals of discipline simplification, namely that the extension of these ideals is destruction, the ultimate simplification and discipline. Obsessions latent in the familiar evil villain are awakened and presented as having contemporary, destructive reality.

Dialogue is the exchange of unadorned responses which proceed relentlessly, logically, here complemented by clashing swords:

> **VICTOR.** I am still alive.
> **ZASTROZZI.** But you are totally on the defensive.
> **VICTOR.** I don't have to kill you. I only have to survive. By merely surviving I neutralize you.
> **ZASTROZZI.** You cannot neutralize something you do not understand.
> **VICTOR.** We are approaching a new century. And with it a new world. There will be no place in it for your attitude, your behaviour.
> **ZASTROZZI.** This new world, what do you suppose it will be like?
> **VICTOR.** Better.
> **ZASTROZZI.** Describe what you mean by better.
> **VICTOR.** More humane. More civilized.
> **ZASTROZZI.** Wrong. Better is when the truth is understood. Understanding the truth is understanding that the force of darkness is constant. (67)

Each answer is a drive toward the "truth," toward seeing clearly. The whole play, full of debates and lesson-duels, has this feel of an endlessly logical argument, which moves toward simplification and clarity, stripping away and reducing issues to their essentials. Given this essential quality of speech, Walker's writing is perhaps just as effectively defined by what it is not, or what it cannot (from the point of view of both author and characters) afford to be. It is not campy, psychological, or evocative. It is lean, spare, and utilitarian. The characters who speak these lines are likewise not so much personalities as they are embodiments, forces, what I will call "absolutes."

Walker's audience is distanced from his characters because their extreme exaggeration and the relentless precision of their logic make identification in a traditional sense very difficult. As was Brecht's aim in "alienating," the play's cerebral qualities can be appreciated without the entanglement of emotional involvement with character and motive. And, as Walter Benjamin wrote of Brecht's epic theatre, "there is no better start for thinking than laughter. And, in particular, convulsion of the diaphragm usually provides better opportunities for thought than convulsion of the soul" (236). The humour is born partly of recognition of a detail faithfully rendered, a pop-culture reference point recognized. But most important and enduring, it is born of the jarring absence of "codedness" in speech, and of the immediacy and size the characters gain as a result. This same purity and exposure make them dangerous because there is no comfort zone of doubt or mystery, no pocket of relaxation for retreat.

In this land of debate, of extreme poles, of simplification, the base unit of language, axiomatic declaration, the sharp, laconic line, acquires special strength. It has the conciseness and boldness of an epigram to match the boldness of statement by which character is represented in Walker's dramatic vision. Such terse, staccato statements carry energy, a thrust which makes them more than empty platitudes, and more than mere pseudo-philosophical, parodic intellectual critiques. They give the characters their size, their pure, absolute quality, and distinguish them from simple masks, types, or emblematic functionaries, mere references to things past. They express things in exaggeratedly summary fashion. Characters habitually present their stance, their essence even, in a single, clear speech:

> **VEREZZI.** I am Verezzi. I am whoever He wants me to be. (*Zastrozzi* 47)
>
> **ZASTROZZI.** I am Zastrozzi. The master criminal of all Europe. This is not a boast. It is information. (*Zastrozzi* 12)
>
> **JULIA.** Madame, I am neither mindless nor a virgin. I am merely a victim of bizarre circumstance. A product of healthy civilization thrown into a jungle of the deranged. (*Zastrozzi* 60)
>
> **ROCCO.** I am the absence of God. (*Beyond Mozambique* 113)

Every efficient, uncluttered line bears (bares), in its sure rhythm and linear procession, the compulsive ordering or shaping of thought. The characters share a propensity for highly organized speech, specifically for enumerations, naming, and the supply of alternate phrasing, of further specification. This speech is the arena where the characters fight the very basic human battle against arbitrariness, against accident and chaos. Their self-conscious cleverness, awareness of their own form, is part of the definition, and hence control, which the speakers crave. This craving, the urgency for definition and passion for exactitude, is Walker's signature. Language is more than an instrument of definition and self-definition: the characters articulate to survive.

Walker's characters, as independent entities or absolutes who do not so much interact as collide, rule out the possibility of harmony, and in struggling to shield themselves against disorder, contribute to it, create it anew. They dictate their own framework. That chaos is the condition of this world is implicit in the power and relentlessness of positive assertions against it, of declarations of singular, final "truths:" The characters themselves identify the crucial function of words in this fight in which the issue of expression itself is often focal:

> **ZASTROZZI.** [I]t is still revenge. But in a larger sense. In fact, it is revenge in its true and original meaning. And, therefore, some other word is probably necessary. It is 1893 and language, like everything else, has become pleasantly vague. (15)

Zastrozzi later rails against Verezzi's "crimes" of "making language pleasantly vague and painting with distorted imagination" (64). The characters are ceaselessly forcing each other to define, to clarify further. Words become weapons which complement the swords, whips, and fists. In their climactic battle, Victor and Zastrozzi demonstrate their ability to "see into [the other's] heart" (65) in a rapid exchange of lines in three different languages. Words are organizers, sense-carpenters, and direct weapons. In this way, Walker and his characters have a very important affinity with Shepard, who compares the use of words in his plays to that in American Indian poetry:

> The roots of this poetry stem from a religious belief in the word itself. Like "crow." Like "hawk." Words as living incantations and not as symbols. Taken in this way, the organization of living, breathing words as they hit the air between the actor and the audience actually possesses the power to change our chemistry. (Shepard 53)

There is also the echo of lonesco, in whose *The Lesson*, for example, the word "knife" itself kills a character. Walker, however, is primarily interested in the organizational capacity of language.

Here, then, is another dimension to Walker's writing, the peculiar demand these characters make on an audience, for all their alienating size and cerebrality. The hunt, that essential clash between the play world's entropy and the characters' hunger for order, is a humanly engaging one. Zastrozzi's most terrifying nightmare is that in which he is capable of doubleness, of containing more than pure darkness. His own name becomes a weapon against himself. His inability to adhere to the simplification, the singularity he demands of others, threatens to rip him apart. He wages territorial warfare against himself with furiously controlled language:

> I am having a nightmare. It involves the final battle over control of the world between the forces of good and evil. It is the most terrifying nightmare I have ever had. Something so extremely unusual has happened that my mind in all its power cannot even begin to comprehend it. I am in charge of the forces of good. And I am winning. I think there is just the slightest possibility that there might be something wrong with my mind after all [...] we are taken to meet the commander of the forces of evil and [...] he looks familiar. And he should. Because it is Zastrozzi. And even though I know that I am Zastrozzi I cannot help but feel extremely confused. And he reinforces this confusion when he opens his mouth and says, I am Zastrozzi. (51)

When Walker was asked about the henchman Bernardo, he said, "He's not stupid. He just exists in a very narrow corridor, and if he goes outside that corridor, he's lost" (Telephone Interview). The same might be said of all the characters, who exist in the narrow corridors of their particular obsessions, defining and defending that territory with appropriately strict language. Articulation offers a chance to build a coherent world of words, a cage of regularity, with rules, syntax, pattern, order.

The play ends suspended: Zastrozzi finally comes face to face with Verezzi after having eliminated the other characters, but spares his enemy because the chase is a source of preoccupation. This lack of resolve, cognitive dissonance, contradicts the truth-seeking, simplifying, fully articulated drive of the characters and the play. Silence has the last word.

Walker's writing calls for boldness of performance style to match the absolutism of his language, the fury of the fight it indicates. The absolutism is both form and subject of his dramaturgy. Believing that the characters say exactly what they mean, and mean exactly what they say, is the necessary starting point from which to build the stage-life of the play. From there, the words can also take on power as mere utterance because they can be given the kind of physical attention (enunciation, projection) proper to incantation. The actors' clarity of delivery is exceptionally crucial because so much rides on the characters' precise word choices. Accordingly, physical gesture can't be allowed to stray from the pattern of precision and bold economy established by the words. Forthright speech here goes hand-in-hand with solid posture and definite, utilitarian moves. These are not the sort of characters who fidget. The directness, efficiency, and size of the line is no accident, no mere aesthetic preference or mimicry. It is a stage direction. The dramaturgical code is the absence of code. This is not meant to imply a mechanical approach to movement and gesture, but an essential one.

In performance, this requires a full, direct act of trust in the text, in the words, a style of acting which Walker has described as "free falling" or "thinking out loud" (Telephone Interview). Since the text itself is the fight, it demands to be accepted as it is, subtext-free, if the stakes are to be allowed to be as high as they are. Only in allowing the characters to be honest, to exist wholly in the moment, will the two prongs of Walker's theatre find their mark: the cerebral, "alienating" extension or turn on the pop-culture reference-point; and the fundamentally human, passionate battle for order which demands the audience's commitment, even identification. In pursuing this performance style, the measure of success is probably not unified audience response, but the fracturing of the audience into shifting, battling clusters, defined and re-defined by the extent to which the "alienation" or "identification" engages them.

After several more plays in the pop-culture vein, Walker turned to his native Toronto as source for the East End plays: *Criminals in Love* (1984), *Better Living* (1986) and *Beautiful City* (1987). The new source brought changes in form and outlook. He took more time to evoke characters who were once thrust whole onto the stage. Language admitted the colloquial, events were hung on a narrative line, individual scenes were longer, and there was something like hope at the end, instead of the pure dissonance of earlier finales. Next came his most evocative piece of all, *Nothing Sacred* (1988), an adaptation of Turgenev's novel *Fathers and Sons.* More than ever, as the nature of the source might lead us to expect, story and psychology came to play a role in Walker's writing. This was followed, in 1989, by *Love and Anger*, another "Toronto" play, which seems to yoke together the old and the new in Walker, perhaps a signal of forthcoming change.

*Love and Anger* is, like *Zastrozzi*, a trial orchestrated by one character around obsessive pursuit of his truth: "holy war." Petie Maxwell, lawyer, has emerged from a stroke reborn and immune to the corrupting forces of his profession. He has moved his practice to a basement in a sad and nearly forgotten part of the city, headquarters for his movement toward the "reorganization of an entire culture" (29). He seeks revenge on Babe Conner, publisher of a "fascist rag" (21), ostensibly for having sent a client's husband to jail, but truly because he sees Conner as a Nazi who exploits the "marginals" of society (15). Petie kidnaps Conner and puts him on trial in the basement, on a charge of "being consciously evil," for his "lack of respect for the essential mysteries of life" (69). On Petie's side are his client, Gail; his skeptical secretary, Eleanor; and Eleanor's schizophrenic sister, Sarah, who presides as judge over Conner's trial. Conner is backed by Petie's ex-partner, Sean Harris, whose campaign for political office Conner supports.

Words have not lost their ballistic function:

> **CONNER.** Hey watch your mouth. Where do you get off, using a word like that to describe me. You know what that word means to people?
> **MAXWELL.** Deep in my heart. At the root of my tenuous connection to the essence of life, I believe you are a Nazi. Your particular place in the historical corridor allows you to modify your behaviour for appearances, but you are still a Nazi. If you were put in a position of power in any society desperate for a violent purging you'd buy yourself a uniform and you'd be a Nazi!
> **CONNER.** I told you to watch your mouth! I hate that word, I just hate it.
> **MAXWELL.** You see a few months ago I had occasion to stare into the benign eye of God. And as God shrugged and gestured sadly for me to come rest in purgatory for eternity unless I got my priorities straight, I made myself some promises. And this is one of them. If it looks like a Nazi, call it a Nazi!! (22)

The power of naming is prominent as ever, and there remain the signature grandiose definition and self-definition, the imperative to establish identities and fix situations, and the over-riding need to drive toward and hold onto precise and simple truth; the dominant need, as in *Zastrozzi*, to make life answerable, to name, to judge, and thereby to order, existence. And the explicit format Walker has chosen in this case is the trial, the purely verbal hunt for truth. There is often, however, in the newly colloquial rhythms, a diverting of that ballistic and territorial function of language, the beginning of a liberation of language into new realms of function. And, as the conclusion to *Love and Anger* also shows, words can even give way, without terror in so doing, to silence.

Walker has begun to address the "arbitrariness" of Zastrozzi's world as "mystery," as possibility. The conclusion to *Love and Anger*, as to *Zastrozzi*, is inconclusiveness. Petie loses the trial, then dies of a stroke onstage. His friends contemplate his dead body, concentrate in order to effect a resurrection, and then become silent.

But where the suspended, silent close of *Zastrozzi* implied hopelessness, a fear of the size of life, of stepping beyond one's "limitations," *Love and Anger*'s ending asserts possibility, through interaction, as opposed to the purely isolated and isolating choice made by the characters of *Zastrozzi*:

> **SARAH.** You hear that, Eleanor? She and I are really going to be friends. And it's going to be exciting. What do you think of that.
> **ELEANOR.** I don't know.
> **SARAH.** Well at least she's not against it. (85-86)

In the Walker-directed premiere, following silence, the basement gave way to a star-filled sky after this final line. This is a far from irresponsibly hopeful comic resolution, but the shift is significant. When coherence and words fail, the complex and indefinite have power by virtue of their mystery which before could be viewed only as threat. It is the "Nazi" villain Conner who boasts, "My whole career is based on offering up simple solutions" (48). Walker is, in his words, "letting in some light" on what has been a predominantly dark dramatic world, allowing his plays to "swirl around" and bring more into consideration, rather than thrust toward a truth by stripping away and simplifying (Personal Interview).

*Love and Anger* might work as a miniature map of the progress of Walker's canon. While initially dominated by its Zastrozzi-like absolute, Petie, the play gradually shifts to a shared stage, occupied, in the end, exclusively by women. Petie voluntarily cedes his dictatorial control over the play's action and submits to Sarah's authority as judge of the trial. From Zastrozzi's clear, sane voice of negative spirituality, Walker turns to a schizophrenic as the source of law. Eleanor explains Sarah's assertion that she's black: "Well maybe she wants us to think she's black. Or maybe she just wants us to think she thinks she's black. It's hard to say. … Or yes maybe in her mind, truly she's black" (35). Zastrozzi's terrifying stability is replaced by Sarah's ever-shifting, unpredictable, and ultimately mysterious, behaviour. When Sean objects to Petie's unspecific use of the word "people," Sarah replies: "Yeah yeah. Objection overruled. […] Calm down. It's just a word. People. I can relate to what he means. Don't worry. This court isn't too crazy about 'the people' anyway. He doesn't get any advantage saying shit like that around me" (73).

This is a far cry from Zastrozzi's outrage at imprecision. Now at the dramatic centre of the play there thrives a sense of expression and comprehension based on grounds other than disciplined verbal communication. Petie describes his visits to Sarah when she was last in the asylum:

**MAXWELL.** All those times I've visited her in the hospital these last few months. We've talked. We've looked into each other's souls. We have this uncanny communication. We don't always use words. Sometimes we just look at each other and nod ... slowly. Very slow nodding. Like this. ... (*He demonstrates.*) It's amazing.
**ELEANOR.** You're worse than she is. (40)

Another especially noteworthy feature on this dramaturgical map is the presence of Eleanor, the first truly agenda-free character in Walker's dramaturgy of colliding obsessions. Moreover, the dominant absolute, Petie himself, is fighting for the "marginals" (15) of society, and against all that is "[i]nsensitive to the nuance of human existence" (13). The ongoing reconciliation of singularity and multiplicity in Walker's plays makes it tempting to explore a new approach to staging them.

Walker has not become a Canadian Eugene O'Neill, in whose plays, as Walker told Robert Wallace, characters "carry their history around on their backs like a knapsack" (222). He still takes no interest in their psychological histories, so that the characters are ardently present-tense, the words just as critically concrete and palpable as ever. But, whereas in *Zastrozzi* the options were singularity or madness, Walker now begins to offer a third option, namely, to embrace multiplicity. This embrace of multiplicity is given concrete form by the final, and now necessary, absence of speech. The isolating, insulating, territorial function of words has opened slightly to admit friendship and shared silence. Walker takes a cautious step toward trusting the unsayable.

(1992)

## Note

1 Dates given in parentheses following play titles are those of first production.

## Works Cited

Benjamin, Walter. "The Author as Producer." *Reflections.* Trans. Edmund Jephcott. New York: Schocken, 1986. 220-38.

Fraser, John. "Walker Turns to Murder with Comedy." *The Globe and Mail* 19 April 1977: 16.

Johnson, Chris. "George F. Walker: B-Movies Beyond the Absurd." *Canadian Literature* 85 (1980): 87-103.

———. "George F. Walker." *Canadian Writers Since 1960.* Ed. W. H. New. Dictionary of Literary Biography 3. Detroit: Gale Research, 1986. 374-78.

Shepard, Sam. "Visualization, Language and the Inner Library." *The Drama Review* 21.4 (1977): 49-58.

Walker, George F. *Beyond Mozambique. Three Plays.* Toronto: Coach House, 1978. 87-135.

———. *Love and Anger.* Toronto: Coach House, 1990.

———. Personal interview. 10 December 1987.

———. Telephone interview. 1 October 1990.

———. *Zastrozzi, The Master of Discipline: A Melodrama.* Toronto: Playwrights Co-op, 1979.

Wallace, Robert, and Cynthia Zimmerman. *The Work: Conversations with English-Canadian Playwrights.* Toronto: Coach House, 1982.

## Out with the Queers: Moral Triage and George F. Walker's *Theatre of the Film Noir*

by Ed Nyman

> A doctor rips a severed human foot from around another man's neck and throws it into the audience. As he does so he says, "What's wrong with you. Have you no respect for human life?"
>
> A drunken young man sits beside the coffin of his recently murdered lover whose grave and corpse he has just desecrated.
>
> A woman narrates a dream of being raped by the tongue of a lizard and lapses into describing the rape of a Catholic school girl by a priest.
>
> A lady proposes a toast and falls dead through a suspended tire.
>
> When the curtain rises, a corpse is suspended above the stage. It remains throughout the play.

All these "sound bites" are opening lines chosen from George F. Walker's plays, which are arguably the most recognised and produced body of theatre texts originating in English Canada. Yet the critical works on Walker's plays are few and far between and uniformly unsuccessful in developing a critical lexis for dealing with scenes such as those described above, let alone the texts' theatrical and political strategies. Terms such as "bizarre," "grotesque," "carnivalesque," "parodic," and "postmodern" are bandied about, but all are an awkward fit. In "The Dramaturgy of the Perverse" Richard Paul Knowles uses the *OED* definition of the word "perverse" to argue that texts, like Walker's, that employ strategies of perversion deliberately "misapply, misconstrue, wrest the purport of" (226) traditional conventions, expectations, and ideas. As the word "wrest" suggests, I would argue that perversity is a pro-active strategy designed not just to subvert, but to take control of a system of representation. A perversion goes beyond the boundaries of what is recognisable within the traditional ways of seeing. If, as Foucault argues, a discourse licenses transgressions, then a perversion is a step beyond what the discourse is willing to accommodate (though Foucault was skeptical about the genuine possibility of "true" perversion). A licensed transgression helps a subject to recognise itself as a subject within a discourse; but a perversion shows a subject to be its not-self—that which it must not be.

The term perversity was commonly used in turn-of-the-century studies of human sexuality (sexology) and has increasingly been re-deployed in contemporary analyses of gender, primarily in the discourse more and more commonly called Queer

Theory. I am *not* interested in adopting Walker as a queer playwright. That would be perverse in quite another sense. I am, however, interested in the ways in which Walker's theatrical and performative strategies are and are not of interest to a queer politics.

As the *OED* amply demonstrates, the root of the word "perverse" implies a "turning away," which as Kaja Silverman, Jeffrey Weeks, and others have argued, assumes a norm or nature that is being turned away from. Freud defined perversity as either: 1) the "lingering" of the subject's attention over objects that were actually steps or stages along the way toward a natural objective or "end" or, 2) the substitution of a different objective for the "right" and "proper" one. Perversion is then delightfully, thanks to Freud, a lingering over the wrong end! To pervert or be perverse, for example, might then be to look away from the centre and to the margins. Perversion denies the *telos*—the end that Freud implied natural sexuality moved toward. In this sense, perversion is anti-essential: it disseminates possibilities that by their very existence challenge what is assumed to be the essential norm (in Freud's case, middle-class, European, male heterosexuality) (see Weeks 14-15). Perversion, as a strategy of desecration, turns away from the "natural" end, inverts the assumed order, substitutes the "unnatural" for the "natural," the absent for the present, the margin for the centre, the bottom for the top; thus, perversion challenges the essential, the hierarchical, and the sacred.

As Richard Knowles argues, Walker's plays deploy perversity as a trope in their playful, persistent warping and reconfiguration of received forms. These strategies work to wrest away *control* of the systems and structures of representation that allow ideologically motivated and media-generated images to masquerade as sacred and essential. Not surprisingly, the theatre's (and the cinema's) own representational forms are the most frequent object of the plays' critical strategies. And though theatrical genres such as the melodrama, the detective play, the Jacobean revenge play, and tragedies, among others, are persistently dismantled and re-deployed in grotesque ways, space limitations and my interest in this paper in *Theatre of the Film Noir* require me to focus on the perversion of cinematic forms primarily.

Walker's perversion of forms such as *film noir* and the B-movie [1] is difficult to describe with precision because these forms themselves appear to be "perverse" already. The darker, seemingly existential versions of *film noir*, with their dangerous femininities and questionable masculinities, appeared to pervert and undermine the ideals of the American culture they were a part of. Indeed, the films were disturbing enough to attract the attention of Joseph McCarthy and the House Un-American Activities Committee (HUAC). Repeatedly, commentators on the B-movie *film noir* argue that these dark, angst-ridden films were a direct reflection of something in the American psyche that could not or was not being expressed in A-movie genres. Just as the cheaper B-movies were intended to supplement the more expensive A-movies, critics argue that the more ironic B-movies supplemented what was lacking representationally in the often superficial and glib A-movies.

In order to understand Walker's use of the *film noir* form this sort of simplistic analysis—in which *film noir* mirrors a "darkness" in the American cultural "Psyche"[2] and is consistently subversive—must be problematised. *Film noir* not only mirrored a culture, but, like any discourse, both represented and produced, both regulated and was regulated by, the cultural phenomena it was said to reflect. Film is not simply a repository; it is reproduced and disseminated and, thus, recreates at each articulation the ills recorded there. In *In a Lonely Street*, Frank Krutnik argues that *film noir* both generated and regulated the cultural effects it "reflected." In *film noir* "culture is made 'comprehensible' for the subject, and the subject made 'recognisable' within the terms of [the] culture" (ix). The subject "recognises" itself in the discourse that produced it. If the *film noir* is indeed a mirror, then perhaps it is so in the Lacanian sense: a mirror in which and by which a subject simultaneously both recognises itself and is produced as a subject. The (*film noir*) mirror becomes, then, not a transparent reflection, but a passage, an entrance into the law of the father.

The B-movies, therefore, were no more subversive than A-movies. As Christine Gledhill argues, the disturbance of genre was an essential strategy in the reinforcement of those same genres. Thus Hollywood produced a carefully controlled "subversion" of its own regulatory economy as part of the institution of that same economy:

> Hollywood genre production tended both to foreground convention and stereotypicality in order to gain instant audience recognition of its type—this is a Western, a Gangster, a Woman's Picture, etc.—and to institute a type of aesthetic play among the conventions in order to pose the audience with a question that would keep them coming back—not "what is going to happen next?" to which they would already have the answer, but "how?" (24)

The two streams merely appealed to different desires in the audience: A-movies to the desire to affirm the national narrative and B-movies to the desire to be titillated by the (containable) disturbance of that narrative. B-movies and *film noir* were the carnival space within the dominant American ideology and, therefore, despite their seemingly subversive effects, no more than a sanctioned disturbance that reinforced a dominant discourse.

In contemporary Western discourse, gender is arguably a principal site of discursive coercion and, therefore, of resistance as well. Thus gender disturbance was a consistent aspect of *film noir*. The potentially subversive nature of gender in *film noir* lay in its construction of women and men in ways that deviated markedly from what was culturally acceptable and common in other Hollywood fare of the time. According to Janey Place, the *film noir* period "stands as the only period in American film in which women are deadly but sexy, exciting and strong" (63). Yet this exciting, dangerous woman of possibilities is only one of the types of women represented in *film noir*. As Tuska explains, there are (at least) two types of women:

> *femmes fatales* and the loving wives and mothers. The *femmes fatales* are interesting, intelligent, and often powerful, whereas the wives and mothers are dull and insipid. Notwithstanding, it is the latter variety which is the ideal role prescribed for women. The *femme fatale* is best characterized by her self-interest, while her opposite is capable of total devotion to a man. (202)

Thus, no matter how subversive the very existence of a woman such as a *femme fatale* is, she is nonetheless proscribed as that which is to be avoided and punished.

Deborah Thomas has argued that this gender "trouble" reflected a post-war anxiety about sexual roles. Although unlicensed heterosexuality, close male bonding, and sanctioned killing were all facts of the war experience, the post-war period offered restricted heterosexuality and forbade male bonding. Repeatedly, even obsessively, *film noir* traverses this loss, yet in doing so, both foregrounds and punishes the transgressions. Films in the "genre" consistently return to those narrow, prescribed limits, punishing women for their sexual freedom and their failure to depend on men. Men are consistently enjoined to flee psychological complexity, homoerotic desire, dependence on or obsession with women, weakness, self-doubt—anything, in fact, that threatened the idealisation of the male as an independent self, sexually free to dominate both men and women, particularly the latter. Nevertheless, even in condemning them, the *film noir* puts into circulation—always a dangerous practice—the unsanctioned male and female.

Problematic women in *film noir* encroach on the masculine. Their appropriation of exclusively male characteristics puts back into circulation that which must be excluded from "masculinity": passivity, emotion, erotic desire for the male body, all that which has been excluded under the heading "feminine." Therefore, as Tuska argues, the punishment of the deviant females and the occasional punishment of the unregenerate male served to restore the balance in the threatened patriarchal system by shoring up the "proper" (i.e. not perverse) hierarchical binary difference. Ironically, *film noir*, as dark, dangerous, and exciting as it appeared to be, consistently returned to the safe, conventional life it appeared to challenge. Thus *film noir* was not, as so many commentators have attempted to argue, a perverse form. Their disturbances merely served to reinforce the hegemonic norm. This recuperation is the site at which Walker's plays attempt to pervert the seemingly perverse form.

Walker's plays challenge the *film noir* form's gender ideology but fail to pervert its compulsory heterosexuality; yet in foregrounding the tenacity of a heterosexual patriarchy, a play such as *Theatre of the Film Noir* nonetheless opens itself to a queer re-reading. *Femmes fatales*, or potential *femmes fatales*, for example, appear frequently in Walker's B-movie plays: Rita in *Beyond Mozambique*, Ramona from *Ramona and the White Slaves*, the women in *Gossip*, one of the Scott sisters in *Filthy Rich*, Matilda in *Zastrozzi*, Lilliane in *Theatre of the Film Noir*. Yet a scrutiny of this list immediately exposes the plays' perversion of this convention. Though the plays do put women in dangerous, seductive roles, the *femme fatale* identification remains an unstable category; and even when a female character is genuinely dangerous, she is not punished for her gender-transgressions. Women such as Margaret in *Gossip*, who appear to be the loving, safe, domesticated women that *film noir* valorises, turn out to be neurotic and dangerous (the *femme fatale* role of Susan Long, for example, is one of Margaret's recurring alter egos). Brigot Nelson, on the other hand, turns out to be less of the *femme fatale* than she appears and more of a crank. In *Filthy Rich*, the difficulty of distinguishing which of the Scott sisters is faithful and which is a *femme fatale* suggests the absurdity of the convention. Walker's plays consistently blur the two roles for women that are so clearly demarcated in *film noir*.

In *Beyond Mozambique*, Rita is living out the role of Rita Hayworth, one of the most famous *femmes fatales* actresses; yet at the end of the play Olga, living out the role of the loving, faithful, eternally optimistic Olga of Chekhov's *Three Sisters*, is treated to the fate normally reserved for *femmes fatales* in *film noir*. Not only is she destroyed (she dies after complaining that Tomas took her in the rectum with his monumental erection [132]); she also becomes a visual metaphor of the subjectless woman: her corpse is manipulated as a puppet by Rocco and mouths Chekhov's words.

*Theatre of the Film Noir* most clearly employs the *noir* conventions and yet perverts them in the most complex and significant ways. Set at the exact cultural moment that *film noir* tends to retrace (the immediately post-World War II years), *Theatre of the Film Noir* recreates the situation of moral ambiguity, the blurring of the "normal" and the "deviant" that many commentators see as the cultural crises replicated in these films. Like *film noir*, the play begins with a framing monologue by the jaded "hard-bitten" detective who must negotiate moral ambiguities; it offers a number of unsanctioned sexual variations; obsession and alienation figure heavily; patriarchally sanctioned concepts of masculinity are challenged by homosexual transgressions but reassert themselves at the end; the lighting and staging styles call for the low-lighting chiaroscuro effects of *film noir*.

Yet the play's transgression of these conventions is signalled almost immediately in the consistent tendency to exaggerate these same *noir* effects. In Walker's own productions, at least, the visual echo of *noir* films has been overdetermined in the shadowed lighting, the clipped dialogue, the posing of the actors, and the upturned collar of the inspector. *Film noir* conventions such as homosexual challenges to compulsory heterosexuality are equally exaggerated. The homosexual liaisons far outnumber the heterosexual ones and are associated, uncomfortably, with necrophilic and incestuous relationships. In fact, the only heterosexual liaisons, actual or suggested, in the play other than the incestuous one between Lilliane and Jean, are performative masks designed to hide the males' true identity (national identity for Eric and sexual identity for Bernard).

Lilliane, at first glance, appears to be the *femme fatale* of the play. Yet Lilliane's construction runs counter to the spiderwoman pattern. Rather than being lured to their doom, the male characters flock to Lilliane for the protection that her sexuality offers them (she offers a heterosexual cover for Bernard and material and political advantages for Eric). Her sexuality is not a threat but a haven. Indeed, at the end of the play, Lilliane is not punished for her independent sexuality—both unlicensed and incestuous—but is brought by the inspector's influence into the American *film noir* industry to become, perpetually, the very *femme fatale* she has not been in the play. Thus the central strategy of recuperating the *status quo* that was characteristic of *film noir* fails entirely in *Theatre of the Film Noir*. Renegade female sexuality is not punished and the attempt to contain transgressive male sexual identities is only ironically successful: the patriarchal order must act with such naked and calculated aggression that its own status as "natural" is undermined.

In terms of a very simplistic gender dichotomy of male versus female, the *film noir*'s ideology *has* been perverted in the play. However, if gender is considered in a non-binary and far more complex way, it becomes clear very quickly that what the play has failed to de-essentialise, de-hierarchicalise, and de-sacralise is the heterosexuality of that patriarchal order. The *film noir*'s typical reinscription of compulsory heterosexuality is not perverted in the same way that its binary gender categories are. Indeed, the play contradicts its own trope of perversity by making the overtly homoerotic (especially any homoeroticism in the submissive posture) an image of decay and distasteful perversity. The association of homosexuality with negative imagery (as opposed to the characterisation of homosexuality itself as negative) need not necessarily be read as homophobic, though the reinscription of traditional metaphors of decadence and pathology, popular since the days of Oscar Wilde, would require a very carefully nuanced deployment to be useful—and I don't think *Theatre of the Film Noir* achieves that (see Gilman, *Difference* and *Disease*). While I want to give Walker, in his anti-naturalistic theatricality, the scope necessary to create a travesty of traditional constructions of gender and sexual orientation, I also want to emphasise the dangers of failing to undermine the stereotypes radically enough. In the case of Bernard in *Theatre of the Film Noir*, the figure of the homosexual can be seen to make a crucial point about compulsory heterosexuality and the dominance of the patriarchal moral order. But achieving this recuperation requires reading into the text's own absences so as to supplement the play's transgressions.

Bernard's construction is more complicated than that of most of the other Walker plays' homosexual characters and more easily recuperable. Such a recuperative reading is initially problematic in that homosexuality in *Theatre of the Film Noir* appears as co-symptomatic with incest, fraternisation, necrophilia, murder, and the moral decay of post-World War II culture. This perspective is, however, that of Inspector Clair, who, as I have argued above, represents the heterosexual male patriarchal order. This creates a chicken-and-egg critical problem—if one reads the play as de-valorising Clair's discourse, then his homophobia is de-legitimised as well; but if one reads the play "straight"-forwardly, then his homophobia is underscored. I choose, of course, to perform the former.

Bernard, as the figure of the homosexual male, works throughout the play to situate the heterosexual "norm" by his difference. Thus, on the one hand, Bernard is used to achieve the play's perversions by challenging the heterosexual order: he manages to wrest the focus of the play away from the traditional detective protagonist, forcing the supremely "heterosexual"[3] Clair to share the spotlight with his Other. By the end of the play, Bernard's "perversions" have become the central problematic of the play and have threatened the other characters to the point that they act aggressively to reassert the patriarchal order. The moral problem in the play is thus revealed to be not who murdered Jean, but whether and how the patriarchal moral order will be re-established. All the other characters are implicated in this act of moral triage, but the inspector, of course, actually performs the operation. What tends to remain a subtext in *film noir*—the defence of patriarchy—becomes the text of *Theatre of the Film Noir.*

On the other hand, though Bernard's destabilisations have permeated the play, he is, in the end, sacrificed to the patriarchal heterosexual order. This heterosexual order is revealed to be an abstract, even sterile, one—indeed, there are no "traditional" heterosexual relationships in the play at all. Unlike a traditional *film noir*, Lilliane is neither destroyed nor do she and the inspector form a relationship in the end. The inspector is, in fact, curiously asexual. The moral order he represents is thus implicitly impotent even though, ironically, it has all the power. Despite the Inspector's quest for moral clarity, he opts in the end for the *status quo.* Sexual desire, uncompromised by material or political gain, is pointedly absent from all the characters except the queer Bernard. The moral battle in the play is between the Inspector's sterile discourse and a discourse of desire, represented by Bernard.

The queer, as the ultimate threat to the play's patriarchal order, must be eliminated if the "moral order" Clair seeks is to be reasserted. The "American" (note the proliferation of American chocolate bars on stage)—which for all intents and purposes was the social structure imposed on Europe immediately after World War II—is established as the dominant moral order and is consistently represented as heterosexual. For example, though the collapse of moral structures has allowed Bernard to surface, he cannot do so openly; he must have a disguise, specifically because of the homophobia of the American soldiers. He says, "I've seen the Americans and they scare me as much as the Nazis. I know they hate queers. I can tell by the way they chew their gum when I walk by" (10). Bernard re-deploys this normativity in a strategy of mimicry in order to "pass": "I will go as a patriotic Frenchman and a friend of the liberators fluent in their language disguising my queerness as I walk past them chewing gum like they do" (14).

The elimination of the queers answers the moral problem of the play, for Bernard's death is a matter of triage for the Inspector: "Bernard had to die. He was just a part of what we have become." While on the surface Clair refers to Bernard's "broken brain," he also refers to Bernard's unsanctioned desire, which represents an even greater threat to the moral order: "How could the rest of us survive and prosper with him out on the streets making other people sad and unpredictable too" (48). Bernard's expendability is self-evident to Clair. Bernard's identity is positioned as Other to the heterosexual norm; if he were allowed to survive, he would threaten that norm by questioning just how "Other" his desires really are (the Inspector, after all, is the only male in the play who does not participate in homoerotic desire). Ultimately, the play suggests that the homosexual as Other is a carefully constructed fiction, for the play represents homoerotic desire as permeating the entire patriarchal order yet remaining effectively unrepresented within that order—as the love that may not, rather than dare not, speak its name. Clair deliberately re-constructs the fiction of a heterosexual patriarchy at the end of the play, making Bernard the necessary sacrificial goat to achieve it.

The compulsory heterosexuality represented by the Americans assigns economic value to each character's sexuality. Bernard's is of no value. All the men in the play, however, seek to possess Lilliane's sexuality because her position, as the heterosexual female, has the greatest economic value in this new world order. Lilliane becomes a disguise and a source of goods from the American soldiers. In Eve Kosofsky Sedgwick's terms, she becomes a form of currency in a male homosocial economy, an object of exchange by means of which the men interrelate.[4] She confers the status and privileges of heterosexuality on the men she chooses to favour. They need her gender to complement their own so that they will have available the gender-currency that is in demand for trade. Rather than having the men at her mercy, Lilliane is "spent" by them. Lilliane functions as the medium for inserting the sexually "deviant" males, including the Nazi as a related deviant, into the heterosexual American social, moral, and economic order. In the end, the inspector extends this by reifying Lilliane into an American screen star to be commodified by millions. The inspector's seemingly disinterested actions work to reassert a moral order that depends on the exclusion of Bernard and the reappropriation of Lilliane. It must reject Bernard's desire and reassert the sole validity of heterosexuality; it must contain Lilliane in order to preclude unsanctioned forms of heterosexual desire. Thus Clair "rescues" Lilliane from the dangerous reaches of Paris society where all her lovers appear to be of uncertain sexuality and brings her into the American order where, on the surface at least, heterosexuality is stable if only because all Others are discharged or eliminated.

Thus Walker's perversions of the cinematic genres' constructions of gender re-configure male and female identities, but in failing to account for queer subjects, re-inscribe a compulsory heterosexual discourse. The irony, of course, is that in identifying that recuperation, the play opens up to a queer politic. The perversity of Walker's plays thus demands, itself, to be perverted. For perversion has no *telos*; it simply goes on, always desecrating what has been made or left sacred.

(1996)

## Notes

1 "B-movie" is a term referring to a material mode of production and consumption. "*Film noir*" is a *style* or tonal quality that could be applied to any genre. The "tough" and the "gangster" are genres that are typically, but not exclusively, B-movies and often given *noir* treatments.

2 Problematic in any case, as though there were such a monolithic and quantifiable entity.

3 In terms of discursive orientation rather than orientation of sexual practice.

4 See, for example, "*The Country Wife*: Anatomies of Male Homosocial Desire" (49-66) and elsewhere in Sedgwick.

## Works Cited

Gilman, Sander L. *Difference and Pathology: Stereotypes of Sexuality, Race, and Madness.* Ithaca: Cornell UP, 1985.

———. *Disease and Representation: Images of Illness from Madness to AIDS.* Ithaca: Cornell UP, 1988.

Gledhill, Christine. "*Klute* 1: A Contemporary Film Noir and Feminist Criticism." Kaplan 20-34.

Kaplan, E. Ann, ed. *Women in Film Noir.* Revised and expanded ed. London: BFI, 1998.

Knowles, Richard Paul [Ric]. "The Dramaturgy of the Perverse." *Theatre Research International* 17 (1992): 226-35.

Krutnik, Frank. *In a Lonely Street: Film Noir, Genre, Masculinity.* New York: Routledge, 1991.

Place, Janey. "Women in Film Noir." Kaplan 47-68.

Sedgwick, Eve Kosofsky. *Between Men: English Literature and Male Homosocial Desire.* New York: Columbia UP, 1985.

Silverman, Kaja. *Male Subjectivity at the Margins.* New York: Routledge, 1992.

Thomas, Deborah. "How Hollywood Deals with the Deviant Male." *The Movie Book of Film Noir.* Ed. Ian Cameron. London: Studio Vista, 1992. 59-70.

Tuska, John. *Dark Cinema: American Film Noir in Cultural Perspective.* Westport, Conn.: Greenwood, 1984.

Walker, George F. *Beyond Mozambique. Three Plays* 87-135.

———. *Filthy Rich. The Power Plays* 73-132.

———. *Gossip. The Power Plays* 15-72.

———. *The Power Plays.* Toronto: Coach House, 1984.

———. *Ramona and the White Slaves. Three Plays* 138-90.

———. *Theatre of the Film Noir.* Toronto: Playwrights Canada, 1981.

———. *Three Plays: Bagdad Saloon, Beyond Mozambique, Ramona and the White Slaves.* Toronto: Coach House, 1978.

———. *Zastrozzi, The Master of Discipline: A Melodrama.* Toronto: Playwrights Canada, 1979.

Weeks, Jeffrey. *Sexuality.* New York: Tavistock, 1986.

# The Role Power Plays in George F. Walker's Detective Trilogy

by D.A. Hadfield

George F. Walker's second published trilogy, provocatively entitled *The Power Plays* (1984), revolves around the adventures of Tyrone M. Power, whom the audience first meets as a nihilistic political columnist who has been forced to become an investigative reporter and given six weeks to solve a murder which has stymied the police for six months. Much of the subsequent criticism of these plays has, therefore, examined them in the light of murder mysteries, with Power as the detective who will uncover "whodunnit." And while the plays, especially *Gossip* and *Filthy Rich* do contain many of the elements of traditional detective mysteries, they inevitably fail to sit entirely comfortably within the generic expectations of the whodunnit. This leaves critics most often making excuses for Power's inability to provide a clearly satisfying resolution in the first two plays, and improvising a different frame of reference for discussing the third play, *The Art of War*, in which the murder is seemingly insignificant to the remaining action. This unsatisfactory focus on Power as a detective intent on exposing wrongdoing or corruption obscures an important structural and thematic anxiety that all three plays do share, about the relationship between art and reality, the power of art in shaping reality, and the question of whose power controls art.

The sources which provide the material for my investigation of these plays do not include actual performances, and this essay is not an attempt to postulate or recreate the dynamics of a specific performance or production. Instead, it uses the textual residues of the original production—photos, reading scripts, house programs, reviews—as well as the published volume of the playtexts and their scholarly criticism in an attempt to examine the role of the historiographic record in constructing readings of plays and performances. These textual remains are of interest specifically *because* of their status as that which survives the ephemeral nature of a particular theatrical performance to be inscribed, for better or worse, into theatre historiography.[1]

As I have already indicated, the texts of the Power plays are most often read in the light of the murder mystery tradition, with T. M. Power as the more or less reluctant detective. Marvin Carlson succinctly summarizes the main characteristics of plays in this genre:

> The often rather isolated setting where the murder has occurred will shelter a number of characters, one of them, preferably the least likely one, the unknown murderer. A detective arrives and after shrewd cross-

> examination, observance of clues, careful comparison of alibis, and/or reconstruction of the crime, announces in the final moments of the play the identity of the murderer. The centrality of this quest and unmasking is suggested by the common sobriquet for such narratives: a "whodunnit." (5)

These are more or less the rules by which critics like Denis Johnston expect Power to play. The final scene in *Gossip*, according to Johnston, is straight out of the book: "In a time-honoured device of murder mysteries, Power invites all the suspects to an elegant dinner" (198). When the scene subsequently fails to fulfill its traditional whodunnit function, Johnston uncomfortably apologizes that "[w]hile the dénouement may be thematically sound, it is not theatrically consistent. [...] Although the final scene is ragged, the ending is appropriate" (199). Fortunately, according to Johnston, things get better. "*Filthy Rich* is a dandy detective yarn, a considerable improvement over *Gossip*" mainly because "[t]he audience grapples with the mystery as Power does, accumulating facts as he does, being tricked or supported by other characters as he is. This greatly augments the audience's involvement with the central character, a crucial element in the mystery genre" (200). *The Art of War* is structurally the odd play out, not fitting into the mystery genre at all because "[u]nlike in the previous two plays, there is no hard evidence of a crime having been committed, nor any palpable motivation for Power's investigation" (202). This change in genre ostensibly reflects a greater seriousness in the play: Power and his sidekick Jamie "have come down to reality with a bump, although they disagree as to what reality is" (202).[2]

Tim Wynne-Jones also begins his analysis of the Power plays by placing *Gossip* firmly within the tradition of the whodunnit. Having decided on this genre, he is even more glib than Johnston in his dismissal of the elements that fail to fit the pattern: "*Gossip*'s popularity undoubtedly comes from its structure as a detective story: the movement of the story is recognizable even if the details get fuzzy—and they do. Multiple identities proliferate but it doesn't matter. The conventions are all in place" (13). Beginning with the assumption that *Gossip* is a detective story, Wynne-Jones ignores the fact that a mystery depends above all on the detective's ability to clearly unravel and arrange the details into a plausible solution, and he never considers the implications of the multiple identities assumed by various characters in a setting where no blatant display of role-playing can be considered innocent.

Clearly, then, the Power plays are not conventional detective mysteries. Marvin Carlson, in his recent book *Deathtraps*, offers a new context for considering the "whodunnit" aspect of these works, in a genre he calls "the postmodern comedy thriller." He traces the emergence of this new genre to the 1970s and 1980s (i.e. precisely the period when Walker was writing the Power plays), when the tricks and devices of more traditional detective mysteries were being used in "combination [with] theatrical productions that emphasized such postmodern concerns as self-reflexivity, epistemological incertitude, and subversion of traditional codes (both within the performance and governing its relationship with the audience)" (12). According to Carlson, the postmodern comedy thriller emerged as a result of the need to keep one step ahead of an increasingly sophisticated postmodern audience. The reaction of playwrights to a genre based upon the stability and predictability of its codes is to create "a machine for increasing destabilization of generic givens and creating their replacement by ludic experimentation" (Carlson 15), in which no aspect of the theatrical event remains sacred. In the traditional detective play, the audience is presented with a narrative world fully created on stage, which circumscribes the entirety of the murder and its solution. Exposure of the murderer and his crime restores order and rationality to this world before the curtain falls. The comedy thriller, on the other hand, by definition respects no such careful distinction between the "fictional" world on the stage and the "real" world of the audience: "Since the goal of the comedy thriller is to keep surprising its audiences with new variations of a form that, even in its surprises, moves always toward codification, this interplay of reality and theatre has continued to be the area of increasingly elaborate and complex development" (62). What is really at stake for the postmodern comedy thriller, then, is the question of how far a performance can extend its horizon of control, and how effectively it can undermine the audience's power to distinguish illusion from reality. Unsure of the ontological foundation of the performance, the audience is less likely to be able to interpret generic codes and predict the outcome of the plot.

The problem of the Power plays cannot be explained merely by calling them "postmodern comedy thrillers" instead of "detective plays," but Carlson's generic reinscription does provide useful clues for refocusing the framework of the discussion of these plays and examining the ways the trilogy is unified around a central concern with the relationships between art, reality, and power.

"In the new world there won't be any acting. Just reality," prophesies the crazed visionary poet Brigot Nelson in *Gossip* (26), ironically summarizing one of the key issues in the play. Nelson implies that there *is* a difference between acting and reality, but this distinction is not operational in her current world—a world which is, to the audience, a play, where the only "reality" is acted. Such dialogue is by now a commonplace technique for foregrounding the metatheatrical concerns of the theatre, and for encouraging the audience into a questioning of what ontological distinction, if any, they can make between art and reality. In postmodern comedy thrillers, Carlson points out, this "play of reality and fictionality [is] a constant concern [...] not only for the audiences, but frequently for the characters themselves" (65). The playworld of *Gossip* is one in which multiple identities proliferate, as characters assume a variety of roles, where Power must, according to director William Lane, "penetrate those disguises and assess motives" (10). Implicit in Lane's description of Power's role is a belief that there is a distinguishable level of "reality" in the playworld, where disguises can finally be discerned and differentiated from the coherent self of the character. In this, Lane echoes the essentialist notion of a unified human character, which theatre makes manifest; or, as Ann Wilson writes in a slightly different context: "The impulse of theatre seems predicated on a particular conceptualization of human subjectivity which is rooted in the notion that each of us has an 'authentic' or 'true' self which ought to be coherent and unified" ("Bored" 36). As she points out, however, "[a]s much as we might yearn for a theatre which affirms an essential humanity [...] this position seems like a nostalgia for a world which doesn't exist, if indeed it ever did" (33). And, true to a poststructuralist sense of consciousness, *Gossip* puts more roles into play than can ever be accounted for in any unified sense before—or after—the curtain falls.

While Power is busily trying to sort out the bizarre cast of characters he meets on stage, he also has to contend with a less visible—but apparently no less active—cast of characters who exist somewhere near, but not exactly in, this play. Crucial to Power's murder investigation are Pedro Puchinsky, the artist, and Phyllis Lazer, the murdered secretary of Margaret's politician brother Paul, while Paul himself presents a constant thorn in Power's side, both personal and professional. While all of these characters are integrally involved in the chaotic scheme of subterfuge and fraud that Power uncovers, none of them ever explicitly appears on stage; they exist mainly on a diegetic, rather than a mimetic, level. These "ghosts" are joined by two more characters, both of whom do appear on stage to play out their parts, but only as masks or alter-egos of other characters. Power first hears of Susan Long from the Lewis brothers, who try to implicate her in Bitch Nelson's murder. When she eventually shows up in Power's office, offering to reveal the identity of the murderer, the stage directions describe her as "*A stunning lady in a blonde wig, a sexy dress and sunglasses* [...] *It is obviously MARGARET*" (52). Having Margaret play this role isn't fun for Power, presumably because he loves her (and therefore, possibly, desires the myth of unified selfhood for her) and reads this blatant roleplaying as the pathological disorder of a fragile mind:

> **POWER.** You're the one who needs help. [*He grabs her.*] Don't you know who you are? Don't you know what they're making you do?
> **SUSAN.** I get it, you want to play identity games. [*Puts her arm around him.*] I can be whoever you want. I can be a movie star. I can be your mother. [*Kisses him.*] Do you have any favourites? (54)

While Power doesn't like playing identity games with Susan/Margaret, he does play them with far too many characters, who are only too willing to be whoever they want to be for him, or, as he puts it: "So much has been done for my benefit. Too much" (63). The final player in this semi-cast of characters is Norman Lewis, who is initially presented to Power—and to the original audience—as exactly who he says he is: one half of the zany Lewis Brothers law firm, Bitch Nelson's lawyers. There is nothing, apparently, to alert the audience that anything is amiss. A quick glance at the program provided by Toronto Free Theatre informs audience members that the actor playing Norman Lewis is named Ian Beckthorpe. This listing in the program is particularly important because of the program's use as an orienting tool for the audience on at least two levels. Through its content, the program provides necessary information for the audience, somewhat like "a menu indicating what will be served—various characters—and the order in which they will appear" (Wilson, "Starters" 50). In its ideological function, it traditionally allows audience members to encompass, at a glance, the entirety of the theatrical world, "a space which is defined by its own set of conventions, most of which arise from the terms of theatrical performance viewed as distinct from everyday life" (Wilson, "Starters" 50). As far as the audience can be concerned, Norman Lewis is as "real" as his brother Sam, played by actor Maury Chaikin. It is not until the final scene, the dinner party where he finally stages the answers to the mysteries he's created, that Power reveals that Norman Lewis has "been dead for six months. [*Takes the photo. Passes it around.*] Peter Bellum director was once Peter Bellum actor. A bit of make-up. And he becomes Norman Lewis. Definitely not well enough for anyone who knew Norman but enough to pass for my benefit" (63).

Here the status of the historiographic record becomes extremely duplicitous. Basing his analysis no doubt on some of the textual remains of the play, Denis Johnston blames this incongruity of character on an authorial slip: "While the dénouement may be thematically sound, it is not theatrically consistent; for example, the revelation that Bellum had been impersonating a murdered Lewis brother is inconsistent with the Lewis's private conversation in an earlier scene. Perhaps to conceal this dramatic flaw, Bellum is glibly poisoned near the beginning of the dinner, then just as glibly resurrected later" (198-99). However, it is unlikely that a playwright so overtly concerned with theatricality and roleplaying would "accidentally" cast an extra character. And, indeed, closer scrutiny of the program reveals an inconsistency that would likely escape more casual reading: in the listing of actors provided on the first page, Ian Beckthorpe's name *does not appear.* Carlson, in fact, documents this "conflict between program practice and thriller subversion" (125) as one of the devices the postmodern comedy thriller uses to extend its horizon of theatrical control beyond the action on stage.[3] The published volume of *The Power Plays* both adds to this confusion, as well as subtly clarifies it. Throughout the text of the play, all of Norman Lewis's speeches are credited to the character called "NORMAN." However, a production photo included with the scene in which the Lewis brothers perform their zany song and dance for Power identifies the actors and characters as "Stephen Markle (PETER BELLUM), Maury Chaykin (SAM LEWIS) and David Bolt (T. M. POWER)" (40). Reading the photo and caption against the playtext, the reader may eventually realize that what the picture shows is, indeed, Peter Bellum impersonating Norman Lewis.[4] The "private conversation" to which Johnston refers is, in fact, a critique of each other's acting, hardly proof that "Norman Lewis" ever existed as a unique individual. The revelation of Norman's "real" identity is theatrically consistent once the reader understands that the program and its cast list have been co-opted into the theatrical performance.

Lest any audience members might think, like Johnston, that the confusion of identities or the characterization of people who don't appear in the play is the result of sloppiness on Walker's part, Power brings them dramatically to the attention of the audience and the other characters during his tell-all dinner party by setting three "extra" places at the table and having food served to the empty chairs. He also summarizes the dizzying dubiousness of existence enacted in the play: "Now what have we got so far. Pedro Puchinsky does not exist. Argentina does not really exist. The copper mine is not supposed to exist. And Phyllis Lazer and Norman Lewis were forced not to exist. Almost an existentialist's utopia, isn't it?" (66). Yet, in his summary of the characters who have been "murdered" somewhere near, but not exactly in, the play, Power omits the one character whose murder *was* enacted in the play: Bitch Nelson, who dives dead through "Pedro Puchinsky's" tire in the hilariously minimalist opening scene at the art gallery. This is not the first time Power has forgotten about her; throughout the play, his investigation gets off track so often that characters repeatedly have to remind him he's supposed to be solving her murder. Brigot Nelson puts it perfectly when she admonishes Power: "We live in a complex age. Truth is a relative commodity beyond your grasp. Come to grips with your limitations, man. Solve one simple murder. Take the applause. And retire!" (48-49). It is only incidentally, after he has sent the majority of the characters out to meet the police, that he extracts a confession from his boss. William Lane describes Power as "a reluctant stage manager with a deep dislike for the cast—setting demented traps for them, giving them unlikely scenes to play, and putting outrageous words into their mouths as he forces them to perform for an audience of their peers" (10), and it does appear, when all is said, that Power is, like a stage manager, the one who had the power to control the world of the play. With the climax of his detective dinner party, he does have the last (if not definitive) word on who these characters are and what they have done. Which is all the more reason to wonder why Power, who has been referred to throughout the play by his last name, all the while insisting on his inherent powerlessness, would deliberately drop that loaded appellation during the dinner party, telling the suspects: "Call me Tyrone. I want you all to think of me as one of the gang. Everyone, please call me Tyrone. [*They all look at him oddly.*]" (58).

Once again, Carlson provides a possible solution to this mystery. By becoming obsessed with his investigation of everyone other than Bitch Nelson, Power tacitly forces the Bitch into non-existence, a position from which he haphazardly recuperates her just before the curtain falls. Were this a conventional detective mystery, the actress who played the role would be "resurrected" in time to take her curtain call. Carlson describes (119-21) a production of a thriller entitled *Reserve Two for Murder*, in which there is no evidence in either the program or production notes that such closure ever took place. Like *Reserve Two for Murder*, Walker's original production of *Gossip* has left no clues behind[5] as to who played Bitch Nelson, or whether the audience ever saw her alive again after the first scene of the play. This is not only a problem of historiography almost twenty years after the production took place: the theatre program handed out to the audience in 1977 at the Toronto Free Theatre contains absolutely no listing for the actress who played the role. Once again, the program becomes an "accessory after the fact" in a murder: the character of Bitch Nelson is forced not to exist as effectively in "real life" as she is in the play. Which brings us back to Tyrone and how much power he really has.

One of the defining characteristics of the world onstage is its capacity for gossip and rumour: the (usually malicious) talk that has the power to make or break someone's "character." Characters abhor it when it hurts them, use it when they think it can help them, and can't deny that "rumours seem to be what makes the world run these days" (39). Bitch Nelson "lived" in a world where the only necessity of life was to be talked about and gossiped about; to be in the newspapers was all.[6] Much the same can be said in the world of theatre history, where only being talked (or written) about grants a type of immortality to a performance. Power's very first lines to the audience are the questions, "Who killed Bitch Nelson? [...] And who the hell cares?" (17). Within the world of the play, he blames Baxter. In the world of the theatre, it is the program that engineers her non-existence. In the "real world" of the audience, it is the audience members themselves who must in some way share the blame for her demise. Despite her character's spectacular death being the impetus for the entire play, the actress who played Bitch Nelson never appears in any of the textual remains—programs, photos, scripts, and especially reviews—that constitute the historical record of this production. History records the same fate for actress and character. By not noticing her absence, by not making her an object of discussion, the audience had the power to perpetuate the murder game on a different ontological level.

And, to return to the beginning once more, it is the audience who seems to have always already had power. As Walker himself said: "I wrote *Gossip* right after *Ramona* [*and the White Slaves*]. I wanted to reach out to a wider audience and give them more of the goods. [...] I see myself as essentially a comic writer and the trick with *Gossip* was to find the discipline to write the kind of play that would have a direct appeal. [...] People should be entertained and if they're not, then *Gossip* will be a failure. Plain and simple" (Fraser 16). In the beginning was an audience, and it begat Power.

Once he had put Power into play, it became almost inevitable that Walker should revisit him. The second installment in the trilogy, *Filthy Rich*, finds Tyrone M. Power grappling with many of the same issues of role-playing and identity that he encountered in *Gossip*, but this time the emphasis has shifted from discerning character "reality" from "acting"—the question of *who* people are—to a focus on *how* who they are affects their reading of "reality."

*Filthy Rich* plays its onstage action in a single set, a dramatic structure which, according to Johnston, "contributes to the tautness of the suspense" and makes it "a dandy detective yarn, a considerable improvement over *Gossip*" (200). The focus on a single set, according to Johnston, allows the audience to watch Power at work accumulating and interpreting clues, instead of waiting for his *faits accomplis* in a final exposition scene. However, in defining the locus of action, Johnston elides the boundary between onstage and offstage, perhaps because, unlike in *Gossip*, the offstage action is not a dark lacuna where Power detects without being detected. This time, most of the important clues that are gathered offstage are reported by the characters as soon as they arrive in Power's office, which, as one reviews points out, is nonetheless not the same as being there: "We were pinned to Power's office, indeed pinned down by his endless conversation while infuriatingly, everything exciting seemed to be happening elsewhere" (Mallet, "Misfire"). Instead, the status of this information *as* reported—already mediated by a character's discursive subjectivity—serves to underscore the play's concerns with the collusion between power and reality.

In making a distinction between mimetic and diegetic space in theatre, Michael Issacharoff points out that "[w]here mimetic space is fixed (when a single set is used), the odds are that the diegetic space will be non-fixed, that is to say, manifold" (222). In *Filthy Rich*, the audience hears about not only manifold diegetic spaces, but also an entire cast of diegetic characters, who play their major roles from somewhere offstage, unseen by the audience except through the descriptions furnished by the characters onstage. In his semiotic analysis of space, Issacharoff maintains that "the modes of reference in the case of mimetic space are more varied and complex than in the case of diegetic space, where reference is *confined* to the realm of discourse" (216, emphasis mine). While this may arguably be true for descriptions of peripheral places, it is a formula that is inadequate in the world of a play where discourse is never neutral, where words have the power to create—and change—"reality." Far from being referentially transparent, the descriptions characters give of the offstage action in *Filthy Rich* are exposed as being shaped by their own predilections: who they are creates the "reality" they read.

Whenever a new character appears on stage, it doesn't take long before another character asks, "Who are you?" a question that has less to do with names than it does with the roles they play, a vital factor in determining the way the characters will read the "reality" around them. Power's first two meetings with Jamie McLean immediately focus attention on the necessity of "reading" others correctly. On both occasions, Power's cynical misanthropy leads him to misinterpellate Jamie into places which the latter refuses to accept. However, the question of determining identity is not always as easy as asking "who are you?" When Power meets Detective Stackhouse, the audience gets the first clue that characters can't always be trusted to represent themselves truthfully:

> **STACKHOUSE.** I'd like to ask you a few questions.
> **POWER.** Would you mind telling me who you are first.
> **STACKHOUSE.** I'm the law, Power.
> **POWER.** Oh. You mean you're a policeman.
> **STACKHOUSE.** That's what I said.
> **POWER.** No. You said "I'm the law." Which is sort of like saying I'm the truth. Or I'm wisdom. Or I'm the god of the Bountiful Harvest. (84)

Power cuts through Stackhouse's meaningless clichéd abstraction, but still hasn't identified Stackhouse's real role: the detective is not acting in his "official" capacity, but is on leave from the force while in the personal employ of the mayor. All of this confusion surrounding the roles characters play sets up the central stumbling block to solving the mystery of Michael Harrison's disappearance: "One of the Scott sisters is innocent, the other guilty. The plot see-saws gently between the two alternative hypotheses, as the Scott sisters perform their strange and mysterious double act" (Lane 11).

It is Jamie McLean, "the working-class hero of these plays" (Lane 10), who best embodies how and why this see-sawing takes place. After his first meeting with Anne Scott, Jamie spells out his reasoning for presuming her innocent: "Process of elimination. Anne Scott is a classy lady. Direct. Self-assured. Not the criminal type.

Susan Scott is an unknown quantity. […] We've got to make a decision. And since Anne Scott is the one who is going to be paying us I'm all for giving her the benefit of the doubt" (97). When Jamie follows Anne from the bus station and intercepts Susan about to shoot someone, he reads the scenario as conclusive proof for his theory. After he describes the scene—which takes place offstage—to Power, Power turns the detective's logic back on Jamie to posit an alternative reading: "Look. It's very simple. Anne and Duvall are the bad guys. Susan was going to shoot them. Therefore, Susan is the good guy. Process of elimination. Get it?" (109). While the audience quickly learns that Power might not wholeheartedly endorse the rereading he has just offered, Jamie, apparently, does not. Audience members may watch in dismay as Jamie, influenced by Power, and by Susan's wealth and sex appeal, naively leaves for a romantic tryst at the Scott family guest house, while Susan exhibits her guilt by stealing the note Jamie leaves behind for Power. When Jamie reappears three scenes later jauntily sporting an expensive new shirt given to him by Susan and claiming they have fallen in love, Power has a harder time convincing Jamie that Susan "was using her sweet voice and her good looks on [him] […] a girl like her could see nothing in someone like [him]" (125). Even after Power gives Jamie the "definitive" reading of the Scott sisters' identities, Jamie insists he knows the "real" Susan: "She won't do anything. Intuition. She's not a killer. I can tell. Duvall has her in some kind of a trap or something" (129). Jamie's naiveté in the face of wealth and sex appeal inevitably culminates in the tragedy of his death.

At least, it could. Fortunately for Jamie, the dirt-poor delivery boy was not as naive as he led the audience to believe. Jamie's "resurrection" defers the end of the play long enough to expose his plot to stage his own death, pointing out to the audience that what they see is no more "real" than what they hear. In this way, the structure of the play enacts a paradigm of its central concern with how we create reality from what we see and hear.

The dual ending forces the audience to reread the scenes leading up to it, to reinterpret the characters' actions and motivations—in short, to engage in exactly the same type of interpretive activity they have just witnessed the characters perform onstage. This is not in itself a groundbreaking new strategy. Keir Elam summarizes a semiotic theory of reception which reads all performances as "an offer or invitation to the audience, paraphrasable in the performative phrase 'I offer myself for interpretation,' or perhaps 'I invite you to interpret me.' The performance or performers, then, send out a kind of polite visiting card to the spectators bearing the message 'come and interpret me'" (46). However, Elam further insists that "[i]n practice, the visiting card […] is no more nor less than the founding convention of the theatrical transaction itself: the spectator knows as part of his elementary theatrical competence that he is called upon to interpret what he hears and sees. So that if each performance does no more than renew this statutory invitation, then the overall act it performs is at best tautological, not to say feeble" (47). Instead of issuing an invitation to mere cognitive interpretation, a performance must, according to Elam, effect some type of pragmatic response in its audience. By placing so much emphasis onstage on the processes of reading and interpretation, and the powers that influence them, *Filthy Rich* conflates the cognitive and the pragmatic and offers spectators a model of the perceptual strategies operational in their own readings of reality, enacting on- (and off-) stage a model for the "general politics of truth" as defined by Foucault: "Each society has its régime of truth, its 'general politics' of truth: that is, the types of discourse which it accepts and makes function as true; the mechanisms and instances which enable one to distinguish true and false statements, [...] the status of those who are charged with saying what counts as true" (131). The removal of so much of the action into diegetic space enables the audience to "see" how malleable "reality" is. This strategy is reinforced by the activity in the mimetic space, where it becomes clear that what the audience "sees" there is also not referentially transparent, but can be read in different ways by characters as well as themselves, or, as Anne Scott sums it up, "It says more about how people like you form your ideas than anything else" (115).

For the characters in the world of the play, the politics of the city as well as the politics of "truth" are governed by money:

> It's about the way the cities in this country were first formed. Through pay-offs and favours and double-plays and connections between a handful who never let go and who can't be gotten rid of because they were in there from day one. So even when you get an honest man like my employer is, the best he can do is hold the compromise as close to the level of decency as possible. (103)

Jamie regularly extends the benefit of the doubt to those who have money, and even Power appears not above taking it when it drops into his lap. Ultimately, however, money does not become Power in this play. While Jamie is "the working-class hero of these plays," he is more than just "a cute stereotype" (Lane 10, 11) and his ability to see through the ruses of the rich is the difference between life and death for him. Moreover, it is Power, rather than the filthy rich, who has the last word in the play. When Whittacker dies leaving the suitcase full of blackmail money, Power considers it "a reward. So maybe I should earn it" (104). Anne Scott, however, astutely points out that Power will not remain virtuous among the filthy rich:

> **POWER.** [...] I've become a rich man. Independently wealthy.
> **ANNE.** Congratulations. Let's see how long *you* manage to remain clean and innocent.
> **POWER.** Money doesn't corrupt everyone lady.
> **ANNE.** No. But it will sure as hell corrupt you. You've got too many grudges. [*Pause.*]
> **POWER.** You're right.
> **ANNE.** Yes. Yes, I'm damn right.
> **POWER.** Shut up. You didn't know you were right. It was an accident. (117)

Sure enough, once Power has decided to keep the cash, he oozes into a world of slightly-drunken self-disgust, forgiving everything he's ever detested, even forgiving whoever killed his friend Whittacker. At the moment he possesses the kind of money that ostensibly conveys power, it is notable that he explicitly loses it, and begins to address himself as merely "Tyrone." When Jamie follows suit, he snaps out of his self-pity with the most energy he's mustered throughout the entire play: "[*Sits up suddenly. Angry.*] Money can't buy everything you know!! [...] Forget everything I've just said. We're starting over. I hereby dedicate the solution of this case to the memory of Fred Whittacker" (125). The solution to the case from this point is purely a function of Power: He stage-manages the scenario that finally ends the see-sawing hypotheses of the Scott sisters, and provides the definitive reading of what has "really" happened onstage and off. He corroborates Duvall's and Susan's implication in the Harrison plot with the documents in Fred Whittacker's envelope, the ostensibly "empirical" bit of evidence that also validates Power's version of the truth.

Power also accuses Duvall and Susan of murdering Whittacker, but can offer no evidence to support it, telling Stackhouse that it would be the detective's job to find the proof. This almost arbitrary off-handedness might be considered especially odd in the light of Power's earlier bold dedication of the solution to the memory of his murdered friend. A possible solution to *this* mystery lies where Bitch Nelson does: in the question of where the memory of Fred Whittacker does (or doesn't) live. Like Bitch before him, Whittacker exists in a liminal space between cast and characters; while he appears onstage to take his fatal dive (through a window rather than a tire), and his legs even reappear briefly, departing on a stretcher in the next scene, the program, published play, and other historiographic remainders never acknowledge the identity of the actor who must have portrayed him.[7] Once again, the murder victim blurs a boundary between "fictional" theatre and "real" audience. Carlson documents the premiere production of Rupert Holmes's thriller *Accomplice*, for which a program note echoes Power's sentiments: "'The cast of ACCOMPLICE dedicates their performance in this production to Crystal Matthews'" (137). The audience of *Accomplice* eventually learns that this notice, as well as the program that contains it, are elements of a fictional theatrical world. Whether or not the audience particularly noticed "these departures from traditional program practice" doesn't change the fact that they "actually marked an encroachment of fictionalization into the real world of the theatre event" (137). For the audience of *Filthy Rich*, being implicated in the "murder" of Fred Whittacker means inevitably being implicated in the "battle 'for truth,' or at least 'around truth' [...] it being understood also that it's a matter not of a battle 'on behalf' of the truth, but of a battle about the status of truth and the economic and political role it plays" (Foucault 132).

The battle "around truth" has especially important economic ramifications in the world of theatre, where the readings of a production, once put into circulation, can have a tremendous impact on its life expectancy. Walker wrote the first Power play in order to reach out to and entertain his audience, but the audience, apparently, never came—a phenomenon which threatened to repeat itself with the sequel. Toronto Free Theatre, which premiered both *Gossip* and *Filthy Rich*, laid the blame squarely on the critics, who have the power to make, or break, an audience. Among the many factors that constitute a theatre audience, only criticism and advertising specifically target people *before* they decide to attend a show. And, while advertising is by definition intended to entice potential audience members, critics who write reviews "don the guise of objectivity, and mask themselves by claiming that they speak on behalf of theatregoers" (Wilson, "Deadpan" 16) while they pronounce the "truth" about the value of a production. For the Power plays, this could have disastrous results, as this special letter to Toronto Free's "preview club members" indicates:

> It's happened again. We've presented what we think is a fine, amusing production of an exciting new play by George F. Walker, and the critics of two Toronto papers have turned in a verdict that's not very flattering.
>
> We might be inclined to listen—if it hadn't already happened like this before. *Filthy Rich* is a sequel to *Gossip*, a play we presented back in 1977. *Gossip* wasn't very well attended—and we had to close it early. One of the reasons was the press coverage. Gina Mallet dismissed the play in the *Toronto Star*. [...] But this impression was somewhat rudely discredited when the same play saw production in Seattle, Chicago, and Williamstown. [...]
>
> What's going on here? This time around, the critics can hardly ignore Walker's growing international reputation. But they still refuse to pass the kind of verdict that might help give this play the long Toronto run it deserves. [...] We don't quite understand the problem. But we do know that the attitude of the critics is going to keep a lot of people away from an entertaining and rewarding evening in the theatre.
>
> [...] This work needs your support. Come and make up your own mind. We think you'll be glad you did. (Kinch and Hendry)

Tyrone M. Power may have the final word within the play world of *Filthy Rich*, defying the corrupting influence of money, but as Whittacker slips across the boundary between theatre and reality, he becomes a reminder that the play exists within the same network it portrays, where the politics of money and power influence how (or even if) the "reality" of a performance is read. As Power gives away the $500,000 in a grass-roots appeal to undermine the political stronghold of the filthy rich, Toronto Free Theatre gives away tickets to *Filthy Rich* to undermine the power of the critics, who disguise the privilege of their position to encourage an unquestioned, and unquestioning, acceptance of the "truth" of their judgements.

Finally, in *The Art of War*, Walker lays his cards out on the table, much to the apparent relief of the critics. It is helpful, no doubt, that the play was originally commissioned as the keynote address to the Conference on Art and Reality, held at Simon Fraser University in August 1982. In *Gossip* and *Filthy Rich*, Walker "played" with the relationships between art and reality, making a deliberate spectacle of them by emphasizing metadramatic devices like character performance and staging, and trusting the audience to infer the connections between the art that shapes our reality, and the powers that control art—with, as it turned out, dubious success. In *The Art of*

*War*, Walker does away with this playfulness, foregrounding explicitly the role power plays in dictating the state of our art.

Much of the playfulness in the first two plays resulted from their structure as detective plays, or, as I have argued, something more akin to the postmodern comedy thriller, a genre that by definition hinges on the destabilization of the distinction between art and reality. While critics have pronounced *The Art of War* as odd play out because it is not strictly a murder mystery, it does have a murder as the impetus for its action, and like *Gossip* and *Filthy Rich*, bears looking at in light of the genre.

The murder in *The Art of War* takes place more or less in plain view of the audience, and by the beginning of scene 1, there is no mystery about the identity of the killers. Marvin Carlson borrows the term "howdunnit" to more accurately describe the operative strategy of many postmodern comedy thrillers, in which the emphasis has switched from uncovering the identity of the murderer to "set[ting] up a very specific plot and center[ing] the interest on whether it will succeed" (68). The focus in *The Art of War* is not on whether Power will successfully uncover the identity of his friend's murderer (Power somehow intuitively "senses" what has happened to Reinhardt), but whether he will let Hackman get away with it. However, according to Carlson, the postmodern comedy thriller did not stop with the shift from "whodunnit" to "howdunnit." As it moves towards consuming every aspect of theatrical exchange, it calls into question the boundary between the theatrical performance and the everyday "reality" of the audience: "As is often the case in comedy thrillers, we are never in any doubt about who done it, but we are quite unsure about what has been done, or upon what level of fiction or reality it has been done" (Carlson 81). Within the world of the play, we witness the murder of Paul Reinhardt, "*[c]horeographed to heartbeat-rushing music*" (135), the most detailed and explicit murder scene in any of the Power plays. As soon as the lights go up on the next scene, the mystery of who killed him is solved, as Hackman and Brown discuss the artistic merits of the murder while burying the body. However, any fan of Tyrone Power should know by now that things are not always (if ever) as straightforward as they seem. Power may not have to solve the mystery of Paul Reinhardt's murder because the audience already has, and with far more conclusive proof than any Power had previously offered. At least, the mystery is solved in *The Art of War*. However, in the tradition of Bitch Nelson and Fred Whittacker before him, Paul Reinhardt slips between the worlds of performance and reality to disappear as effectively from the historiographic remainders of the production as he does from the remaining action of the play: again, neither published play, archival production records, nor original theatre program contains any clue to the identity of the actor who splays himself against the translucent wall of Hackman's bunker as the lights go up, before being stabbed twice by the henchman Brown. Once again, the murder victim acts as a point of slippage between "theatre" and "reality," implicating the audience in the same political, economic, and artistic network that frustrates Power.

In *The Art of War*, the battle between Hackman's forces and Power's is a battle over the role of art in everyday life. Hackman may define art as "the leisurely reflection of an elite society" (162), while Power considers it "the leisurely reflection of a dying society," (159), but they both agree that the main cultural practice of art is something superfluous, to be presided over by the biggest joke in government, "an insignificant minister of culture" (157), whose activities would never make the front page. In the original production, the climactic dinner party confrontation between Hackman and Power contained "a kind of robotic yet animal dance between the insidious Hackman and the appalling Karla" (Wynne-Jones 13), which one critic likened to "opening night of the Stratford Festival: stuffed shirts strutting: the essential truth of government attitudes to art. Art is an occasion to dress up for, to be seen at, to express the *power* of government money and government presence" (Mallet, "Art"). This is the type of art Hackman is in a position to perpetuate, but it is not the type of art in which he ultimately believes. Only the art of war has the power to change anything, and Hackman proves the more committed artist in that medium, as he explains to Power before leaving: "You're indignant. You're outraged. You just don't understand, do you. Anger is a weapon. Allowing you to be brutal. Brutality is another weapon. Allowing you to take action. [...] No chance, Power. You had no chance. [Karla] hates you. She'd risk everything to beat you. You have to risk taking action!" (182).

Critics have pointed out that this is the only one of the Power plays in which Tyrone M. Power does not, finally, "get his man": the inevitable outcome of the battle between liberal idealism and autocratic power. Within the world of the play, artistic victory appears to tilt in favour of the politically influential Hackman and his stylish but superfluous spectacle that glosses over an actively brutal coercion. As the curtain falls, however, the play's first victim of Hackman's artistic brutality, Paul Reinhardt, slips across the threshold between "theatre" and "reality," projecting the battle onto a different ontological level. Power may have let Hackman get away unpunished for the murder of his friend, but Reinhardt's duplicitous status defers any possibility of closure when the curtain falls.

The argument in *The Art of War*, then, becomes part of audience "reality," where the battle has a rather different outcome. As critics have noted, *The Art of War*, like *Gossip* and *Filthy Rich* before it, is a far cry from classically-constructed drama; instead, its ambiguity and unpredictability results in precisely the kind of theatrical experience that Hackman would hate: "In performance, the Power plays demand to be bumptious and fractious, calling up a whole range of reactions in no predictable order, rather than smooth and efficient, like Hackman's insidious 'art of war'" (Lane 13). Critics (and audiences) eschewed this difficult style in *Gossip* and *Filthy Rich*, implicitly displaying their preference for the smooth and unchallenging type of spectacle of Hackman's "leisurely reflection of an elite society." This is not an unusual position for a theatre critic to take, as Wilson has pointed out (writing specifically here about *Toronto Star* theatre critic Gina Mallet):

> Apparently, only intelligence defines Gina Mallet's imaginary theatre-goer. Just as she replicates the stance of the New Critics when she suggests that reviewers must evaluate each production as a self-

> contained entity, she indicates that position when she identifies theatregoers as among the company of "educated individuals." This position renders her (or anyone operating from these assumptions) virtually incapable of discussing theatre which doesn't aspire to the standards of "high art." [...] Reviewers like Mallet, who unquestioningly employ conventional aesthetic standards, dismiss this form of performance [i.e. theatre of social action] because it doesn't adhere to their notion of "good" theatre. Thus their critical stance, although presenting itself as apolitical because it is concerned only with the quality of each production, is actually highly political for it reinforces the power of elite notions of "high" culture. ("Deadpan" 16)

Lane's description of the "bumptious" shape of the Power plays likens them to a form of social theatre: "They are, after all, the Power plays. And like the man himself, their ability to surprise an audience into new recognitions about the world is their greatest strength" (13). Reviewers who failed to pick up the connections between the medium and the message in the earlier two plays could hardly ignore them in *The Art of War*, in which Walker explicitly spells it out for them. Mallet, who pronounced that *Gossip* "simply rambles off into remote absurdities" and *Filthy Rich* had "a dead hole in the centre of the play [which] doesn't work," found *The Art of War* "brilliantly on target [...] [Walker] makes his points with a light but deadly sting, and he has also produced a play that in its laconic acceptance of the absurd projects an authentically Canadian sense of self-mockery." One negative review, on the other hand, is steeped in the language of critical distance and elitism exposed by Wilson:

> None of this troubles Walker's fans who love his unlikely wit. His comedy comes from the timeless pleasure of enjoying unavoidable human foibles. His special flair is for the SCTV sort of comedy—off-beat, contemporary cynicism that leaves middle class intellectual poseurs content in the knowledge that *they* would never stoop to being so well-intentioned. (Neil)

After everything that Power, Hackman, and their audiences have been through, such a review suddenly does "[say] more about how people like you form your ideas than anything else."

The audience that Walker (and Power) set out to find in *Gossip* had finally materialized. The original production of *The Art of War* was successful enough that it became the only one of the three Power plays to be canonized when the three major anthologies of Canadian drama were published in the mid-1980s, and reviews of the publication of *The Power Plays* trilogy repeatedly echo assertions like Conolly's that "[t]he subject matter of the third of the Power plays—*The Art of War*—is quite significantly removed from that of *Gossip* and *Filthy Rich*, and its level of seriousness is on an altogether higher plane" (111). Beyond the world of the play, artistic victory appears to tilt in the other direction, in favour of the type of quirky, indiscriminate style embodied by Power.

One of the key differences between the detective play and the postmodern comedy thriller as defined by Carlson is the latter's commitment to destabilizing the distinctions between "theatre" and "reality," in order to perpetuate the mystery and questioning on a different ontological level. The Power plays make ample use of this instability, especially through the recurring tactic of having the murder victim slip across the line between character and cast, clearly indicating that the game does not end when the curtain falls. Instead, these characters become a site of conflation for "theatre" and "reality," embattling the audience (mainly represented historiographically by critics) in the same networks of art, reality, and power demonstrated in the plays. The first two skirmishes apparently go to the critics: Power gets his murderer, but Walker fails to get his audience. The third battle resembles more of a negotiated cease-fire, with Walker giving up the playful superiority of Power in exchange for connection with a wider audience, an arrangement with far happier results for those of us who are thereby enabled to enjoy at least published Power.

Carlson notes that comedy thrillers almost invariably end in death, usually the death of the "trickster protagonist" (187) who has been responsible for the mayhem and disorder in the play. In the Power plays, where the play worlds leak into the world of the audience, it is not farfetched to consider Walker himself as the trickster protagonist. To say, "Whodunit? Walker" (Wynne-Jones 13) is to acknowledge that the problems in these plays extend far beyond the time and place portrayed in any one of them, but are as epic as the battle between Hackman and Power. If there is an ongoing war around art, a struggle for power in the face of governmental preference for superfluous spectacle, a struggle for funding on behalf of art that actively challenges the status quo of a cultural elite, surely it is more appropriate in this case that the trickster protagonist will go on instigating mayhem and disorder. Walker, like Power, must survive, because "[i]t would be more interesting if you lived and we met again."

(1997)

## Notes

1 For some interesting insights into the differences between reading and watching these plays, see Wynne-Jones. While his analysis of the actual texts of the plays is full of frustratingly unproblematized distinctions between "art" and "reality," he does offer some useful commentary on ways in which the original production dramatized aspects of the text.

2 Conolly, in his review of the published trilogy volume, echoes Johnston's assessment, making even more explicit this significant distinction between *The Art of War* and the other two plays: "The subject matter of the third of the Power plays—*The Art of War*—is quite significantly removed from that of *Gossip* and *Filthy Rich*, and its level of seriousness is on an altogether higher plane. The two early plays amuse us with their convoluted murder plots, whereas *The Art of War*, while still amusing, poses some troublesome questions about the nature of 'liberalism' in the face of autocratic power" (111). However, unlike Johnston, Conolly does not place *The Art of War* entirely outside the detective genre, but cites Power's inability to solve it as crucial for the play's "serious" message: "[Power's] ultimate triumphs in solving murder cases in *Gossip* and *Filthy Rich* are not matched in *The Art of War*, where political manipulation and corruption are shown as too strong for Power's good intentions" (111).

3 In a perfect postmodern irony, Carlson also details how the subversion of the program, effectively turning it into an additional aspect of performance, has had very serious implications for "reality" outside the theatre: "The disjuncture that this sort of experimentation has introduced between the program and its presumed referent, the physical performance, has affected not only the security of the audience reading of the program text, but other readings beyond the performance itself. The professional organization, Actors' Equity, which used to require a copy of the program for its records of professional participation in specific productions, now requires further depositions or sends representative to productions to be sure that the Actors' Equity records show who is actually performing" (125).

4 It is interesting to note that playwright Carol Bolt, whose husband, David Bolt, created the character of Tyrone Power for the original Toronto productions of all three Power plays, wrote her own thriller, *One Night Stand*, at around the same time Walker was bringing *Gossip* to life, and explicitly documents her desire to take advantage of the technique of program subversion: "I'm an admirer of the thriller form and I wondered if I could write one. [...] Now in *Sleuth*, the two people dress up as other characters, so I couldn't do that, but I decided to have a corpse! And we'd put this character's name in the programme and the audience would think that she'd be showing up eventually and it would keep them hooked!" (Rudakoff and Much 179). And, as any hockey fan knows, a power play occurs in a hockey game when either team has one player missing—a player who will eventually be released from the penalty box offstage to defuse this potentially dangerous situation.

5 According to production and administration files, photos, prompt scripts (examined in the University of Guelph Archives), and the published text of the play.

6 Scenographically, this idea was cleverly brought across in the original production by constructing the set out of sliding panels covered with newspaper. As one reviewer described it, "As each actor or actress moves on or off the stage via a sliding door, they are, in effect, rustling the pages of a newspaper—a motion that is paralleled in a literal sense, for these characters are celebrities whose every transgression makes it to the gossip columns" (*Entertainment Weekly* 28 April 1977).

7 Unlike Bitch Nelson, Fred Whittacker at least has his existence as a character acknowledged by reviewers. Bemoaning the play's structure, Gina Mallet writes, "We never met the most interesting people, the candidate and a murder victim called Whitaker [*sic*]" ("Misfire"). Mallet fails to note that while Harrison remains purely diegetic, she did "meet" Whittacker onstage briefly as an embodied actor. The prompt script for the original production, viewed in the University of Guelph archives, indicates that Whittacker's murder scene was performed onstage; however, the script contains likewise no clues to the identity of the actor who played him. Sandra Souchotte, reviewing for CBC radio, makes Whittacker's body *the* crucial element in the play—"The play is on the verge of tedium when suddenly the stage crackles with menace and the sound of gunfire. A body comes crashing through a window, clutching a briefcase containing $500,000 and some secret documents. The man is dead but the play is instantaneously much alive"—while awkwardly skirting the issue of who exactly the audience has to thank for this dramatic "rescue."

## Works Cited

Carlson, Marvin. *Deathtraps: The Postmodern Comedy Thriller*. Bloomington: Indiana UP, 1993.

Conolly, L. W. "Dramatic Trilogies." Rev. of *The Power Plays*. By George F. Walker. *Canadian Literature* 112 (Spring 1987): 110-12.

Elam, Keir. "Much Ado About Doing Things with Words (and Other Means): Some Problems in the Pragmatics of Theatre and Drama." *Performing Texts*. Ed. Michael Issacharoff and Robin F. Jones. Philadelphia: U of Pennsylvania P, 1988. 39-58.

Foucault, Michel. "Truth and Power." *Power/Knowledge: Selected Interviews and Other Writings 1972-1977*. Ed. Colin Gordon. New York: Pantheon, 1980. 109-33.

Fraser, John. "Walker Turns to Murder with Comedy." Rev. of *Gossip*. By George F. Walker. *The Globe and Mail* 19 April 1977: 16.

Issacharoff, Michael. "Space and Reference in Drama." *Poetics Today* 2 (1981): 211-24.

Johnston, Denis W. "George F. Walker: Liberal Idealism and the 'Power Plays.'" *Canadian Drama/L'art dramatique canadien* 10 (1984): 195-206.

Kinch, Martin, and Judith Hendry. Letter to Toronto Free Theatre Preview Club Members. 25 January 1979. Toronto Free Theatre Archive. XZ1 MS A837011. Archival and Special Collections, University of Guelph.

Lane, William. "Introduction." *The Power Plays.* By George F. Walker. Toronto: Coach House, 1984. 9-14.

Mallet, Gina. "*Art of War*: A Light but Deadly Sting." *Toronto Star* 24 February 1983: E1.

———. "Misfire at Free Theatre." Rev. of *Filthy Rich*, by George F. Walker. *Toronto Star* 21 January 1979: B2.

Neil, Boyd. Rev. of *The Art of War.* By George F. Walker. *Canadian Forum* 63 (May 1983), 38. Rpt. in L.W. Conolly, ed. *Canadian Drama and the Critics.* Rev. ed. Vancouver: Talonbooks, 1995. 301.

Rudakoff, Judith, and Rita Much. *Fair Play: 12 Women Speak. Conversations with Canadian Playwrights.* Toronto: Simon and Pierre, 1990.

Souchotte, Sandra. "Something Germaine." Rev. of *Filthy Rich.* By George F. Walker. Toronto Free Theatre. CBC Radio. Toronto Free Theatre Archives, University of Guelph. XZ1 MS A825033.

Walker, George F. *The Power Plays.* Toronto: Coach House, 1984.

Wilson, Ann. "Bored to Distraction: Auto-performance and the Perniciousness of Presence." *Canadian Theatre Review* 79/80 (Fall 1994): 33-37.

———. "Deadpan: Ideology and Criticism." *Canadian Theatre Review* 57 (Winter 1988): 11-16.

———. "Starters: A Theatre Progam and its Audience." *Canadian Theatre Review* 71 (Summer 1992): 49-54.

Wynne-Jones, Tim. "Acts of Darkness." *Books in Canada* (April 1985): 11-14.

## A Conversation with George Walker

by Carole Corbeil

George Walker has been writing plays for over twenty-five years, and his works have been produced around the world. His early plays, *Beyond Mozambique*, *Zastrozzi*, and *Theatre of the Film Noir*, played with the conventions of B-movies and film noir and were populated by obsessive, mad, but excessively articulate creatures. Inspired by his upbringing in the east end of Toronto, Walker went on to write what he calls his "East End plays," *Escape from Happiness*, *Criminals in Love*, *Love and Anger*, to name a few, plays featuring anguished characters in dire situations, but all looking for a way out. *Love and Anger*, in particular, struck deep chords in Toronto, addressing as it did the struggles of haves and have-nots in the neo-con eighties. Walker has now written the *Suburban Motel* series, a cycle of six plays, all set in the same motel room. While each play is meant to stand on its own, some of the characters appear more than once; the characters are desperate, the plays dark yet mordantly funny. In *Problem Child*, the first play in the series, a young couple, Denise and R.J., are in the motel room waiting for a call from the social worker who will decide whether they will get their baby back from state custody. In *Adult Entertainment*, two middle-aged cops, Donny and Max, take the law into their own hands. *Problem Child* and *Adult Entertainment* had already been produced at Toronto's Factory Theatre when I met George. He was rehearsing *Criminal Genius*, which was about to open. We spoke in the run-down splendour of the Factory's green room.

**CC:** You know, *Beyond Mozambique* is the first show I ever saw in Toronto.

**GW:** Is this true?

**CC:** Yeah.

**GW:** Wow—that's a long time ago!

**CC:** I was thinking I don't remember anything about it except that the feeling was wild and reckless. And I still have that feeling about your work! That wildness. Do you ever think back, Oh I did this phase and then I did that phase? Do you think of your work in terms of an arc or …

**GW:** I think sometimes in interviews you're made to think those things. When I first talked to Ken Gass [artistic director of Factory Theatre], when they made me resident playwright when I was twenty-three years old, all I felt that I wanted to do, even then, was make a body of work. And he said he would protect me so that I could do that—that it wouldn't be about one play or even one phase—so that falling in and out of fashion or having harder times and easier times would never be the issue.

**CC:** That's an extraordinary gift to give somebody.

**GW:** Oh, for sure. It was a big deal, a big, big deal. He said, You write, we'll protect, and you'll do it. That's an investment in the writer. And once we're investing in you, then we've an obligation to let you do the work. I think of it in terms of a benchmark in self-confidence. The second benchmark was when my work first started to get done in the States, that was a big thing, because I knew they weren't doing it because the [Canada] Council said they had to. I was always suspicious up till then. Just something underlining all Canadian choices. I think I still have this suspicion to some degree.

**CC:** Do you ever think that you kind of swung back and forth between two approaches in your writing? In *Beyond Mozambique* you had a sort of surreal—

**GW:** It could be called speculative writing—I think the work started outside of myself. I don't think there were two things. Part of it was because I was really young when I started, I had no artistic background and always was very suspicious of theatre, even when I was in it. There were all sorts of reasons for it, but I think those were the two big ones: being suspicious of it and not knowing what it was. Then just kind of growing and not leaving. I thought: I may as well start giving more of myself to this, more of my life, I started to let that come. I just opened the door and let it come.

**CC:** Do you think it was a process of maturation?

**GW:** Generosity. I think that's the most important thing in theatre, the most important quality you can find in an actor, and therefore the most important thing you can find in a writer. And you have to be able to feel like an idiot, in theatre, the way actors have to—you're going to go out, totally exposed: I'm an asshole. This is it—the feeling of coolness falls away—I never felt a great cool, but the little cool I felt continued to fall away. And you put yourself out there. One critic in Washington said that the politics in *Love and Anger* were naive, and I remember thinking, well they would be—if they were politics! What they are are desperate emotions!

**CC:** Exactly—"Love and Anger"!

**GW:** They're not a cool, political view of the world. This is what happens to people when they get frustrated—they go nuts! This boy [Petie, the protagonist of *Love and Anger*] is *nuts*. That's what I think is important about that—you're marginalized and you get desperate. You can put yourself out there in that way and look as foolish and naive as the characters, which in fact, I am! Why wouldn't I be? So I had to come to grips with the idea that there are no *ideas*, per se, worth exploring in theatre. I don't have any great ideas. I don't know anyone who has great ideas or has come across a great idea. The only time I came across an idea that made any sense to me was that we're all really, really pathetic, but we should try anyway! And I thought, well, that's enough. It's the trying anyway part that was the active part of that, and that's all you need to hold onto in theatre—try anyway.

**CC:** Do you think that *Love and Anger* was a real turn-around for you, in terms of connecting with the audience on that visceral level?

**GW:** I think there was a lot of connection. I had the same thing happen with *Escape from Happiness* from women who go, "It's me, it's my sister!"

**CC:** I wanted to talk to you about that, the thing I've always loved about your work—the women get to the boiling point so quickly, and that's so familiar to me—having a very quick cooking temperature! So that there's an incredibly aggressive—

**GW:** They get to act out.

**CC:** Does that come from sisters?

**GW:** It comes from sisters, for sure. I've been around women.

**CC:** How many sisters do you have?

**GW:** I have three. Yeah, I'm not used to women who think of themselves as victims. You start writing strong women and you come across a whole generation of women actors who have been asked to play victims for a long, long time. I remember doing this early on, with some of these actors, going, I still don't understand why, when your script says you're angry at him, it comes across like you're angry at yourself. What's that all about? It's okay to be angry at yourself sometimes, but sometimes it's just okay to be angry at someone else. That was a big thing. So the actors worked that out. Now I think they know. If the woman in a Walker play is mad, she's *mad!* She's not feeling like she's a victim, she can be mad. You don't have to carry the weight of the world with you—you can just be pissed off. My friend Danny [De Raey]—an American director—did a little intro in the published book of this, and he says that women in these plays get to get in touch with their wilder, more intense sides (5). They don't have to walk whatever that line is that women are asked to walk in literature, so often, or in a play—

**CC:** Where women are reacting to things.

**GW:** Reacting to things!

**CC:** The women in your plays all drive the thing. In *Problem Child*, Denise, who is trying to get her child back, just drives that play from beginning to end.

**GW:** Exactly. She is the power, she is where the stakes lie, and she is the force. I said to Shawn [Doyle, who plays R.J., Denise's husband], that's a male thing too, that's okay. I said, you can be okay, you're not weak. It's a very generous, powerful thing that you're doing there! It's like supporting this *power*, that needs to act out, this feeling of sadness, this rage, and just giving it licence.

**CC:** And there are so many men like that, who are never given that portrayal struggling to be good, to be part of it, and not—

**GW:** And not in charge. I know! I used to say, Shawn, this is my problem! I know what it's like. Women will talk about the problem, in all of its diversity. Men will think, well, what's the point, you've got to solve it right away! No, you've got to *live* it, is what she's saying. So they're different. You know what's great for me is that a writer is putting them centre-stage. In some way all these characters are secondary, or even walk-ons, in a lot of other plays, they don't get any lines, and sometimes they're not even there, they just get referred to. Like scum of the earth or people we met over there or the neighbours—you bring them on centre-stage. So I'm bringing Denise into the middle of the play and letting her act out the things that she wants. She's formidable. I find it liberating as a writer.

**CC:** I find it exhilarating. It's like a whole bunch of oxygen comes into the room and people just go!

**GW:** I think it's got that quality because now, more than ever, I'm not trying to do anything. I'm not trying to go anywhere, I don't have any place I'm trying to get to, I don't have anything I'm trying to accomplish. I'm just there. It's something to do with the way actors work—some of it's method, in a sense, kind of getting inside and whatever happens is valuable in some way.

**CC:** Very few playwrights direct their own work. You do, and the quality that you bring as a director is that there's going to be that intense engagement between the actor and the character. It's almost Zen, it's about that moment of being totally *there.*

**GW:** Totally there, totally connected. I talk about that all the time—it's the connection. You can't be wrong, you can only be connected! We're all wrong, if there's such a thing, but it's connected. I've learned a lot about connecting the writing by understanding how actors work, and putting all the things together, putting them in this room where there's nothing else around—no terrain that you have to crawl around, there's just this, nothing between the actor and the character. It's sort of like music, not worrying about where it's going. There's some kind of narrative—he wanted this, she wanted that, that's what happened and that's it, I can't do any more. I'm not trying to create great art. I'm not trying to create *any* art, actually, but I want something very alive in the room. That's all.There's a moment in *Problem Child,* a part where they look like they're going to kill each other, when they're fighting about something. Denise just wants, she says I want this baby, I'm going to have this baby. It can only happen if it's invested and a bit dangerous.

**CC:** I don't think there's a greater plot in the world than a mother separated from her child.

**GW:** It comes from where the character starts. I have, I want this. Basic stuff! I want this, I can't have it, I want her.

**CC:** You're always working with the element that's pure theatre.

**GW:** Basic need, *really* basic need and want. Again, I think the room helps with that. I've never stopped myself when I was writing, never said, I think this should be more about this and more about that. I guess that comes with a certain confidence. You live on a planet, you have a life, therefore the whole thing, or even an aspect of it, is worth writing about. It contains elements of heroism and simple confusion, whatever—but that's it, that's all you're going to get.

**CC:** Watching *Problem Child* though, you understand how people end up. With Denise's last speech, you understand that if those conditions are not met, that basic condition of having your child, the sadness is for life.

**GW:** Mm-hm. And the anger.

**CC:** The anger, and the killing of self. That's extremely powerful.

**GW:** I felt that she wanted to share some of that, directly, with the audience. To end a play on a speech like that, it just sort of happened. And I thought, What a very generous thing for her to do! Also, when you write these plays, they don't have endings ever. In *Love and Anger* in particular, I'd go Stop! and then I'd go, Oh, there's a bit more! It's really me saying, if the work is getting closer and closer to the bone, then it's the ending which seemed the most artificial, if you look for it, if you find it. I try to avoid that by not having endings.

**CC:** Because the closure is the lie, right?

**GW:** Exactly. I always feel kind of sloppy and confused at the end of my plays. I go, I just feel kind of fucked up. Oh, wow, I felt fucked up! So this is as close as I can get to an ending for *Problem Child*, because I felt more fucked up than anywhere I can remember. At the end of the speech, I became more fucked up than I was, but I tried to say, but we can't sit here all night, and things are not going to get any better.

**CC:** But there's another beautiful twist there, when she goes on the bed and tries to make R.J. feel all right. She hides that despair from him, for that moment.

**GW:** Yeah, and she says in the speech, I can't do that or he'll die!

**CC:** Yeah! So even though we know the despair and the bitterness that's to come, there's still that human thing of protecting someone from one's own despair, which is beautiful.

**GW:** It's just a little thing, but I thought, again, that it was important that she went back to him, to say this and this, because that's who she is as well. She has all this other stuff, despite the rage and everything. I was sort of there with her. There's a critic at the *Washington Post*—who's actually a big fan—who has problems with my endings. A friend of mine got tired of hearing about it. He said, the same stuff you liked about his work is why he's having a hard time ending his play—don't you see that? They're all part and parcel! There are no endings, he's saying that, you can't do that—have that emotional mess—and then go, Aha! But here's the satisfactory ending. It becomes, How do I get out of this, now that I'm in the middle of it? In *Criminal Genius*, they all die—that was my solution. They all fucking die! I was stunned by this, I was truly stunned.

**CC:** It's a very Canadian ending!

**GW:** Well, I thought, How are they gonna die? I don't know. They lived by this and they're going to die by this. And I thought, There's an ending. No one can talk now—they're all dead!

**CC:** *Adult Entertainment* seems a much darker play to me.

**GW:** With *Adult Entertainment*, I just let it go where it had to go. I felt it going down and down and down. The next cop play, the other cop play, *The End of Civilization*, is darker. It's the bleakest thing I've ever got anywhere near. And again, it's just going there, I'm not pushing it there. But these two cops start opening their mouths, about what they think about work and their lives and their families' lives and everything else, and you just kind of let them do that.

**CC:** *Adult Entertainment* seemed to be about the hell of middle-age ambivalence! Nobody's really where they want to be and nobody has done what they really wanted to do.

**GW:** I think it's probably true in a lot of that, there's a lot of me in there—me and those guys—middle-aged men in their underwear walking around going, This is it. This is it! It's also a special treat to see in the theatre, eh? Middle-aged guys in their underwear. We kept saying to people, people, Now *this* is beautiful—middle-aged men in their underwear, this is beauty, look at this! Take it in guys, you're never going to see it again!

**CC:** I loved that. The exposure on that level has always been female.

**GW:** Exactly.

**CC:** And the men have never run around, in their little BVDs, in their paunches—

**GW:** Well, they get to have it, it's their play in a lot of ways, so they have the responsibility to say, It's our play, here we are in our underwear.

**CC:** What's wonderful about it is that it's actually really attractive, in a funny way!

**GW:** Because it's not—

**CC:** It's human.

**GW:** Yes, human, and then it's not anything other than what it is. Layne's [Coleman who plays Max, a cop] in that underwear for a long time, in that first scene. Then you get Ron [Lea, who plays Donny, another cop] and I felt really good about the acting. Here I am, doing this stuff, and here are these guys doing their stuff. We're meeting each other in some way that's very interesting. But it gets to the point where—I think that chilling moment when he straps on the gun and goes off to do what he's gonna do to the kid. Without a lot of fuss, just—And his final speech I found chilling, really chilling. I just let him go, thinking, well this is how they think. So it seemed all right. I wasn't stopping anything. That's mostly what I remember. I wasn't putting the brakes on anything.

I hadn't been writing theatre for a while, so when I went back I thought, I'm just going to do what I want! And when I finished those two, I thought, yeah it's different. There's some kind of shift in the writing.

**CC:** Yeah, because there's no crusader figure in either of them, like the thing in *Love and Anger* where Petie is standing up for the good fight.

**GW:** Remember we talked about this around *Love and Anger*, or even *Escape*, that I was looking for the light, I was actually searching for it. In *Escape from Happiness* it was important to me to look for some kind of resolution in that family. I was looking. So that got in. And then to let all that drop away, if you're going to let that drop, then everything has to drop away. Then you just write it from the character's point of view, and god knows what their point of view is going to be about certain things. So I have no point of view, I wasn't looking for anything. And it's that way in all six plays, I think, to varying degrees, but it's basically it.

When you get to *The End of Civilization*, which is about this middle-class couple—a middle-class couple from the suburbs and they are fucked—they can't be saved, they are economically fucked. He's frustrated. And it ends with this bleakness, with the wife sitting on the bed for ten minutes, in silence, because she can't find anything to say. I wanted to give the audience a feeling of what that would be like. I don't know if we can do that, but it felt not necessarily a healthy thing to do. I wanted to be healthy, for a long time, in and around *Love and Anger*, I wanted to contribute, to be the good citizen. Now I suppose it's okay to say, I don't give a fuck. I'm that way. So I'm in this thing where I'm not responsible for saving the world, or making it better or anything else. I'm going to write these little plays, and they're going to go where they're going to go. They'll be zanier than usual, sometimes, and sometimes they'll be darker than usual. But that's the power of the room, to just open the door and go, Oh, this is this one! Maybe that's the point of view that you'll be able to address, and I felt better as I was writing them.

**CC:** What brings the couple to the motel room?

**GW:** They've come looking for work. They've come to a bigger city, from a small town. He hasn't had work in a long, long time. Middle management, laid off, he's been out of work a long time. They've left the kids with her sister, they're on the verge of losing their house, everything. They've got nothing. It's been a couple of years. And the cops are there, Donny and Max are there because, where this guy has been going to apply for work, people have been getting killed. The fact is, he's killing people. He's fucked. The husband. He's gone.

**CC:** He's snapped?

**GW:** He snaps; in a very interesting way. At first the wife says, Who's died? Management? They go, No, other guys that have been applying for work. She says, well, he'd kill management. I could see him doing that. But it turns out he kills them because he calls them disgusting toadies, sucking up! What he calls a process of degradation. Donny knows her from school, from high school, so there's a kind of connection. And it just gets bleaker.

**CC:** Are you saying that we have an illusion that we are something or someone, but it's actually certain conditions that create us?

**GW:** Exactly. And I think as long as conditions support who we think we are, everything will be more or less okay. If conditions get relentlessly bad and keep changing, then I think it's all up for grabs. I really do. I think it comes all up for grabs that this middle-class guy can go, They disgusted me! I'm depressed, it's degrading, and I'm disgusted, I'm mad, I'm really, really mad!

**CC:** Do you see it as a condition of late capitalism?

**GW:** There's something going on there. I feel really connected to it. I feel connected to it as part of the world and the middle-aged thing, also the economic thing.

**CC:** I think that's fairly new, isn't it? I mean, in the last half of our century, that the snakes and ladders of life are really tricky right now. You see people on the street who do say they were managers and—

**GW:** I think that's definitely true. We've had a couple of decades of it now. I think that's starting to sink in. That this is actually possible. There's an elite that is probably protected from that, but not many people are.

**CC:** As you're describing it to me, I know that sense of marginality—

**GW:** Artists in particular, people working in the arts, feel that kind of lack … The guy in *The End of Civilization* says, I went to school, I went to work, I did this as part of my social contract. His contract is broken and all the rules are off. So he says, It's finished. The rules, behaviour, everything. His wife says, You're nuts. He says, Maybe. This is how I take it, this is how I sense it. I have rage, and I feel like acting on it. I'm writing this, and I'm going, Oh, neat! In a way. What would he do?

**CC:** But you're picking up on the zeitgeist. There's no question that the elite is getting more and more removed and smaller and stronger—that's what the feeling is in society, anyway, that even with environmental ruin, we know the elite will build their ark.

**GW:** For sure. And we'll be left. It's certainly right, that feeling was there. But I felt kind of bad, having written it. It was like, bring people into the theatre and make them feel bad.

**CC:** But there's a mirror aspect to theatre, right?

**GW:** Yeah—you feel good about feeling bad. You feel good about voicing the concern, is how I think about it. Here's something that's obviously on my mind—is it on your fucking mind? So maybe now we can start worrying about it together.

**CC:** The very act of showing your cards is a kind of hopeful thing?

**GW:** I think so. Maybe we should listen to these people, who are sending out warnings about this stuff. Maybe that's what it was, acting out the fears of these things. It's interesting when you come across a character who says something alarming, that alarms you, you go, No—where did that come from? You go searching for it in yourself, and you think—It's all public knowledge, it's all public domain, and you've just filtered it in. But there's a couple of times—in *Adult Entertainment* and in this—that I think it's got to do with middle-aged men and has to do with all sorts of stuff. I'd just as soon not go there, but I went there.

**CC:** In *Adult Entertainment*, I find it very moving when Donny says, I go home and this is the family and it's all very nice, and I know that's not the world, and I can't stand the discrepancy.

**GW:** Again, he's outside of a protective layer, so he can say and feel just about anything. That's why it's scary. He mocks all that progressive stuff and says things like, Maybe I have to get some counselling and shit like that. That's a moment I find chilling. This is what he thinks about counselling: shit like that, pleasant shit. Meanwhile he likes sex this way, he lives this kind of life and that's what makes sense to him. I had a feeling like that, walking through Parkdale. How can you separate those lives? How long can you separate life with a family and our big, long Toronto streets full of debris and homeless, fucked-up people? How long can they be really separate? How separate are they now? How are they going to get entwined, finally, down the road? They can't do it, can't have all these parallel lines, it's wrong in some way. I don't know if it's a moral, but it's wrong.

**CC:** Do you think the time you spent working in TV made you freer, when you went back to theatre?

**GW:** Yeah, because I thought if I'm going to go back to theatre, then I'm really going to go back and I'm going to *do* it. Because what's the point? There's no money—I've learned that about theatre—I think I'll go back to theatre and make no money—seriously no money!

**CC:** I'd like to talk about pacing, for a bit. Do you think you have a different pace than other directors?

**GW:** It's interesting—Ken [Gass] went to see *Problem Child* in New York, in a small off-off. He said, I certainly didn't think it was a small production because the director was doing it down there—the guy's done my work a lot. It was fifteen minutes slower than my production. This production of *Problem Child* is fifteen minutes faster than the New York production, and I know it wasn't slow down there. Yeah, it is [different].

**CC:** You're fast.

**GW:** I believe the audience takes in the information faster than we think they do. But more importantly than that, I'm trying to get the actors to the same place where

I am when I've written it. I think the actors bond with the material—I'm trying to get them close to how I wrote it. It sounds primitive but it's right in a way.

**CC:** So they're never thinking about what's coming next.

**GW:** Exactly. I wasn't thinking, so why should they? In that way. But I'm getting them closer to the pulse of it. I also say to actors, When you get there, you'll know, because the play then comes in behind you, stiffens your back, and that's where the play helps you. No, it's not about fast, it's where it lives, where the stakes are, and keeping you not thinking but listening. I'm only saying this because of what you just said. I'm not saying this because I have some thought. I'm responding and I'm taking it farther. I'm also the writer, so I get impatient. I'm not there trying to create great moments. I have no respect for the work, in a way.

**CC:** You don't have to have your directorial ego impose a vision on it.

**GW:** No. It's about acting. For me, when the work disappears into the actor, that's when it's successful. There is no text. Someone said that the best is when actors are doing it and you think they're making it up. Because there is no construction. There's response and listen. Then you go to the next thing, and you go, I thought they were making it up, how come they're doing exactly the same fucking thing, and how come it looks like they're making it up again! You know? To commit to the mess, too, before you try and look for solutions of clarity. Take the mess just as far as it will go.

I'm learning stuff. I feel with actors that they keep raising the bar on each other. It's there to get the actor and the text as close as they possibly can be, together. It's really just them. I know that feeling when the text is gone, the play is gone. It's just performance now. That's when I'm happy.

**CC:** I find that in all the arts, when you forget that there is a writer, when it's completely transparent, you're in it and you're not thinking about how it was made, that's what is always wonderful for me.

**GW:** Yeah. And I think when actors are acting on stage they're required to do so many things. In my plays there's a lot of stuff. There's a mind/spirit/body connection, there's athleticism, there's a lot of text, the body's involved in it. It thrills me to ask them to do more, all the time.

**CC:** That reminds me of something. When I saw *Escape from Happiness* and also *Love and Anger*, I felt that having children had changed your writing. What you witness when they're very young, their tantrums, the directness of their wants and their needs had come into your work in a big way.

**GW:** I think so too. Except I couldn't put it any better than that. That's probably what it is. Asking someone like Barbara Gordon, who's also gone through motherhood, to tear that kitchen apart—that's all I had to say: Tear it apart!

**CC:** What do you think about the fact that all the big theatres in Canada are not available to playwrights?

**GW:** I think that this particular generation of artistic directors is pathetic, I really do, coast-to-coast, all these artistic directors of those regional theatres. I think that on that level—and a couple of other levels—they seem to be passionless dweebs.

**CC:** How do you account for it?

**GW:** I don't know. It might be generational, it might just be a response to a crisis, that they've all gone looking for a board-friendly artistic director. Do you know that Thompson [director Paul Thompson] calls them The Gentles? I love that line. But it's sort of what they are: perfectly fine people, but I don't feel any kind of passion. To put new work up requires a commitment, and an ability to take a risk that I don't think they're willing to take.

So I think it's worse now than it's ever been, on those stages, because these people are gutless. It could come back again. They're all around the same age. But if you look coast to coast … they're all pleasant people, but they should not be running the flagship theatres of these towns.

**CC:** It means that there's a generation of Canadian playwrights who can't make a living. You could make a living if you were playing in those houses and getting those royalties.

**GW:** Oh, sure, exactly. They're actually big. When you start getting those American regional theatre productions. *Nothing Sacred* was done all over the west coast, Seattle Rep, American Conservatory in San Francisco—1,600 seat house.

**CC:** That's nice.

**GW:** Yeah! That's TV money! [*Laughter*] Really, when you do that. But if you don't have access to the big stage, then you're asking the poor to produce you. … And you're right, they could bring in a whole generation of Canadian playwrights, making a living, reaching a wider audience. The audience in that size of theatre challenges you back. Playwrights learn from that kind of exposure to the larger audience, the subscription audience. You've got to reject or accept certain of what they ask. They're going to go, Oh, we didn't like this, and we've got to go, Well, maybe you should like more of the other thing. Or maybe I should listen to you a bit, too. But whatever it is, you don't get that chance.

**CC:** You're not only deprived of money, you're deprived of an opportunity to grow.

**GW:** For sure. And you stay in a small house, and you hear the same thing over and over again, I loved your work, in relative terms. And yeah, that's bad. You just give up on those guys. Unless they change how they behave and what they do, I really don't want to go play with them. I think it's not so much the language in my plays that offends them. I think these guys, this generation of artistic directors, don't even know who these characters are. I don't think they even get close enough to reject them. I think they look at Denise and R.J., and they don't even know who they are. Some part of them is going, Why is George writing about these people?

Who are these people? It's become such a middle-class activity, this group of people who are running this stuff.

**CC:** Yes, so the success of Canadian theatre is that it's become bourgeois and it no longer does Canadian theatre!

**GW:** That's right—as we always expected would happen! [*Big laughter*] Good work! We could have just skipped the last twenty years, and said "The play you want is in America!"

**CC:** Are we going to end on this note? Find the light, George.

**GW:** I'll find the light. Now, either they'll grow up—these people—or they'll just be replaced. Maybe the ones under them are going to take those chairs again. So a handful of theatres—Factory and Passe Muraille and a few other theatres—year after year, are going to do the work.

(1998)

## Works Cited

De Raey, Daniel. Introduction. *Suburban Motel* 4-6.

Walker, George F. *Adult Entertainment. Suburban Motel* 50-104.

———. *Beyond Mozambique. Three Plays by George F. Walker.* Toronto: Coach House, 1978. 87-135.

———. *Criminal Genius. Suburban Motel* 105-56.

———. *Criminals in Love.* Toronto: Playwrights Union of Canada, 1984.

———. *The End of Civilization. Suburban Motel* 213-63.

———. *Escape from Happiness.* Toronto: Coach House, 1992.

———. *Love and Anger.* Toronto: Coach House, 1990.

———. *Problem Child. Suburban Motel* 7-49.

———. *Suburban Motel.* Vancouver: Talonbooks, 1997.

———. *Theatre of the Film Noir.* Toronto: Playwrights Canada, 1981.

———. *Zastrozzi, The Master of Discipline: A Melodrama.* Toronto: Playwrights Co-Op, 1979.

## From *The Theatre of Form and the Production of Meaning: Contemporary Canadian Dramaturgies*

by Ric Knowles

### from "Modernism and Its Containments"

The early absurdist plays of George F. Walker and Michael Hollingsworth, the Beckettian one-act plays of Michael Cook, and Tom Cone's explorations of modernist forms drawn from painting all emerged in Canada between 1971 and 1976 and presented recognizable if often inventive variations on familiar European modernist models. Thus, Hollingsworth's *Strawberry Fields* (1973) and *Clear Light* (1973)—although, because of their tendency toward violence, scatology, and sexual "perversity," they have most often been discussed in terms of Artaud and a theatre of cruelty-style catharsis that, in its ideological effects, is like its Aristotelian counterpart (Hancock)—are perhaps best seen as typically modernist theatrical images, however violent, images that, to paraphrase Archibald MacLeish on poetry, do not mean but simply are.[1]

Cook's Beckettian plays, *Tiln* (1971) and *Quiller* (1975), are similarly memorable less for their language, themes, or characterization than for their riveting images: of Tiln as a self-appointed god of light, accompanied by the screeching of gulls, moving through a land- and seascape peopled only by Fern, who is buried to the neck in a barrel of brine and dying in a lighthouse at the edge of an apparently empty universe; and of Quiller in his dilapidated longjohns on the stage of his clapboard house/coffin arguing with and cajoling the Lord or anyone else who passes by.

Walker's earliest plays, *Prince of Naples* (1971) and *Ambush at Tether's End* (1971), have been described by Chris Johnson in "George F. Walker: B-Movies beyond the Absurd" as "exercise[s] in the theatrical techniques of the Absurd" and compared, respectively, with Ionesco's *The Lesson* and Beckett's *Waiting for Godot* (90, 89-90). Renate Usmiani, like Johnson, interprets these plays as making "a negative statement about the human condition" (37). But neither Johnson nor Usmiani engages in any detailed structural analysis or comments on the significance of Connie Brissenden's observation that "the characters George [Walker] creates seem to hang suspended in space, and they [the plays] are all set somewhere and everywhere" (*Now* ix). The combination of existential despair with the lack of specific social referents and the use of an essentially closed formal model seem to replicate the modernist self-containment of the theatre of the absurd. Even in these plays, however, Walker's characteristic irony creates a formal fissure indicative of the discomfort that Canada's most modernist playwrights have frequently felt with the form. *Ambush at Tether's End*, closely modelled on *Waiting for Godot*, works structurally, as does its model, to contain signification and resist referentiality, but it nevertheless inserts at its outset the self-consciously sardonic premise that "evasiveness is next to godliness" (89) and insinuates the possibility of human choice or agency by creating a portrait of Max's conscious (if posthumous) manipulation of Galt and Bush, the play's Vladimir and Estragon characters. In *Prince of Naples*, similarly, there are moments that rely on a self-consciousness—about interpretation and inscrutability (64), about phrases such as "existential conundrum" (72), about the play's own use of Nietzsche (the titular "Prince of Naples" [74-75]), about the theatre (99), and about the 1960s (78-79)—that serves structurally to open the play outward in a way that the metatheatrical references in Beckett, which tend to fold the audience into the play's modernist enclosure, do not.

The references to the 1960s in *Prince of Naples*, in fact, place the 1971 play in a historical moment when existential angst was a popular component of the "disaffection among young adults" that the Local Initiative Program (LIP) and Opportunities for Youth (OFY) grants that funded Factory Lab and other alternative theatres were created by government in part to reduce (Johnston 7). The same 1960s disaffection also ultimately points toward Walker's more direct engagement with his society in his later plays. Overall, however, the ideological work performed by these plays is culturally affirmative, serving to deflect disaffection into existential inertia in which audiences are directed to "suffer" (*Ambush* 89) or, as in Walker's *Zastrozzi* and the best "art-for-art's-sake" tradition, "occupy yourselves" (55).

### from "Aristotle, Oedipus, and the Bible: Forms of Naturalism"

Aristotelian *peripeteia* and *anagnorisis* derive from an analysis of a specific kind of drama in a specific historical place and period reflecting specific ideologies; as analytical tools, however, they have been adapted, reconsidered, interpreted, and used with universalist claims throughout the history of Western dramatic criticism, with the result that these structures and the ideologies that they embody have remained privileged, in Canada as elsewhere. In his discussion of Shakespeare's "problem comedies," Northrop Frye points to survival and deliverance as underlying factors in the "unifying social ideologies" of all cultures, and he sees these dominant "myths of concern" reflected in Aristotelian reversal and recognition:

> We notice that some words in religion, such as "conversion" in Christianity or *paravritti* (turning around) in Buddhism, or "revolution" in political ideology, emphasize the fact that one thing necessary is a reversing of the normal current of life. Other words, such as "enlightenment" or "salvation," emphasize rather the sense of recognition that accompanies this process. Reversal and recognition, then, seem to be structural principles outside literature. (*Myth* 13)

It is clear from this account that, as structural principles that function to affirm "unifying social ideologies" in the realms of literature, religion, and politics, reversal and recognition, like conversion, revolution, enlightenment, and salvation, are linear and dialectical concepts that invoke social containment and dramatic closure. And, as Frye remarks elsewhere,

> as far as his main historical influence goes Aristotle points straight ahead. He worked out the organon of a deductive logic [...] and provided a technique for arranging words to make a conquering march across reality, subjects pursuing objects through all the obstacles of predicates, as the Macedonian phalanxes of his pupil Alexander marched across Asia. (*Great Code* 9)

Frye's argument and his metaphors strongly suggest that the ideological weight and endurance of reversal and recognition as structural principles—particularly as articulated by Frye and other modernist critics and as inherited by Canadian students, scholars, critics, theatre professionals, and audiences—render them difficult to avoid completely and useful only through active and creative perversion as shaping structures for those interested in alterity, contingency, or heterogeneity.

In the introduction to *Endangered Species: Four Plays* (1988), Margaret Hollingsworth claims to have written the short, experimental plays "out of perversity" (7). Although she makes the comment in passing, it strikes me as a good starting point for a discussion of what I think of as "the dramaturgy of the perverse" in a number of contemporary Canadian plays, including [...] plays by George F. Walker [...].

The definitions cited for "perverse" in the *Oxford English Dictionary* range from "selfwilled or stubborn (in error)" to "untoward, froward; disposed to go counter to what is reasonable or required; hence, wayward, petulant, cross-grained." For "pervert," they include "to misapply, misconstrue, wrest the purport of." As a structural principle, perversity may usefully be seen as a revisioning of Aristotelian *re*versal (and recognition) as well as an intertextualist (or "interstructuralist") rejection of modernist purity, clarity, and self-containment [...] Unlike the more familiar concept of *sub*version, however, the perverse is not simply arranged in an oppositional (and therefore affirming) relationship to the dominant. Perversion is dialogic in Bakhtin's sense,[2] more variously disruptive and less simply reactive than the concept of subversion suggests.

As a structural device, the perverse revisions the romantic and post-romantic conceptions of unified subjectivity and of unified character and action. It focuses on the *constructed* nature of identity; it displaces the symbolic authority of structural principles such as reversal and recognition; and, while acknowledging and employing engagement with character, plot, and dramatic ritual, it disrupts the complacent, voyeuristic, oedipal, or ecstatic satisfactions and containments provided by dramatic catharsis.

Among the clearest and most prominent contemporary Canadian examples of the creative perversion of neo-Aristotelian dramaturgy are the plays of George F.

Walker, in which what he calls "the Walker twist" [3] replaces reversal as a structural principle; in which recognition, at the least, is a more complex and less comfortable concept than in more traditionally linear dramatic structures; and in which the satisfaction of closure is rarely provided. Indeed, if Walker follows any tradition, then it is that of dramaturgical perversity as established by Christopher Marlowe, that most "wayward, petulant, cross-grained," and unsettling of the Elizabethans, whose plays have disturbed drama critics almost as much as his life and opinions disturbed Elizabethan authorities. Walker's *Zastrozzi*, in fact, in its unimpeded and unreversed rising action, echoes the structure of Marlowe's *Tamburlaine*, in which expectations based on the Christianized Aristotle of the *de casibus* tradition are aroused and, together with all sense of poetic justice and dramatic containment, disappointed. Like Marlowe in *Tamburlaine*, *The Jew of Malta*, and *Dr. Faustus*, in which religious, legal, and political authority as well as classical dramatic structure are both invoked and denaturalized, Walker neither rejects nor revises (nor, as he consistently insists, parodies [4]) neo-Aristotelian structures; rather, he perverts them, using them in ways that acknowledge their cultural authority while fracturing and misusing it.

The final scene of Walker's *Love and Anger* uses a trial, perhaps the most conventional of dramaturgical devices for the achievement of reversal and recognition, but it does so in a most unconventional way. Near the end of the play, the publisher of a sensationalist newspaper ("a fascist rag" [21 and passim]) is kidnapped and tried by a lapsed lawyer on the charge of being evil before a makeshift judge who has just escaped from an institution where she was confined as a practising schizophrenic—a condition that the play posits as more normal in its response to the world than the well-adjusted balance of its capitalist "greedy pricks." [5] The trial in *Love and Anger* is inconclusive, there is no reversal in the play's action, and, in spite of the central character Petie Maxwell's best intentions, there is no revolution in the play's plot. But there are fissures in the play's legal and philosophical systems based on binary opposition and "objectivity"; there is the beginning of a new community among the play's variously marginalized characters; and there is a "twist" to the proceedings that is characteristic of Walker and of the dramaturgy of the perverse, which (as I see it) typically *foregrounds* the expectations of its audience in order to disappoint, disrupt, or fracture them. There is also an implied rejection of the concept of "recognition" as the self-discovery of a unified subject, especially in the characterization of the schizophrenic Sarah, who emerges as the unlikely hero of the play. [6] "Character" in this play comes to mean something close to a series of temporarily adopted subject positions that are continually subject to reversal but allow for no final or permanent recognition of an essential self.

If Walker's *Love and Anger* productively perverts the neo-Aristotelian structures of reversal and recognition, then his *Nothing Sacred* (1988) does something similar with the oedipal narrative that it borrows from Turgenev's novel *Fathers and Sons*. Like David French before him, but characteristically with more ironic self-awareness, Walker seems to be conscious of the role of his play in working out his own father-child relationships:

> It's funny that I'm writing about Bazarov at this time because I read *Fathers and Sons* when I was 17 years old, and I related so strongly to that character then. That I should get around to writing about him when I'm 40, and still relate to him so strongly, is odd because I'm no longer just a son; I'm a father, too, and I have to come to grips with that, to understand that as well. (Wallace 27)

Walker's anxieties of influence, however, although they echo those of French and Cook in the oedipal pleasures of writing the plays, are considerably and refreshingly free of real angst. The program notes to the 1994 revival of *Nothing Sacred* at Toronto's Wintergarden Theatre quote his 1988 account of writing the play: "Do you know the feeling you have when you hear a song or read something and say, 'Oh, I wish I'd written that'? Well, I wished I'd written *Fathers and Sons.* So I did. [...] It was very liberating." It is not surprising, given both this tone and the play's title, that *Nothing Sacred* treats its oedipal model with something less than reverence; nevertheless, its perversions are not without purpose or seriousness, and its (re)structuring of the narrative of generational conflict might usefully be seen as *anti*-Oedipal in Deleuze and Guattari's sense.

The play is structured around fathers and stories of fathers, with most of its central male characters at one time or another measuring themselves against their fathers or father substitutes, mostly constructed as authority figures (army doctors, military men, gentlemen farmers, or, among the play's peasant and working classes, bailiffs and one's betters). Thus, Bazarov and Arkady rebel, if not always against their actual fathers, whom they know love them, then at least against "the Law of the Father" and the institutions that it represents and reproduces; conversely, the brothers Kirsanov and Pavel struggle and fail to maintain the traditional societal and familial order represented by their father:

> **PAVEL.** Remember the way father conducted his business ...
> **KIRSANOV.** Business? Father was a general in the army, Pavel.
> **PAVEL.** The business of his life. He conducted it with dignity. He behaved well because he knew what he came from. And he knew what he came from was respected. And so it followed that he showed respect [...] Remember the holidays. Each holiday marked by the same traditional routine. It gave you strength. It gave you memory ... Oh I ruined that part of my life myself. Ruined any chance to have a real family. I got carried away by love. [...] Does everything turn dark in this world, Nikolai.
> **KIRSANOV.** Yes. Darkness. Then ... what?
> **PAVEL.** Death. [...]
> **KIRSANOV.** I know now that I wanted a wife and child to live for. Too late though. (87-88)

The oedipal failures of these characters are accompanied, moreover, by some intriguingly Freudian resonances. To both his shame and his comfort, Kirsanov, for example, has fathered a child with the daughter of his former housekeeper, Fenichka, and he deflects (or transfers?) his concerns from one kind of flow (of desire) to another: "I should have just said something affectionate to her. Fenichka I love you. I love you Fenichka. Just like that. [...] So it's up to me. All right then I'll do it ... (*He starts off.*) But not now. I have to supervise the distribution of fertilizer" (61). When he calls to her later and she asks "What?" he can only answer "Nothing" (70).

"Nothing" is an important word in this play It may seem like special pleading to recall in this context that the word in early modern English could mean the female genitals.[7] But there does seem to be a link in the play between an obsession with fathers, with inappropriate, absent, or threatening objects of desire, and with "nothing," which, as the title tells us, is "sacred." Kirsanov's apparent death wish in the passages above is linked, of course, to his supposed failure to assume appropriately the role of the symbolic father and to his inappropriate obsession with "nothing." In addition, the obsessive and fetishistic love of Pavel for Anna Odintsov's mother, now transferred to Anna herself,[8] is explicitly linked—in the passage quoted above and elsewhere—to a failure of (re)production on his part—reproduction in the biological sense and in at least two social senses: capitalist production (surplus value) and the reproduction of his father's traditional order. Pavel's story, moreover, is structurally parallel to that of Bazarov, who as a nihilist, of course, has a different investment in "nothing."

Unlike [some of] the plays [of David] French and Cook [...], in which father-son relationships figure so prominently and women play minor, exchange, or brokerage roles, *Nothing Sacred* concerns itself with the psychological struggles of its characters only peripherally, or perhaps perversely, preferring to critique the socially repressive role of "Oedipus"[9] as it plays itself out in the class struggle. Apart from occasional moments in which Pavel elicits a perverse sympathy, his psychological malaise is seen for the most part to be less sympathetic than simply pathetic.[10] Walker, like Deleuze and Guattari before him, conjures up Oedipus as a psychological complex primarily to mock it and the authority that it has been granted. Socially, however, the play presents a serious criticism of Oedipus, whose myth (as Deleuze and Guattari have demonstrated) has served to reinforce the dominant order by inhibiting the *an*oedipal flows of desire and production and creating docile subjects (in both psychological and social senses) and workers.

The play opens with the savage beating of a peasant by Kirsanov's bailiff, a representative of law who later admits to enjoying the process: "I don't know why. I didn't make human beings. Human beings enjoy beating other human beings. That's a fact" (58). The bailiff also argues, in an evocative conflation, that, if left unbeaten, the peasants will "rob you blind. They'll get drunk and do damage to the machinery. They'll eat their children" (58). Throughout, the play offers criticism of surplus production—most notably as embodied in the sartorially and otherwise superfluous Pavel; of class divisions both explicit and implicit—Bazarov, for example, insists that Kirsanov's "problems regarding his feelings" for Fenichka are in fact "problems [...] about class. His class. Her class" (40); and of oedipal social institutions, including the family:

**BAZAROV.** Why do people think that what goes on in a family is somehow beyond the criticism of society in general. Is a family above the civil law? No. Then should it be above the natural law, the laws of behaviour?

**ARKADY.** Only when those laws are being imposed by a man who is not only outside the family but outside of society as well. (64)

In the final scene, the dying Bazarov—killed accidentally over a matter of archaic "form ... That's all" (90)—speaks of the reciprocal love between himself and his parents, making it clear that his brand of revolutionary nihilism (versus Pavel's fetishistic "nothing") is neither oedipal nor pathological. The scene and the play conclude when Bazarov's last words, "You are the ... ," spoken to the play's assembled servants and peasants and failing to be the play's final words, are completed by the very characters whom Bazarov sees as "the future." Perverting the tradition of giving the play's last words to its most noble characters, *Nothing Sacred* ends with the servant, the bailiff, and the two peasants planning their future to the accompaniment of Anna Odintsov's laugh of "*light joyful recognition*" (99).

(1999)

## Notes

[1] MacLeish's famous argument, of course, in *Poetry and Experience*, which summarized modernist poetics and served as a kind of manifesto for much modernist criticism, was that a poem does not mean but be (see 3-88). In reference to Michael Hollingsworth's plays as theatrical images, Geoff Hancock notes the playwright's sense of the importance in contemporary theatre of the visual (versus verbal) image.

[2] Bakhtin uses "dialogic" to suggest a "polyglot" polyphony of voices, opposing it to the "monologic," in his discussion of alterity and polyphony as revolutionary in potential. See Knowles chapter 7 and Bakhtin, *Dialogic* and *Problems.*

[3] Used in conversation with the author, 29 October 1987.

[4] In conversations and classroom visits 1984-90 and in Johnson ("George F. Walker Directs" 170), who says that "'Parody' is anathema to Walker as a description of his work." Walker is thinking of parody in the usual sense as ridiculing imitation rather than in the specialized sense of "repetition with critical difference" that Linda Hutcheon uses in *A Theory of Parody* (7). Hutcheon's "parody" is related to what I am calling "perversion," but I am focusing on intertexts that operate on the level of structure and semiotics without necessarily conjuring up any conscious reflection of specific texts.

[5] The classic case for schizophrenia as an entirely appropriate response to a capitalist society is Gilles Deleuze and Felix Guattari's delightfully anarchic and distinctly perverse *Anti-Oedipus: Capitalism and Schizophrenia*, a book that resonates with Walker's plays in a variety of ways (including its anger, its love, and its intriguing observation that "Schizophrenia is like love" [5]). At one point, for example, Deleuze and Guattari offer a discussion of schizoid behaviour that reads like a commentary on the character of Sarah, particularly her strategies for coping with the play's "greedy pricks":

> The schizo has his own system of co-ordinates for situating himself at his disposal, because, first of all, he has at his disposal his very own recording code, which does not coincide with the social code, or coincides with it only in order to parody it. The code of delirium or of desire proves to have an extraordinary fluidity. It might be said that the schizophrenic passes from one code to the other, that he deliberately *scrambles all the codes*, by quickly shifting from one to another, according to the questions asked him, never giving the same explanation from one day to the next, never invoking the same genealogy, never recording the same event in the same way. When he is more or less forced into it and is not in a touchy mood, he may even accept the banal Oedipal code, so long as he can stuff it full of all the disjunctions that this code was designed to eliminate. (15)

R. D. Laing, in *The Divided Self*, which concerns itself specifically with female schizophrenia as an intelligible response to the "double bind" of invalidation within the family, includes an account of Ophelia that is also compatible with Walker's Sarah.

Sharon Pollock's *Getting It Straight* also presents a scathing critique of patriarchal structures from positive, feminist, and schizophrenic perspectives, in ways that are considerably more sophisticated and subversive than those of her earlier oedipal drama, *Doc. Doc*, of course, has reached a much larger audience than has *Getting It Straight*, in part because, although it regenders the central character(s), as an autobiographical therapeutic memory play in the tradition of [David French's] *Of the Fields, Lately*, it presents no *formal* or deep-structural challenge to a mainstream audience.

6 I am indebted in my discussion of Sarah and Walker's characterization to Mary Pat Mombourquette 130-35.

7 See Eagleton 64 and 107, note, where, however, he notes that "It need not be supposed [...] that when Lear asks Cordelia what she can say to win his favour, she replies 'female genitals, my lord.'"

8 It is significant that most of the play's men are obsessed with, or "in love" with, Anna, who (as both a woman and a nihilist) has an overcoded connection with "nothing" and who (as a terrorist, we are told) has used "one or two" bombs and plans to use more (81).

9 "Oedipus" is the term that Deleuze and Guattari use, *tout court*, as a conflation of the various functions played in psychoanalysis and society by the Greek myth of Oedipus, "the" Oedipus complex, and various oedipal mechanisms, processes, and structures. See their translators' note (3).

10 The most explicit statement of the nature of Pavel's obsession comes from the character himself, in a letter that he reads to Anna in an attempt to explain the emotional "terrorism" (another connection to the Bazarov/Anna plot) that he had carried out on her mother and is now directing toward her:

> "The love I felt for your mother was my life. It came to be my entire life. No thoughts in my head. No world in front of my eyes. No friends. Or family. Or profession. I only lived in my love for your mother. Which drew me to her, so close that everything in the world came through her and I was just an aura, not solid, not heard ... and finally not felt. And when she was gone from me ... I began to dissolve ... (*He looks at her.*) And then I saw you and stopped dissolving and after I stopped dissolving I began to hope that I could become real again." (75)

## Works Cited

Bakhtin, M. M. *The Dialogic Imagination.* Trans. Caryl Emerson and Michael Holquist. Austin: U of Texas P, 1981.

———. *Problems of Dostoevsky's Poetics.* Ed. and trans. Caryl Emerson. Minneapolis: U of Minnesota P, 1984.

Brissenden, Connie, ed. *The Factory Lab Anthology.* Vancouver: Talonbooks, 1974.

———. *Now in Paperback: Six Canadian Plays of the 1970's.* Toronto: Fineglow Plays, 1973.

Cook, Michael. *Tiln and Other Plays.* Vancouver: Talonbooks, 1976.

Deleuze, Gilles, and Felix Guattari. *Anti-Oedipus: Capitalism and Schizophrenia.* Trans. Helen R. Lane, Robert Hurley, and Mark Seem. Minneapolis: U of Minnesota P, 1983.

Eagleton, Terry. *William Shakespeare.* Oxford: Blackwell, 1986.

French, David. *Of the Fields, Lately.* Toronto: New, 1975.

Frye, Northrop. *The Great Code: The Bible and Literature.* Toronto: Harcourt, 1983.

———. *The Myth of Deliverance.* Toronto: U of Toronto P, 1983.

Hancock, Geoff. "Michael Hollingsworth." *The Oxford Companion to Canadian Literature.* Ed. William Toye. Toronto: Oxford UP, 1983. 362.

Hollingsworth, Michael. *Clear Light.* Toronto: Coach House, 1973.

———. *Strawberry Fields.* Brissenden, ed. *Factory* 285-313.

Hutcheon, Linda. *A Theory of Parody.* London: Methuen, 1985.

Johnson, Chris. "George F. Walker: B-Movies Beyond the Absurd." *Canadian Literature* 85 (1980): 87-103.

———. "George F. Walker Directs George F. Walker." *Theatre History in Canada/Histoire du théâtre au Canada* 9 (1988): 157-72.

Johnston, Denis W. *Up the Mainstream: The Rise of Toronto's Alternative Theatres.* Toronto: U of Toronto P, 1991.

Knowles, Ric. *The Theatre of Form and the Production of Meaning: Contemporary Canadian Dramaturgies.* Toronto: ECW P, 1999.

Laing, R. D. *The Divided Self: An Existential Study in Sanity and Madness.* 1960. Harmondsworth: Penguin, 1965.

MacLeish, Archibald. *Poetry and Experience.* Cambridge, MA: Riverside, 1961.

Mombourquette, Mary Pat. "Walker's Women in the East End Plays." MA Thesis. U of Guelph, 1990.

Pollock, Sharon. *Doc.* Toronto: Playwrights Canada, 1986.

———. *Getting It Straight. Heroines: Three Plays.* Ed. Joyce Doolittle. Red Deer: Red Deer College P, 1992. 85-126.

Usmiani, Renate. *Second Stage: The Alternative Theatre Movement in Canada.* Vancouver: U of British Columbia P, 1983.

Walker, George F. *Ambush at Tether's End.* Brissenden, ed., *Factory* 89-183.

———. *Love and Anger.* Toronto: Coach House, 1990.

———. *Nothing Sacred.* Toronto: Coach House, 1988.

———. *Prince of Naples.* Brissenden, ed., *Now* 61-102.

———. Program notes. *Nothing Sacred. Curtain Call Theatre Magazine.* Elgin Winter Garden Theatre Centre. Fall 1994.

Wallace, Robert. "Looking for the Light: A Conversation with George F. Walker." *Canadian Drama / L'Art dramatique canadien* 14 (1988): 22-33.

# Escaping the "Savage Slot": Interpellation and Transgression in George F. Walker's *Suburban Motel*

by Reid Gilbert

As the Postcolonial critique moves from ethnographic projects based in settler culture and Imperialist influence to a wider conjecture that, as Edward Said puts it, reflects a "contrapuntal" discourse between centre and margins (259, 336), examinations of who is colonised and by whom also broaden. At the same time, such investigation demands that attention be paid to the receiving subject (as, indeed, the critiquing subject) and the intricate web of colonising forces (including and most especially language) that enwrap the object(s) of study.

In theatre, these notions are particularly concrete: the *dramatis personae* are clearly specular objects though they operate in a fictional world in which they are apparent subjects. Playwrights manipulate these fictions according to various criteria of their own positions, but always as colonising subjects; and spectators constitute themselves as viewing subjects, but are also determined by the playwright's design and the greater metanarratives in which they live. Such a matrix of positionality illustrates the Poststructural assumption, by now widely held, that identity is non-essential, negotiated, and contingent.[1] It also illustrates the contemporary notion that "[t]he 'us and all of them' binary [...] is an ideological construct." However false, this binary is "implicit in the symbolic order that creates the West" (Trouillot, "Anthropology" 39), a fact reflected in many of George F. Walker's plays. Walker repeatedly examines the control of created subjects, and he regularly explodes his audience's complacent assumption that colonial control remains stable. Walker, then, is representative of a Postcolonial drama in Canada which recognises the manoeuvres of power but subverts, or, in Ric Knowles's use of the term, "perverts" them. In doing so, and in creating both colonised and resistant characters and themes, Walker orchestrates a contrapuntal design. As Said warns, to think and to write this way is "more rewarding—and more difficult" than to think only about "us" (336) but this is the task Walker sets his audience.

Although much of Walker's success can be attributed to the commercial viability of his plays—partly because of the contemporaneity of his cynical sense of humour, partly because of the fast-paced action within urban settings—his plays primarily engage contemporary audiences because they interrogate the largely unconscious fears of bourgeois theatre spectators about the tenuous control they maintain on their own subjectivity and about that of subjects over whom they hold imperial sway. As always, it would be dangerous and wrong-headed to generalise across audiences. Reception is a function of individual spectators in particular venues at particular performances. Yet common in many contemporary spectators is the growing realisation of the instability of all classifications and a congruent urgency on the part of some spectators to reformulate categories that can still contain identity, or a desire among other spectators to escape any such fixity, to "queer" the pitch.[2] Walker's plays urge spectators to do either or both, often simultaneously, layering contradictory desires of the audience into a polyphonic pattern, "making up a set of [...] intertwined and overlapping histories" (Said 18). The plays, then, open up audience subjectivity, though, at first glance, they appear to support the determination of many Western viewers to maintain the anthropological myth of a "savage" (as an "exotic") slot, the eagerness to fabricate an Other against whom to measure. In Walker's work, such others are drawn from a palette of urban types (of different ages and socio-economic groupings), whose variety and consistent subjugation to (varying) ideologies pose problems for reception and containment. Walker's dramaturgy relentlessly plays with reception, refusing easy identification even as he paints characters who appear, on the surface, to fulfill expectation as "savage" or—at least—as failed.

The group of one-act plays collectively called *Suburban Motel*, especially the companion plays *Problem Child* and *Risk Everything*, reflect these theoretical notions. An analysis of these plays, then, may stand to illustrate a post-modern and post-colonial dramaturgy increasingly evident in Canada.

The two plays—first produced by Rattlestick Productions at Theatre Off Park in New York on 13 May 1997 and 15 June 1997 respectively, and first produced in revised versions by Factory Theatre in Toronto on 25 October 1997 and 17 June 1998—present characters who, as the original director, Daniel De Raey remarks, "are usually presented [...] marginally, if at all [...] On the fringes, these characters are barely visible, never audible, seem vaguely cloddish and are certainly easy to miss. In Walker's center [sic] stage light, however, they are seen to be vivid, articulate, perceptive and never to be forgotten" (4). In the same motel room in the two plays, the protagonists, Denise and her husband, R.J., engage in highly verbal and generally frantic action with a social worker, a chronic alcoholic, Denise's gambling-addicted mother, and the latter's lover, a pornographic film director.

Walker first contemporises the colonial Other in *Problem Child* by presenting representatives of the Canadian underclass as victims of the totalising narratives of capital, class, and government. In this play, the protagonists seem to be figures from the "savage" slot and partly complicit in their own victimisation. Walker, however, reveals the fragility of any construction of reality and the danger in allowing the negative half of any binary to be seen. Diane J. Austin-Broos points out the split that accompanies any identification by summing up Trouillot's notion of European identity as "a double image of the Reason that it was, and unreason that it might encompass" (297; see Trouillot, "Culture"). Denise is read as an unreasonable Other who must be contained, but the very acts of conjuring her (as well as R.J. and the alcoholic Phillie) within the specular field and of controlling these characters, allows the category of the unreasonable to exist—indeed, requires it in the action of *Problem Child*, and opens the door for its subsequent personification in Carol in *Risk Everything*. Kathryn Woodword has suggested that "discourses create what it is possible to think by articulating different elements into a discursive formation at particular times" (255); Walker routinely gathers together diverse elements (characters, themes, moral attitudes) to create a discourse which at once amuses and challenges his audiences. Once the unreasonable is conceived in a Walker play, it threatens quickly to take over. An intertext of television-as-substitute-reality underscores these themes while also foregrounding the more intriguing question of the role of all theatricality (including the plays themselves) in the delicate matrix of reality and performativity, voyeurism and participation.

In *Risk Everything*, Walker first seems to validate the very normative system he has just repudiated by presupposing a "savage slot" to which his protagonists can return, and by having them transfer the same false binaries into this under-world of petty crime and pornography. The world of *Risk Everything* is established on a moral hierarchy parallel to that of the social worker in *Problem Child*, though "black," affirming Alan Sinfield's contention that "Subcultures should not be envisaged [...] as having clearly defined boundaries" (68). The unreasonable becomes reasonable, though inverted. In this apparent imitation, Walker shows the seductive power of those regimes of mainstream society and of etiquette that he has previously depicted as cruel and constricting; in doing so, however, he reveals them as contextual, shifting, and subject to rupture. In this second play, Walker also extends the trope of television, continually questioning layers of reality. And, finally, he does show a contingent escape through "perversity" in the manner Knowles discusses. He gestures to this possible hegira through the character of Carol who, significantly, is a mother.

*Problem Child* concerns the plight of Denise and R.J., a couple who have lost their baby to the state, ostensibly because Denise's mother has reported alleged child neglect to "the government" (20). Living in the city, Denise became "a drug addict [...] when [the social workers] took my baby away"(26), and has "turned a few tricks" (24) to pay her rent while R.J. was in prison. While incarcerated, R.J. has also become addicted to television, especially to daytime talk shows that present "Mothers who confront their cross-dressing sons" (8) and similar aberrations in a bourgeois world. The set indexes their life as the play opens: in the dingy motel room, "*R.J. REYNOLDS is watching TV* [...] *There are two old suitcases on the floor and a small baby crib up against the wall*" (8). The cramped space is important not only to Walker's characterisations and tone, but within the colonial critique. As Said reminds us, "In too small a space, you cannot see clearly, you cannot think clearly, you cannot have regulation or attention of the proper sort. [Such limited space] renders very precisely the dangers of unsociability, of lonely insularity, of diminished awareness that are rectified in larger and better administered spaces" (88). Agents of The Law in *Problem Child* and of the criminal boss in *Risk Everything* are free to roam, and to speak from the larger world: it is the colonised protagonists in both plays who are trapped in an isolated environment that is controlled from afar and by the voice of the absent Father/Law. The resemblance to the history of imperialism seems clear.

The farcical plot is too complicated to summarise, but involves the attempts of the two protagonists to convince a social worker, Helen, to return their child; Denise's outrageous decision after "thinking it through" to "bury" Helen "alive" (41) when the latter cuts herself and swoons; Denise's subsequent decision to engage the motel employee (who is literally falling down drunk) to steal back her child from its foster parents; a confrontation with the revivified social worker, and the capitulation of the pair to authority as Denise slides into a deep depression, "trapped in a sadness and an anger so deep I know I'll never get out" (47).

Denise is driven by nervous desperation in her efforts to reclaim her child; she is "in hell" (47). R.J., who is "disgusted," who feels "Life is disgusting" (10), has opted out to watch television, and has consented to "make the effort to impress [the social workers]" (27) by moving the family to a small town, getting a menial job, and joining a church "to make points with you people" (43).

In falsifying himself, R.J. accepts the practical power of The Law, but Walker makes clear the active cynicism and self-defeat with which he views this new self-inscription. That "Life is the place that fucks people like you and me up" (10) is the pivot of R.J.'s self-image. He suffers a deeply embedded sense that "I can't do anything about life" (10), despite the fact that he is striving to pass as a member of mainstream society and has obtained the necessary documents to testify to his submission to Foucault's "strategic unities" (103) and their attendant agencies of control: "we've got doctors' papers. We've got a social worker's letter. We've got a letter from our landlord" and "from my boss" from whom he is learning "a trade" (14). His attempts to satisfy the social workers affirm Jonathan Dollimore's observation that "the subculture, even as it imitates, reproducing itself in terms of its exclusion, also demystifies, producing a knowledge of the dominant which excludes it" (287). Althusser warns that there is always "a reproduction of submission to the ruling ideology" (132) and R.J.'s attempts to reinvent himself in the image of the social worker (and of, and against television characters) represent examples of such repetition. To view such transparently hollow self-construction, however, assails the spectators' own careful masquerades. This "reproduction of submission" on stage may trigger either the distasteful realisation that we all act out our abjection and that any stability of self requires that we continually repeat such performance, or the unsettling recognition that those who submit to us are not only playacting, but are thereby also constructing us mimetically. Denise understands the necessity to act out "reality" within known conventions and media in order to win acceptance:

> I don't know, maybe I should go on TV and sit on one of those stupid chairs. Cry. And then you'll see me and hear my story and your heart will go out to me and you'll understand. But if I just tell you how it happened and I'm just me and you're just you [...] I don't know, I don't know ... (31)

Giving up any attempt to fabricate an identity outside a normative citational chain, R.J. has traded any attempt to interact with "real" life with a passionate engagement with television. In this world, he not only escapes persecution, but can take what *feels like* positive action, attempting to redress the abuse of guests by talk show hosts, aiming to "write that show a letter" (10), and telephoning the producer to complain. The hopelessness of his actually changing the TV world, however, throws into high relief his inability to change his "real" life. That R.J. is actually a fictional character trapped between the "real" and the make-believe reminds the audience again of the instability of categories: all that might finally be possible is to take what *feels like* action, to become what *feels like* an independent subject. Lacan has pointed out that "feeling like" an ideal who is a creature of the symbolic is, in fact, an identification with the *moi* (in the famous mirror) and a loss forever of the *je*" (304).[3] It means to become a character in a drama; it entails an escape into language that assumes its own degradation.

As Helen points out, however, R.J.'s "letters" contain "no reference" to Denise "at all" (26). They attest to his male adherence to a normative world, but say nothing about the central issue of Denise's fitness to be a mother. Foucault argues that the female body and its reproductive capacity is the primary target of control, that the "hysterisation" of the Mother constitutes a key mechanism for the bringing of human sexuality into consciousness and under control (104-07). In these two plays, Denise, her mother, and even her grandmother are presented as women whose bodies are sexualised but maverick. In Foucault's view, the regulation of parental sexuality by various regimes of power is fundamental to corporate regulation of the body politic, to the "homeostasis of the social body" (107). R.J. and Denise have failed the test of acceptable parenthood ultimately, it seems, because Denise has exactly failed Foucault's rubric for socially acceptable womanhood and motherhood. As Helen outlines her shortcomings, Denise does not cook for her husband, does not clean the house adequately, does not seek religious values, and wants her child only because she is "mine" and as a "friend" (27), not so that she can educate the child or complete herself as woman. On R.J.'s talk shows, examples of Foucault's "perverse pleasures" (105) and failed families abound, each of them being brought to ridicule and justice by a studio audience. While the theatre audience sees through the circus of these shows—Walker makes sure no spectator can take them seriously and differentiates them from the "real" world of his protagonists—it also sits in judgement of Denise and her mother. Helen uses Carol's testimony against Denise who insists that "We've got to investigate my mother's part in this" (25). Whether any given spectator believes Denise is a fit mother or not, each is part of the web of regulations and binaries that ultimately control each spectator as surely as they do Denise. And, again, the stage world also comes across as a fiction, which causes a doubling of audience reaction. If TV is false, but the stage is "real," what epistemological foothold remains available to the spectator in daily life?

Cast by the legal gaze as an unfit mother, and delivered to the law by her own mother, Denise is pushed into the role of the "hysterical woman" by the medical gaze of the social worker. (It is a wonderfully retributive touch, and typical of Walker's wry humour, that her "hysteria" should reach its peak when she overreacts to Helen's faint and "buries her alive.") Yet the play makes clear that her excitable actions are a necessary response to a subjectivity that interpellates "people like us" (48) for whom "things don't work out" (47) and her own articulation of self. Austin suggests that conversation not only carries fact, but also functions as speech act to hail both speaker and auditor (see Austin). Denise reads herself backwards from her own pronouncements of self: to R.J.'s claim that they "could have gotten a lawyer," and in response to his Foucaultian certificates of respectability, Denise replies, "No. No lawyers. No law [...] It's not our route [...] We're doing it our way. The only way we've got" (34). Denise's speech is excitable, partly because, as Butler suggests, "speech is always in some ways out of our control," (15) but mainly because of the psychic tension which she inflicts upon herself by the circular path of her discourse. She defines herself by a statement which presupposes itself—the Lacanian "effect of retroversion" (Žižek 102-05), to which I will return in detail.

While R.J. is becoming one of many constituting subjects who, as Althusser puts it, "work by themselves," (169) Denise is a "bad subject"; indeed, Helen tells her, "You're a bad girl, Denise. That's all you are. Someone should have told you this a long time ago. You're a very bad girl." With her "smart-ass mouth" (26), Denise replies, "Ah, shut up" (41), railing against The Law, attempting to resist its power while also rejecting R.J.'s substitute reality: "That wasn't life, R.J. It was a TV talk show" (10). Beneath it all, however, the Denise of *Problem Child* operates out of the conviction that she is indeed, and only, a "bad girl."[4] However revolutionary she may at times fancy herself, Denise knows that any supposedly anterior self (the "old" Denise [15]) was always already "scum," already figured in the negative and, again, read backwards from the "Denise" she now speaks into being. (This self-identity in the future anterior is a central Lacanian principle [86].) In the end, she has nothing left but language—the play ends with a forty-three-line soliloquy in which she admits, "I'm not really there" (47). She knows that if "I" could speak out how "I" "really felt and what I really wanted to do [...] maybe they'd just cancel the fucking show" (47). The elaborate performativity of human life, however, depends upon a mute *je* and a vocal *moi* to prevent its cancellation.

Denise and R.J. "speak" themselves, then, but only within an interpellation as beings in the objective case "suspected of being inadequate" (24). Their bitterness reflects their sense that they cannot escape a fate that is in the hands of others—"Listen it was over before [Helen] fell. We were finished as parents. Our life. Our future. Everything we wanted to do was over" (33)—but it also raises the question of whether they were somehow destined to such a fate even before they took independent action. An audience might well dismiss their plight as the inevitable predicament preordained by their family background, breeding, and what Helen calls their "senseless self-indulgent life style" (41), but Walker prohibits any such essentialist assumptions. In *Risk Everything*, Carol knows the newly docile Denise is merely acting and that a "real you, Denise, the dangerous adventurous Denise, not the scared suspicious Denise" also exists (299). She insists "there are a few Denises" (278). She attempts to hail her daughter anew, to alter the powerful interpellation which has almost destroyed her in *Problem Child*. R.J. replies that "None of the Denises are going to listen to a word [Carol] says" (299): the power of the state (which holds her child) is stronger than her Mother's call, but both act upon her. In the tug of war for Denise's subjectivity, Walker requires of his audience a "contrapuntal" reading which, Said cautions "must take account of both processes, that of imperialism and that of resistance to it" (66). The characters of *Problem Child* are not simply colonial subjects to whom the dominant culture speaks in fixed language. They are part of a complex hegemony which reproduces itself through constant adjustment and assimilation and which speaks out its own subjectivity in "excitable" language that continuously struggles to maintain control. As "excitable" speech cannot be admitted into evidence, the human subject must learn to speak in a regulated manner:

> **HELEN.** [...] It's important to be polite ... Politeness is a cornerstone of civilised behaviour [...] Politeness. Moderation ... Reasonable behaviour. I don't think people know these things intuitively. They have to be taught. (40)

Even Helen, however, loses verbal control when she is forced into a near-death experience. As a result, when she realises that she is no longer "all right," she must reiterate her sense of self within a reproduction of The Law. By screaming at Denise, she stabilises herself within the chain:

> I was buried alive! I had to claw my way up through garbage and leafy smelly muddy things [...] I won't shut up! [...] I have a job here. I'm a representative of our government. And what government represents to me is the people's will to have a civilized society. And what that means is dealing with people like you and getting you back in line. You're out of line, Denise. Way out of line! (41-42)

It is the voice of The Law that stabilises, both as its message is recited and as it is heard. In *Problem Child*, this voice is electronically mediated through the television and the telephone.

At the outset, Denise and R.J. are waiting for a telephone call that they erroneously believe will announce a decision regarding custody. In typical fashion, they have taken Helen's words to "stay put" (13) literally and haven't left the room for a week. They assume that the utterance when it finally comes will be "illocutionary"—a speech act that constitutes reality in the moment of its utterance—when in fact it will, at best, be "perlocutionary"—a speech act that ushers in effects (Austin 105-09). By misdefining the call, Denise and R.J. reveal their eagerness to hear a voice that will bring them into being even though the same voice will abject them. [5] The actual illocutionary utterance(s) in this play are, in fact, Denise and R.J.'s own. The merely perlocutionary utterances of the social worker will have effects, but none as devastating as the fact of their own entry into a learned system of iteration. Based on his reading of Althusser that "the vast majority of (good) subjects work all right 'all by themselves,'" Alan Sinfield concludes that "ideology does not deceive us, we discover our selves through it" (Sinfield 24).

The audience, too, first mistakes the power of the telephone call, hearing it described only by Denise and R.J. Spectators appear quite willing—like the couple—to accept that they must await an important message (from the playwright, if not the "real" Law) in order to understand and to participate in the drama. When spectators learn that the couple has been overly obedient, and also that the phone has been out of order all along, they either laugh at R.J.'s ingenuousness, feeling superior, or experience a terrible pathos for this hapless couple. Either way, they ignore their own previous anticipation of exactly the same regimes and their own naïve belief in the "well-made" play. In a manner precisely analogous to Denise's surrender to the state's definition of appropriate behaviour, the audience has been tricked by the playwright, using well-established Aristotelian conventions. They are subject to manipulation only because they have previously learned appropriate responses to these very literary forms. Ric Knowles argues that "as structural principles that function to affirm 'unifying social ideologies' in the realms of literature [...] reversal and recognition [...] are linear and dialectical concepts that invoke social containment and dramatic closure" (44).[6]

Modernist and Pre-Modernist playwrights have depended upon such audience expectation. But, as Judith Butler asks, can they—should they—assume that the social structure which controls them, is in fact "static"? (*Excitable* 19) Does an audience have any reason other than convention to anticipate closure? Walker certainly denies it. Denise's self-loathing "performs its deed at the moment of its utterance," but as Butler points out, "The 'moment' [...] is a condensed historicity: it exceeds itself in past and future directions, an effect of prior and future invocations that constitute and escape the instance of utterance" (*Excitable* 3). Walker's plays reveal the power, but also the fragility of such a historicity, and its essentially theatrical nature. Like the television world in which R.J. hides, the "real" world stands revealed as a linguistic and performative construct by Walker's refusal to cement his characterisations or to allow the audience any surety. Neither play is closed. Even the humour is so "black" as to cause sensitive spectators to feel guilty at their own enjoyment.

As Knowles points out in reference to other plays, the "Walker twist"[7] "replaces reversal as a structural principle; in which recognition, at the least, is a more complex and less comfortable concept [...] Indeed, if Walker follows any tradition, then it is that of dramaturgical perversity" (45). Knowles directs our attention to "intertexts that operate on the level of structure and semiotics without necessarily conjuring up any conscious reflection of specific texts" (234.n24). It is also on these levels, Knowles points out, that audience self-identity is interrogated by Walker's "unreversed rising action [...] in which expectations [...] are aroused and, together with all sense of poetic justice and dramatic containment, disappointed" (45). In *Problem Child*, events sweep along to a conclusion which promises the death of the social worker, or the abduction of the child, or the arrest of Denise. Audience reaction cannot be unitary: some will want Helen to die (she is a shallow, insensitive bully); others will agree with her attitude and her formula Christianity. Some will want Denise to regain her child; others will consider her an unfit mother. No one, however, will be ready for the "twist" when Helen returns from the dead. Once she is back on stage, however, the audience will anticipate the reversal such a farcical resurrection promises; none will be forthcoming. Instead, a further "twist" deflates the play in Denise's quiet, anguished monologue and then hints at new action in her understated mention that she might "come up with a way of letting [Helen] know" just how "angry" she is (48).

Knowles suggests that the "dramaturgy of the perverse [...] *foregrounds* the expectations of its audience in order to disappoint, disrupt, or fracture them"(46). Audience response is dislodged: the tone is concurrently hilarious and almost Greek in its pathos, yet the audience must hold both responses without any clue as to which will finally be appropriate. The set and props are easy to read, but fail to fulfill their promise: the gun is not used; the broken telephone does not cause any outcome; likewise, the explosives in *Risk Everything* do not detonate. Indeed, the action does not conclude, but moves from the heavily indexed set to the apron where the audience is left, alone, with Denise's synopsis of inconclusive events and the inescapable evidence that her speech is all that gives her life—as abjected subject, as fictional character, and as actor on the stage. The reality of the play becomes only words, but the power of these words to constitute subjectivity is starkly revealed, intensified by the earlier busy action.

In *Risk Everything*, Walker takes a lighter, less emotionally gripping, but even more stridently disruptive stance. Kate Taylor notes that "despite its title" this play "actually takes the least amount of risk of all the plays in the series," but *Risk Everything* is more complex than it may at first appear. It importantly repositions the serious discussions of *Problem Child*, and it plays with audience reception even as it seems to cater to a desire for easy comedy. (Although the plays need not be presented together, the action of *Risk Everything* flows from and comments upon that of *Problem Child*; I shall therefore take the second play as a sequel to the first.)

The play concerns Denise's mother, Carol, who has cheated on an underworld boss during a gambling deal, has been beaten, calls her daughter to the hospital, and plots to escape the retribution of the angry mobster and to increase her gains. Again, the plot races through farcical business: Carol attempts to con everyone; R.J. is taken by the mob and returns to the motel with explosives strapped to his body; Carol seduces the next door neighbour, Michael, who is directing a pornographic film, and involves him in the action; Michael is also taken by the gangster and he too returns rigged with explosives; R.J. and Denise conceive a reckless plan in which R.J. will go the boss's place and "explode all over him" (310); Denise discovers that Carol has lied and has retained the missing money "to make a fucking bet on a fucking horse" (298); Denise forces Carol to return the money; the men are freed from the explosives; Michael returns to the motel room and to Carol's sexual reward.

This action drives forward at breakneck speed, and the dialogue is often very funny, but under its plot-based action, the play reveals interpellation every bit as strong as that which governs the characters in *Problem Child*: a class of people in Canadian society live outside the mainstream, but, within this class, a hierarchy exists driven by economic power, controlled by punishment and supported by an ideological apparatus. The space between these two societies is more fluid than a simple ethnographic reading might suggest. The difference in *Risk Everything* is that the protagonist, Carol, accepts her interpellation but repudiates normative consequence.

This play brings together the Althusserian notions and colonial critique so obvious in *Problem Child*, but centres on Carol's maternal body. As Judith Butler has remarked, this body is "an effect or consequence of a system of sexuality in which the female body is required to assume maternity as the essence of its self and the law of its desire" (*Gender* 92). Carol simultaneously views herself as "mother," knows such an inscription is illocutionary within the symbolic order, and pierces this act of interpellation with her own desire. In *Problem Child*, the audience learns that Denise agrees with R.J.'s characterisation of Carol as "the biggest screw-up in the universe" (21), and has "sent her in my mind to hell" (21) (where she will later describe herself as residing). In *Risk Everything*, however, we see a much more complex relationship between the two women. Denise—no longer "bad," but speaking from a morality which she is adopting in order "to impress" the authorities—asks, "Jesus, Mom. What's wrong with you?" (293) and calls her a "fucking liar" (313). Carol's responses are important. To the question of why she acts as she does, she reveals the same cynical self-awareness that hailed the young parents before they capitulated: "You can't leave the shit behind. It's a world made of shit. It's everywhere" (272), and describes herself and her children as "beyond blame" (293). To the question of her (dis)honesty, she replies, "Who are you calling a fucking liar, Denise? I'm your fucking mother" (270). As we shall see, this answer is central.

Carol attracts various signifiers of the categories *mother* and *woman*: she tells affectionate stories of rearing Denise, but she would not satisfy Helen's definition of a fit mother; she reports Denise for child neglect, but quite gleefully recalls similar abuse; she calls her daughter pet names, but also rails at her in obscene language; she wears a skirt, but appears in front of her son-in-law with it "around [her] fucking ankles" (270); she turns to her daughter when she is beaten up, but lies about the perpetrator in order to con the daughter; she insists on family loyalty, but responds to her daughter's depression by saying "Ah, who cares. You should just leave" (284). She cries, but is probably only acting to further her plan. She sees herself as a sexualised woman, but rejects any obligation to limit herself to "regulated fecundity" (Foucault 104). In "a blast from the past," she has sex with "a total stranger" (286) in front of her daughter, who rages against her promiscuity, but the ending of the play turns on her unabashed sexual *jouissance*, both in Lacan's sense of desire in loss and in Nietzsche's sense of *affirmation*. She casts herself and Denise as strong women, preferring Denise when she is aggressive and outside The Law (and undermining R.J.'s self-confidence about his masculinity), but she also relishes a potent male sex partner and centres her interest directly on his phallus, an action to which I shall return. She does not, however, simply embody a set of self-contradictions; she is the product of a "quilting" of signifiers which temporarily fixes a shifting variety of *Mother* far outside Helen's ken.

Carol is a rather special example of what Ernesto Laclau and Chantal Mouffe have called a "nodal point" (112). As Slavoj Žižek sums up Laclau, Mouffe, and Lacan, "the multitude of 'floating signifiers,' of proto-ideological elements, is structured into a unified field through the intervention of a certain 'nodal point' (the Lacanian *point de capiton*) which 'quilts' them, stops their sliding and fixes their meaning" (87). Of course, to apply Lacan's theory strictly, this *capitonnage* must reveal the "effect of retroversion" in that the hail as *Mother* that is momentarily fixed can only be a reading backwards onto Carol of normative signifiers from a category already situated within the Lacanian "Big Other (O)." In other words, her actions can be interpreted as rebellion only because such a possibility is already accepted by those who deal in symbolic identifications—namely, everyone in the play except her, as well as the bourgeois humanist audience: hence, the frustration Denise feels. Carol embodies an element of alterity, but only because the audience collectively pretends the Big Other is normative and has an existence other than as structure. Carol's triumph is that she appears to be able to see her identifications as merely performative. Unlike Denise, who slips into an imaginary identification which she acts out for the benefit of the Law (as Žižek reminds us, "imaginary identification is always identification *on behalf of a certain gaze in the Other*" [106]), Carol is aware that her position as nodal point is simply a quilting sought by the others, is by definition unsound, and means nothing to her. While the audience is actively engaged in misrecognition of Carol as an autonomous agent (who makes bad choices), Carol herself breaks through this illusion, knowing herself to be the product of an inauthentic structure, a structure whose symbol is the phallus (of which she makes sport). Žižek alerts us to the paradox in which "*capitonnage* is successful only in so far as it effaces its own traces" (102). Carol, however, refuses to efface the residual effects produced in her moments of quilting—they stream behind her, performing themselves as disruptions of the symbolic order. Carol offers to fix a rebellious meaning of *Mother* that disowns normalising conceptions of that elemental sign, but also refuses to reconstitute the category in the opposite pole of the binary. She is not simply moving to "the place" from which she would feel happier with herself, Lacan's symbolic identification (Žižek 105); she is living (sometimes happily) in a maelstrom of fluid signifiers and shifting subject-positions. She contributes to "a radically contingent process of retroactive production of meaning" (Žižek 102) by her wilful acts of deceit. She "lies," and in doing so she exploits "the open temporality of the speech act [...] Such a loosening of the link between act and injury, however, opens up the possibility for a counter-speech, a kind of talking back, that would be foreclosed by the tightening of that link" (Butler, *Excitable* 15). While Denise has integrated her lifelong interpellation as "scum" with her current designation as "unfit Mother," Carol recognises her own hailing, but fashions a life for herself within it by running with the consequences of her actions, in full knowledge that these actions are already determined by an anterior illocution. Again, she knows that this illocution comes from a place within the Big Other and reads itself back onto her own rebellion so that whatever action she takes turns out to be ultimately pointless. The two women embody on stage the Hegelian couple, "for-the-other"/"for-itself." Denise is hysterical because she unhappily enacts roles for the other;[8] Carol is in control because she knows that she is, already, the other for whom "[she] is enacting a role [...] [her] being-for-the-other is [her] being-for-[her]self" (Žižek 106). She also accepts that she can never escape her symbolic identification within the Other (as none of us can, short of madness) and yet that she is powerless within it. Carol acknowledges the serious consequences of such a revolutionary attitude: she is beaten by men, she is censored by her daughter.

While Carol dodges the attempts of conventional signifiers to adhere to her name as Mother, but accepts her position as perverse and unstable nodal point, she does not accept that her body itself is unstable, or that it must, as Shuttleworth warns, be taken "metonymically" to represent the chaos of her class (54-55). She stands in opposition to the social assumption "that the construction of women [...] helplessly subject to the tyranny of their bodies and in need of medical supervision has functioned as a necessary support for the idea of its opposite: autonomous man" (Harding 28).[9] In this play, the men are far from autonomous and the threat to their bodies is to explode entirely. Carol, on the other hand, presents a punished body still eager for lovemaking (despite the pain of her bruises) and still very much in possession of itself.

Walker plays with the audience's reception of Carol, just as he twists his plot and spurns closure. The TV subplot is intensified to question each of the "strategies" by which the state constructs its reality and each is revealed as theatrical contrivance. Sexuality is linked to television by the fact that Michael directs pornographic films, and is revealed as both a pleasure that is not necessarily reproductive (Carol offers to fellate Michael), nor domestic, nor loving ("the sexual climate I'm used to isn't always happy and spontaneous"[303]). The final image of the play shows Michael returning to the motel room "*One hand casually over his crotch.* [...] *He has a massive erection. CAROL looks at his crotch. Smiles*" and says, "Nice going" (319). In traditional usage, then, Walker perverts his world, but he also "perverts" it in Knowles's sense.

The audience's attention, like that of Denise, is drawn to the erection and to Carol's glee that "scum" like this family and—more important, perhaps—women of this class have managed, in the face of The Law (and its inverse, the criminal boss), to escape control, still to be active, to be sexually alive, to reject decorum, to have fun. The sexual irregularity echoes the *exposés* on R.J.'s television talk shows, and like the TV audience, this audience (while it likely laughs at the impropriety) also shares something of Denise's embarrassment in the final line of the play, "Ah ... Jesus ... " This powerful image, however, works to destabilise sets of conventional icons resonant for the spectators: a Mother pointing "proudly" to a penis that she has caused to become erect and that she intends unabashedly to use for her own pleasure, in front of her son-in-law who is wearing her panties, while her daughter (also a mother) blasphemously invokes the name of Helen's chaste God, the Son of the absent Father/Law and His Ever-Virgin Mother. Indeed, as Žižek observes, "If the Name-of-the-Father functions as the agency of interpellation, of symbolic identification, the mother's desire, with its fathomless '*Che vuoi?*' marks a certain limit at which every interpellation necessarily fails" (121).[10]

Carol reads herself backwards—as, again, Lacan says we must—from the gaze of the spectators, writing alterity onto her sexually charged female body, but simultaneously and perversely teases the audience with its own potent Sign-of-the-Father. She knows she is other to the bourgeois and imperial gaze, but she also seems to know that the spectators' subjectivities (however diverse) are collectively grounded in what Butler has termed the call of the other (*Bodies* 94-95). Her playful actions are not simply "free play nor theatrical self-presentation" (*Bodies* 94), but formative (90-95) of the colonial masters who observe her and dismiss her as irresponsible, or vulgar, or even courageous.

That the spectators misrecognise their own formulation within Carol's (and, even Denise's, R.J.'s and Phillie's) alterities represents the final irony of Walker's seemingly simple farce. And it is fitting that this crucial misunderstanding should be contained in that powerful figure of imperialist misreading, the phallus. As Lacan argues, but as is often forgotten, the phallus is the sign of the ultimate failure of the Big Other. Carol's playfulness refuses a Freudian castration; it refuses to be mortified. It signals enjoyment and, as Žižek reminds us, reading Lacan's graph of *jouissance*, "as soon as the field of the signifier is penetrated by enjoyment it becomes inconsistent, porous, perforated—the enjoyment is what cannot be symbolised, [it] [...] can be detected only through the holes and inconsistencies of this field, so that the only possible signifier of enjoyment is the signifier of the lack in the Other, the signifier of its inconsistency" (Žižek 122). Walker, then, gathers bourgeois propriety, theatre etiquette, theatrical convention, and a much more complex psychological performativity together in his final stage image, and literally points it out to an imperialist audience predisposed to miscomprehend.

Walker presents a world that is alien to the experience of most of his ticket-buying audience, and offers his spectators a variety of possible responses. In the end, however, Carol offers "a blow for our side" that is "a victory over all the negative mingy shit that goes on in this world" (313). Her victory may well suggest to spectators a way out of the interpellations which configure them, a way to ignore the voice of The Law, a way to read the performative as simply that and to admit that "the Real is the writing itself as opposed to the signifier" (Žižek 171), and finally a way to displace psychic construction without pretending such a system does not exist. Walker insists that the spectators notice the implications of such visible theatricality in their own "real" lives. Equally important, however, Walker's dramaturgy disallows what Said calls a "'return' to culture and tradition" (xiii) as "protective enclosure" (xiv). Such retreats to a comfortable "source of identity [...] accompany rigorous codes of intellectual and moral behaviour that are opposed to the permissiveness associated with [...] hybridity" (Said xiii). *Problem Child* shows the grinding power of the call for such returns; *Risk Everything* declines the call, celebrating "hybridity" even in the chthonic icon of the Mother, and disclosing failure even in the apparently potent success of the Father.

As the colonial critique in Canadian drama moves in "counterpoint" with established social regulation and postmodern refiguration, plays like these of George

F. Walker engage their audiences in important new ways, disrupting reception to open a liminal space which allows "new alignments made across borders, types, nations, and essences [...] that [have] been the core of cultural thought during the era of imperialism" (Said xxiv-xxv). In Denise's words at the end of *Problem Child*, these plays "come up with a way of letting [authorities like Helen] know" (48) that this era has ended.

(2001)

## Notes

1 This assumption is, however, not held universally or without qualification. See Diane J. Austin-Broos; as she points out, Postcolonial thought "reflects an important conjunction [which] involves [...] the repudiation of the holism and the autonomy of the 'culture' concept. Also rejected is the essentialism of much cultural analysis, based on notions of cognitive structure or binary opposition. On the other hand, the conjuncture involves casting aside those varieties of Marxist thought that propose a generalised theory of history, economistic in its intent" (295). Since this essay will assume Althusserian neo-Marxist ideas as part of its collateral, Austin-Broos's caution against a simplistic Marxist historicity is salutary advice. Trouillot had previously alerted anthropologists to the danger of easy binary thinking ("Anthropology" 39).

2 Walker's dramaturgy, which I have called "perverse," using Knowles's term, is a prime example of a current notion that the "queer" and the "perverse" need not have directly to do with sexuality, but often arise at the junction of the sexual and non-sexual.

3 See "Completed Graph" (Lacan 315).

4 In *Risk Everything*, Carol tells Denise that nothing she can do will "make those social workers trust you enough [...] Because to them you're a bad girl who's just pretending to be a good girl. And they know it's just a matter of time until you stop pretending and start leading the life you *have to lead*" (299, emphasis added).

5 Consider Austin's famous example of a policeman who hails a pedestrian: "Hey, you there." Many on the street turn in response and each, in that moment, recognises him/herself as now called into being. None, or only one, previously existed as the "you" the policeman sought. Since it is a representative of the law who beckons, each respondent, by turning, accepts guilt as the price of entry into representation.

6 Knowles is quoting Frye, *Myth* 13; Knowles calls for "active and creative perversion" of such shaping structures.

[7] Walker's own term; see Knowles 234, n.23.

[8] In *Le Seminaire III—Les psychoses* (Paris, 1981), Lacan says that the hysteric asks of the Big Other, of the symbolic order, "'Why am I what you're telling me that I am?'—that is, which is that surplus-object in me that caused the Other to interpellate me, to 'hail' me as [scum; failed mother]?" (qtd. in Žižek 113).

[9] Harding paraphrases Shuttleworth 64. Note that the play begins with Carol's departure from the hospital in the care of her daughter and note her refusal to return to that medical institution.

[10] The Mother is asking Lacan's question in the third Graph. A gap always remains in desire and in the residue of any quilting. In this gap persists the question, "What do you want; what are you trying to receive back from the Big Other by naming yourself in this way?" In speech act theory, a similar gap develops between locution and the illocutionary power of any utterance. It is a pivotal concept in the analysis of Carol's role in these plays where locution, illocution, and desire ricochet off one another to fuel transgression.

## Works Cited


Althusser, Louis. "Ideology and Ideological State Apparatuses (Notes Towards an Investigation)." *Lenin and Philosophy and Other Essays.* Trans. Ben Brewster. New York: Monthly Review P, 1971. 127-86.

Austin, J. L. *How to Do Things with Words.* Cambridge, MA: Harvard UP, 1962.

Austin-Broos, Diane J. "Falling through the 'Savage Slot': Postcolonial Critique and the Ethnographic Task (N1)." *Australian Journal of Anthropology* 9 (1998): 295-310.

Butler, Judith. *Bodies that Matter: On the Discursive Limits of "Sex."* New York: Routledge, 1993.

———. *Excitable Speech: A Politics of the Performative.* New York: Routledge, 1997.

———. *Gender Trouble: Feminism and the Subversion of Identity.* New York: Routledge, 1990.

De Raey, Daniel. "Chords: Lost and Vocal. An Introduction." Walker, *Suburban* [4-6].

Dollimore, Jonathan. *Sexual Dissidence: Augustine to Wilde, Freud to Foucault.* Oxford: Clarendon, 1991.

Foucault, Michel. *The History of Sexuality, Volume 1: An Introduction.* Trans. Robert Hurley. New York: Pantheon, 1978.

Frye, Northrop. *The Myth of Deliverance: Reflections on Shakespeare's Problem Comedies.* Toronto: U of Toronto P, 1983.

Harding, Jennifer. *Sex Acts: Practices of Femininity and Masculinity.* London: Sage, 1998.

Knowles, Ric. *The Theatre of Form and the Production of Meaning: Contemporary Canadian Dramaturgies.* Toronto: ECW, 1999.

Lacan, Jacques. *Écrits: A Selection.* Trans. Alan Sheridan. New York: Norton, 1977.

Laclau, Ernesto, and Chantal Mouffe. *Hegemony and Socialist Strategy: Towards a Radical Democratic Politics.* London: Verso, 1985.

Said, Edward W. *Culture and Imperialism.* New York: Knopf, 1993.

Shuttleworth, Sally. "Female Circulation: Medical Discourse and Popular Advertising in the Mid-Victorian Era." *Body/Politics: Women and the Discourses of Science.* Ed. Mary Jacobus, Evelyn Fox Keller, and Sally Shuttleworth. New York: Routledge, 1990. 47-68.

Sinfield, Alan. *Cultural Politics—Queer Reading.* Philadelphia: U of Philadelphia P, 1994.

Taylor, Kate. "Suburban Motel Finale Is More Raucous than Risky.": Rev. of *Risk Everything.* By George F, Walker. At Factory Theatre. *The Globe and Mail* 19 June 1998: C 10.

Trouillot, Michel-Rolph. "Anthropology and the Savage Slot: The Poetics and Politics of Otherness." *Recapturing Anthropology: Working in the Present.* Ed. Richard G. Fox. Santa Fe, NM: School of American Research P, 1991. 17-44.

———. "Culture, Color, and Politics in Haiti." *Race.* Ed. Steven Gregory and Roger Sanjek. New Brunswick, NJ: Rutgers UP, 1994. 146-74.

Walker, George F. *Problem Child. Suburban Motel* 7-48.

———. *Risk Everything. Suburban Motel* 261-319.

———. *Suburban Motel.* Rev. ed. Vancouver: Talonbooks, 1999.

Woodward, Kathryn, ed. *Identity and Difference.* London: Sage/Open University, 1997.

Žižek , Slavoj. *The Sublime Object of Ideology.* London: Verso, 1989.

## From "George F. Walker: Postmodern City Comedy" (in *The Buried Astrolabe: Canadian Dramatic Imagination and Western Tradition*)

by Craig Stewart Walker

### from Closer to the Bone: The Postmodern City Comedies

In 1959, a few years after making his remarks about the suitability of the comic grotesque for the atomic age,[1] Friedrich Dürrenmatt was awarded the Schiller Prize. In his acceptance speech he returned to the question of what sort of dramaturgy suited the contemporary political world. Looking to the shift in Schiller's own work, from early angry rebelliousness to later abstract classicism, Dürrenmatt asks:

> [D]oesn't the realization that the world is in bad shape presuppose an insight into the way the world ought to be, and doesn't it also morally require some indication as to the way in which the world can be set aright again, and doesn't such an indication necessarily involve the demand that one take these steps? Now, if this question is answered in the affirmative, it is not sufficient to describe the world as unjust. It must be described as a world that can be changed, that can be set aright again and in which man need no longer be a victim. But if this is the case, the writer turns from a rebel into a revolutionary. ("Friedrich" 241-42)

Certainly, Dürrenmatt remarks, that is the path Brecht followed, not stopping at mere protest and satire but going on to promote communism. But then Brecht's work arose from his direct confrontation of a "homogenous, centralized, dictatorial empire" (that is, the Third Reich), whereas Schiller, writing after the collapse of the Holy Roman Empire, confronted a disorganized world that is in some respects (here Dürrenmatt lays out a few caveats) comparable to ours. Emerging from the upheaval of communist revolutions, two world wars, and the detonation of the atomic bomb, the political shape of the postmodern age can be seen, suggests Dürrenmatt, as a larger-scale version of Schiller's own post-revolutionary age:

> The old maxim of the revolutionaries, that man can and must change the world, has become unrealizable for the individual, out of date; this sentence is now applicable only to the crowd, as a slogan, as political dynamite, as an incentive for the masses, as a hope for the gray armies of the hungry. The part is no longer absorbed in the whole, nor the individual in collectivity, nor man in humanity. The individual is left

> with a feeling of impotence, of being left out, of no longer being able to step in and influence things, of having to lie low in order not to go under, but also there is the presentiment of a great liberation, of new possibilities, of the time having come bravely, decisively to do one's part. (245)

On this occasion Dürrenmatt is silent about his own dramatic solutions to the problem, though it is clear enough that Brecht's solution would not suit him. As he put it in an earlier essay, "I refuse to find the universal in a doctrine. The universal for me is chaos. The world (hence the stage which represents this world) is for me something monstrous, a riddle of misfortunes which must be accepted but before which one must not capitulate" ("Problems" 857). But, of course, neither is Schiller's solution—a quest for some kind of transcendent ideal through the medium of poetic drama—at all typical of Dürrenmatt's work. Rather, his plays are characterized by a caustic cynicism attacking the complacency of a society that assumes itself to have already transcended its immoral excesses. But the transition from there to more positive solutions—the shift from "rebel" to "revolutionary," as he put it—seems to have remained elusive.

In other words, although his tone is admittedly more savage, the essential ethical attitude of Dürrenmatt's work is comparable to the outlook of the Power plays—the very outlook that, I have suggested, Walker was determined to transcend.[2] Now, on the face of it, writing a non-cynical play may not look like such a difficult matter. But the problem is connected at a deeper level to the integrity and essential character of the playwright's vision. The difficulty is that, having written one's way into a truthful, albeit cynical rendering of the failure of liberal humanist enlightenment to make a better world, it becomes extremely difficult to write a plot that traces a path back out again. The task entails not only a remodelling of one's habitual view of the world but an attempt to answer some of the thorniest philosophical problems of our age. Nevertheless, with *Criminals in Love*, Walker began to dramatize the possibility of transcending cynical critique to emerge with positive values.

In a 1988 interview Walker spoke about this change in his writing over the preceding few years, which had seen the production of the first three East End plays and *Nothing Sacred*:

> For me it was a matter of letting more light into my plays; just naturally, I felt I had to do that, see what sort of hope—that's not a good word; "possibility" might be better—I could find. More than anything, that's the major change I think: I'm getting more possibility, more future into the work. The early plays don't have much hope for the future; their essential concern is "what is the world?"—what is the nature of the chaos there? Now it's more a question of how to deal with it, how to fight through it. (Wallace 22)

Of course, where the scale of the chaos in question assumes the proportions of an imminent Armageddon, as it had in some of the preceding plays, with their international, gothic settings, the prospect of coherently and persuasively dramatizing the "fight through it" looks dismal. But if the question of the future and possible redemption of civilization ultimately rests in issues about basic human nature, there is no reason that the reappraisal of human relationships cannot begin in one's own neighbourhood. Accordingly, Walker returned to a setting like that of his coming-of-age play, *Sacktown Rag*: the East End of an unnamed city resembling Toronto. As he put it in the 1988 interview: "I believe that the East End plays allowed me to get closer to the bone. I started them because I thought I was avoiding stuff in the writing—where I was brought up, notions of class ... I wanted to address these things with my own voice" (28). Apparently he had decided to set his own house in order before extending his solutions, to recover a sense of positive values he could then take out in into the wider world.

At the centre of *Criminals in Love* (1984) are two young lovers, Gail Quinn and Junior Dawson, who are manipulated into joining the criminal world. Junior comes from a family of criminals who are spectacularly unsuccessful in their vocation. Possibly the most inept of them is Henry, Junior's father, who at the beginning of the play is, as usual, in prison. Junior has deeply ambivalent feelings about his father. He wants to repudiate the family legacy of crime, but his father declares that if Junior does not join forces with his Uncle Ritchie and Ritchie's common-law wife, Wineva, he, Henry, will be killed by Ritchie. Unable to turn his back on his father, Junior accedes; loyally, Gail accompanies him. Uncle Ritchie never does appear, but they soon meet Wineva, a domineering, maniacal woman who insists on kissing to establish "family loyalties." Gail's friend Sandy, a waitress who is experimenting with prostitution as a possible career to fall back on, also joins them, hoping to pick up some criminal skills as further financial security.

More importantly, Junior and Gail are joined by a self-appointed protector, William, a derelict former revolutionary who fell into skid row, he says, out of sympathy for the downtrodden. From the beginning the effectiveness of William's protection looks dubious, and it proves all but wholly inadequate when Wineva reveals her true colours. She is a crazed revolutionary armed with a cache of explosives with which she hopes to "destroy the world." Luckily, her plans are as impractical as they are dangerous, and things go no further than blowing up a warehouse. By the end of the play Junior's house is surrounded by the police (tipped off by Henry as a ploy to reduce his sentence). It looks inevitable that they will all end up in jail, but William goes out to face the police, carrying the semi-conscious Wineva and accompanied by Sandy. He stalls the police long enough to give Gail and Junior a few moments alone, in which they renew their optimism and begin to make love once more.

The most important word in *Criminals in Love* is "destiny." A vague but abiding presentiment of destiny is the main problem of Junior Dawson, whose very name seems to insist on his regrettable "legacy" as a Dawson. When he suggests to his father that they should end their "relationship," Henry replies: "What are you talking about you dumb fuck. We're father and son. That's not a relationship. It's destiny" (33).

Much as Junior objects to his father's use of the word (35), privately he concurs: "If you put all the things of life along a ruler," he says to Gail, "legacy is at one end and destiny is at the other" (21). The rigidity of the ruler image shows how much he believes that connection to be predetermined. Nevertheless, he resists his "true destiny"—the idea, as he puts it, that he is doomed to "fuck all"—by clinging to Gail, who is, he insists, his salvation (17). And yet Junior's attachment to Gail, while endearing and sympathetic, finally represents another sort of helpless infantilism, as is indicated by his more than merely adolescent fixation on her breasts.

Junior's conception of destiny is complicated by William, who claims to be "the inventor of the modern connotation" of the word. Where Junior is afraid of "destiny as a concept of mind and soul," William's own understanding of the concept is based in "pure economics, politics, social patterns" (28). He argues for a "historical perspective": for example, the menacing Wineva is part of a "class" that has been "bent from years of repression" (59). In other words, William uses the word "destiny" in a quasi-Marxist sense that assumes the possibility of becoming enlightened about the various material and psychological forces one experiences as "destiny" and thus of beginning to overcome feelings of helplessness. He attempts to enlighten Junior and Gail on this point: "This I stress [...] To understand the possibility of progress you must first identify the force which keeps you static. Is it external. Does it lie within. To find the answers you require self-awareness" (64).

Or, as Stevie Wonder succinctly says in the song from which the epigraph to *Criminals in Love* is drawn, "When you believe in things that you don't understand, then you suffer. Superstition ain't the way." William is determined to demonstrate to Junior that the worst obstacles to his happiness are based in a superstition that is finally educable, and that the ability to choose a better life is chiefly contingent upon an informed will.

Yet there is a paradox here; if William is capable of the kind of enlightenment that not only recognizes adverse social forces but is able to suggest ways of transcending them, why is he in such a wretched condition himself? We are told that William "used to be something big," that "he's been in four revolutions" (82), and, despite appearances, he evidently still has enough money in the bank to consider himself middle-class. William's own account of the matter is this: "I have great sympathy for the truly sad cases of our world. The victims. I have felt so badly that I fell amongst them. This is the truth. This is not melodrama. Their misery made me useless. I fell" (77). William's condition is a version of the malaise described by Peter Sloterdijk in *Critique of Cynical Reason*, the cynical paralysis that arises from "enlightened false consciousness" (5-6).[3] The difficulties William had with helping "victims" through enlightenment may be surmised by considering the (at best) equivocal social justice produced by *any* four revolutions he conceivably might have taken part in—and, of course, by observing the action of the play.

Walker brings home the demoralizing sense of futility that has undone William by making his arch villain, Wineva, a self-proclaimed revolutionary. In a way, Wineva is heir to Sayer, from Walker's first play, *Prince of Naples*: an enthusiast of the violent overthrow of established order who holds no conviction whatsoever that a more humane and equitable world will follow—although, in contrast to Sayer, Wineva is actually equipped with grenades. Superficially, her plans for a violent insurrection present a sort of reckless alternative to the passive acceptance of "destiny," however defined. But, sensibly speaking, this is no alternative at all: not for Junior, trying to escape a criminal "destiny," nor for any philosophical attempt to grapple with the large-scale problems implicit in this play. Indeed, this is approximately the philosophical stalemate described by Sloterdijk: "In a system that feels like a cross between prison and chaos, there is no standpoint for a description, no central perspective for a compelling critique" (xxxiii). With minor adjustments, that sentence could describe the situation of Junior and Gail as the play ends.

Perhaps this sounds distressingly like a step backwards into the existential paralysis that beleaguered the protagonists in Walker's previous plays. But against such an impression we should consider, first, that while the negative forces are by no means wholly vanquished at the end of *Criminals in Love*, they are at least neutralized. Moreover, this play inaugurates a decisive shift in the tone of Walker's work. The most obvious change is spelled out in the title of the play. Junior and Gail are in love—real, vital, earnest love—a concept unheard of in the earlier plays. Furthermore, they are still in love when the curtain falls; indeed, their love has been fortified by their ordeal. As Walker declared in his 1988 interview: "Their love is so strong and clean and clear-headed, especially hers, that it might be able to meet the challenge. As long as she keeps her head and he keeps his heart, they have a fighting chance. I thought the ending was pretty desperate but that there was some kind of hope or, if not hope (I really don't like that word), then possibility for the future" (Wallace 26). So, while it may be true that, as regards social thought, Gail and Junior are trapped in the sort of paralysis Sloterdijk describes, they also possess a faith in one another that promises some means of transcending their problems.

This does not represent a momentary romantic lapse for Walker; it is a key element of all his subsequent work. In *Criminals in Love* itself the theme of love is extended in two important ways. First, there is the character of William. Like Power, he attempts to intervene to foil the plans of social predators, and like Power his cynicism is based in a disaffected humanism. But in his optimism and genuine affection for Junior and Gail he represents a major departure from Power, providing more emotional uplift than acidic commentary. Downtrodden and almost incapacitated by physical decay though he is, William's handicaps only underscore his resilient spirit, as if he were a sort of Fisher King in whom the hope of social reform resides.[4]

To be sure, William does not represent a repudiation of the cynicism associated with the earlier work so much as a slight reform of its essential character. He belongs to the type Sloterdijk calls by the older Greek word, the "kynic," of whom Diogenes the Cynic is Sloterdijk's *exemple par excellence*. Diogenes, probably the funniest of all Greek philosophers, is the eccentric tramp who claimed to be "looking for an honest man" and who chose to live in a tub rather than a home and indigent rather than wealthy—the better, it seems, to maintain a marginal position from which to criticize the mainstream. According to Sloterdijk, the outlook of Diogenes is one of the few ways of avoiding the more destructive kind of cynicism arising from the limitations and misuses of enlightenment. His is what Sloterdijk calls an "uncivil enlightenment," a subversive provocation from the margins of society that sets in motion a "dialectic of disinhibition," a satirical loosening of hardened critical positions (101-03). William shares some of this Diogenic function with earlier Walker characters like Power or Bernard [in *Theatre of the Film Noir*], but in both his more extreme disaffection and his terrific buoyancy, he is a purer example of the type.

Another aspect of the theme of love in *Criminals in Love* is manifest in the tensions attached to the idea of family. Three concepts of family are juxtaposed. First there is Junior's actual family: his father, Henry, and his Uncle Ritchie, both of whom see familial relations solely in terms of the opportunities they present for exploitation. Similar is the idea of family promoted by Wineva: "We're doing it together. Like a family. It's a family business" (53). Comical though she is, this is the idea of family by which the Mafia sets such store: loyalties made absolute through a ritual show of affection, creating impenetrably powerful allegiances. These notions of family are a kind of demonic parody of the sort promised by Gail and Junior's union. Even their alliance with William is closer to a morally true image of what a family might be: a group of human beings who are related to one another not by some pattern of exploitation but by, foremost, an abiding sense of mutual love and respect.

In part because of its functions as the intermediary of the individual and community, family has always provided one of the richest grounds for drama. It is a natural context in which personal and social values meet and conflict, in which individual aspirations are frustrated or supported, and in which human relations must more often be negotiated than avoided. Walker evidently became extremely interested in further exploring his themes in this framework. In his next play, *Better Living* (1986), called a "prequel to *Criminals in Love*," we meet Gail Quinn's family: her distracted and eccentric mother, Nora, her older sisters, Elizabeth, a tough lawyer, and Mary Ann, a nervous wreck, and her Uncle Jack, a jaded and disaffected priest. As the play opens, Nora is digging a new underground room. Mary Ann has returned home from a failed marriage, and Junior, Gail's boyfriend, is spending most of his time in the house.

Into this environment returns the father, Tom, a former policeman who left the family ten years earlier after a succession of violent, lunatic outbursts. Like Odysseus on his return to Ithaca, Tom wants to reassert order in the household. He warns of an imminent apocalypse in which the have-nots of the world will attack and loot the Quinn home. Shortly after he arrives, Gail moves out, breaking off all contact with the family. Meanwhile, despite Elizabeth's plans to assassinate him, Tom establishes his hegemony over the family, turning Nora's underground room into a bomb shelter, surrounding the property with barbed wire, and building up huge stockpiles of canned food in preparation for the expected siege. Nora and Elizabeth become meekly subordinate; Junior is Tom's mindless helper; and Mary Ann is increasingly frustrated. When Gail returns, confident and happy, she announces that she now remembers that Tom beat her: "That was the crime, eh. The secret all these years" (211). She threatens Tom with a gun, but Jack takes the gun himself and drives Tom from the house. In the last scene Jack reveals that he has hired Henry Dawson, Junior's father, to finish off Tom, and that he intends to retire from the priesthood. The other family members are bewildered by their ambivalence about Tom. Though frightened of him, they realize that, as Elizabeth put it, "certain things" that Tom brought into the family "are worth retaining" (190): a sense of order and security that, at some level, they cherish. Tom's tyranny is perhaps too high a price for these things, but they are valued none the less. The family begins to regroup: Mary Ann announces that she and her baby will return to the house, and Nora resumes plans for their "new world down below." But in the final moment of the play Tom reappears at the screen door, holding a large old portable television.

The ambiguity inherent in the final image of Tom standing at the door could serve as a synecdoche for the play as a whole. There is at once both penitence and menace here. The television set is a fascinatingly ambiguous symbol because, for most middle-class North Americans, it arouses profoundly ambivalent personal feelings and memories. Depending on how one interprets it, the television in Tom's arms can represent either a threatening external intrusion into the privacy and delicate ecology of family life or a symbol of family togetherness. It could be a sort of Trojan horse for the inimical forces Tom represents (e.g., patriarchal aggression), or it could be a genuinely good-willed and humble peace offering.

To attach a single conclusive meaning to Tom's gesture would be to ignore the essential ideas of the play. "Has everyone forgotten," asks Elizabeth late in the play, "there are things that go on in this world that aren't easy to understand, aren't easy to take a position on" (214). Chief, perhaps, among things difficult to take a position on is the question of the best response to a threatening sense of social disintegration. The concern causes all the characters some degree of anxiety. Indeed, it pervades their world with the kind of vague yet omnipresent menace we associated earlier with the threat of nuclear annihilation; for some, it results in a similar kind of hopelessness. Mary Ann, for example, ascribes the sense of doom to a malevolent deity, thus burdening herself with a fatalism not essentially different from that from which, in *Criminals in Love*, William was trying to free Junior and Gail.

Even where the characters refuse to be defeated by their premonition of apocalypse, it is a terrifically destructive force. By far the most fanatic in this respect is Tom, who, upon his first entrance, nearly quotes Yeats: "Things just fall apart," he says, adding portentously, "Be careful, the worst is yet to come" (147). While Nora is not possessed of so certain a foreboding, she has been already vaguely resisting the threat of the outside world, trying to extend the protected enclave of her home by means of her subterranean room. In a way, Tom simply brings more force and aggression to the deployment of such measures. Nora's room naturally lends itself to becoming a bomb shelter, and her notion of organizing the family into a unit that will resist external threats slips all too easily into Tom's declaration of martial law within the household. The motives of Tom and Nora are finally quite similar (as is the tenuousness of their sanity); it is their methods that differ—with such drastic, even frightening consequences.

But the play is about more than the struggle between two crazed parents for control of a household. The underlying issue has to do with who can provide "better living" for the family, and what that would mean. To set the idea in perspective, consider Arthur Miller's argument:

> all plays we call great, let alone those we call serious, are ultimately involved with some aspect of a single problem. It is this: How may a man make of the outside world a home? How and in what ways must he struggle, what must he strive to change and overcome within himself and outside himself if he is to find the safety, the surroundings of love, the ease of soul, the sense of identity and honor which, evidently, all men have connected in their memories with the idea of family? (73)

In the East End plays Walker focuses on the most basic version of the problem, asking: How does one make of a *house* a home? How can one provide one's family with the sort of security and assurance that ultimately one would like to extend into the world at large? Yet one eye is still on the larger questions of social reform—so much so, indeed, that the relation of the domestic concerns to the broader social sphere has a consistency verging on allegory or parable.

Tom's Odyssean efforts to re-establish domestic order after his ten-year absence are identifiable with attempts to reassert an older patriarchal governing structure based in a stick-and-carrot combination of demagogic fomentation of fears and paternalistic assurances of protection. Here, as so often in literature, a father represents the authority of the past over the present; more specifically, Tom's re-emergence in the family home suggests the neo-conservative resurgence of the mid-1980s. The popularity of Ronald Reagan and Margaret Thatcher at that time was largely attributable to their promises to re-establish, amidst widespread social anxiety, the security and confidence of an earlier age by taking aggressive measures to defend national interests against putative military and economic threats. In Canada the mandate attached to the Mulroney years was not so definite, but there was abundant evidence of the climate of opinion associated with Thatcher and Reagan. This is not to say that *Better Living* satirizes specific political events; rather, Walker uses parable form to explore the psychological concerns and anxieties that engender the sense of social desperation from which such political events arise.

Among the responses of the others to the anxieties about social dissolution, those of Jack, the disaffected priest, are particularly revealing. Jack is one of the most sympathetic characters in the play; yet, in terms of contributing a positive solution to the underlying social problems, Jack (like Walker's earlier disaffected priest, Father LiDuc of *Beyond Mozambique*) has little to offer, a deficiency of which he is well aware. Tom suggests that Jack is jaded because he has spent "too many years living in the shadow of God. It sucks the free will right out of a man." Moreover, he argues, priests can no longer be effective, "and do you know why?" "Yes," replies Jack. "Because they're perceived as being outside society in the first place and all their actions even the sacrificial ones are perceived as actions, once-removed, of personally motivated non-political symbols" (171). In so far as he is "perceived as being outside society," Jack fulfills a role in *Better Living* comparable to William's Diogenic function in *Criminals in Love*, and to the ethical functions of Power or Victor. Indeed, in Jack we may see something like the last gasp of the "liberal idealism" that Denis Johnston suggests was Power's downfall (201). Jack finally turns his back on the moral restrictions contingent upon being a man of the cloth and forsakes pacifist persuasion for, as Mao put it, the power that comes from the barrel of a gun.

As it happens, Jack is the single character who does not go on from *Better Living* to *Escape from Happiness*. This probably has to do with what was, for Walker, the ultimate untenability of Jack's position. Maintaining any loyalty to a transcendent moral code of the kind Jack represents demands a modicum of detachment from the world. Where this consists in cynical disaffection, yet not quite wholehearted disavowal, the sense of detachment results simply in moral paralysis. True, Jack ends that paralysis by taking action near the end of the play, getting his hands dirty with the real world, so to speak, even if that means embracing Henry Dawson's way of getting things done. Yet doing so not only prompts Jack's resignation from the priesthood but apparently causes the disintegration of his dramaturgical function in Walker's work.

Elizabeth points to the crux of the problem: "Political involvement often causes moral confusion. I mean, unless you're mentally rigid" (189). Her point applies to more than the compromise of Jack's pacifist convictions. In a different way Tom's pursuit of personal security and order for his family represents a kind of mental rigidity that finally must be confounded. Nevertheless, the family's contact with Tom proves that the notion of his being purely and utterly villainous is mental rigidity of another kind. Confusion in such matters may feel demoralizing, but is less dangerous than moral certainty.

Ruthless certainty appears in different guise in *Beautiful City* (1987). While Walker retains the East End setting, he sets the Quinn family aside to focus on the architect Paul Gallagher and his relations with three other families: the wealthy, corrupt Rafts; the stupid, criminal Moores; and the charming, eccentric Sabbatinis. The play opens with Paul in a state of crisis as Tony Raft involves him in plans for a monstrous Harbourfront mall linked by tunnels to other major commercial buildings. Paul collapses in pain, fearing, by turns, appendicitis, heart failure, or an anxiety attack. In hospital Paul meets Jane Sabbatini, a young volunteer who introduces him to her mother, Gina Mae, a benevolent witch who works at Bargain Harold's discount store and heals people by forcing them to face "the simple ugly truth."

Meanwhile, Tony and his intimidating mother, Mary, bribe Paul's brother, Michael, to persuade Paul to return to work for them. For insurance Mary Raft hires Stevie Moore, a moronic small-time crook whose father, Rolly (an only slightly less moronic small-time crook), has been embezzling from the Rafts's pornography business. The Moores, though close spiritual cousins to the criminal Dawsons, are actually distantly related to the Sabbatinis, so Gina Mae undertakes Rolly's reformation to prevent his disgracing the family name. When the incorrigible Stevie, accompanied by Michael and Tony, detonates a bomb under the Sabbatini house, Paul and the Sabbatinis escape, taking Tony hostage. There is an armed showdown between the two matriarchs, Gina Mae (representing the forces of good) and Mary (representing the forces of evil), but before anyone is seriously injured, a *deus ex machina*, Dian Black, an unorthodox police officer, arrives. Illegally, she negotiates a settlement in which the Rafts will fund the rejuvenation of poor sections of the East End in a socially responsible and financially unprofitable manner. In a coda Paul shows up at Bargain Harold's and humbly proposes marriage to Gina Mae. Eventually she accepts, though both are left shrugging awkwardly at the final blackout.

If architecture is, as Mies van der Rohe suggested, "the will of the age conceived in spatial terms" (qtd. in Harvey 21), then it provides a uniquely rich figurative battleground for ideas of social reform. Architectural planning is a form of social engineering; thus she who controls the architects is she who directs "the will of the age" (and in the matriarchal world that, in *Beautiful City*, has succeeded the dissipated patriarchy of Walker's earlier plays, it is definitely a "she" who ultimately calls the shots). Hence, the contest to determine whose influence over Paul will prevail, Mary's or Gina Mae's, is symbolically crucial. The connection between the Rafts's moral outlook and the architectural vision they are hiring Paul to realize is spelled out by Tony: "My mother was born in a police state. Eventually she escaped. [...] But when she lived in a police state she had values. I got my dream for this city from the part of my mother that's still under siege. It's based on family. Family and safety. Everything indoors. My motto is 'No more strangers in your life'" (234). The kernel of this vision—"Family and safety. Everything indoors"—is related to Nora's "new world down below." And just as Tom's "consumer socialism" amplified the acute paranoia latent in Nora's domestic vision, so are Tony's xenophobic urban plans a grotesque extension of the protective values forged in his mother's youth. In either case, once an ordered defence against a sense of external threat is extended beyond a certain point, it becomes a species of fascism. Construed as a pointed sociological critique, this is fairly solid; National Socialism, in the first instance, established its roots in the besieged psyche of a people who had been badly battered and humiliated by war and economic hardship. Germans tried to exorcise their fear and resentment by protecting themselves from the so-called alien element in their society, and ended up creating the Third Reich.

However, set against the Rafts's etiolated urban vision, as Saint Augustine set the City of God against the city of Rome, is the vision of Gina Mae:

> I want a community centre. I want two new parks. I want low cost housing. I want a shelter for the homeless and the mistreated. I want big bright wonderful stores where people get useful products at reasonable prices. I want halfway houses for people who are trying to re-enter the world from the unfortunate darkness of their circumstances. I want a throbbing, connecting, living, creative neighbourhood. (314)

What she wants, in short, is the socialist vision: accessible, publicly owned space that would provide whole communities with the comfortable sanctuary that, under laissez-faire capitalism, remains the exclusive preserve of the wealthy. In Canada, with its long-standing liberal-socialist traditions, one would be hard pressed to find someone who would not pay at least some lip-service to such ideas; as Dian says of Gina Mae's vision, "it seems deeply connected to a kind of popular fantasy" (315). But few are willing to dislodge their first priority of undaunted pursuit of self-interest in favour of such communal values. So Gina Mae provides not only the moral centre around which this play revolves (charitable, quirky, self-righteous, angry, ironic, afraid of sentiment, utopian but a little embarrassed by this, and accordingly, defensive); she also serves as a moral conscience for the others.

The paradox of characters like Gina Mae is that, central as their moral function of critique may be, they are usually depicted as being outside the social order. William's place on the social margins was guaranteed by his homelessness; Gina Mae's is guaranteed by her status as a witch. As Jane comments, "The power is awesome but it kinda removes you from the rest of the world. Puts you in opposition" (236). Inherently, most moral touchstone characters are self-righteous like Gina Mae, though seldom do they emit the whiff of sanctimony; their ironic detachment means that their more usual contribution is, again like Gina Mae's, humorous. Depending on whether the play ends with a successful achievement of social integration or a failure, the alienation of the moral touchstone may be (a) finally fatal and therefore tragic, as with the Fool in *Lear*; (b) perpetually frozen and therefore ironic, as with the savage moralist Thersites in *Troilus and Cressida*; or (c) temporary and therefore comic, as in the case of Feste—whose nature is, as his name suggests, to bring about the festivities with which *Twelfth Night* ends. Prototypes for this character may be found in two holy fools: Prometheus, who is forcibly exiled and tortured for his moral role, though with the hope of eventual emancipation and integration; and Jesus, whose martyrdom is meant, ideally, to prompt a massive penitence leading to the absorption of his moral view into an integrated, redeemed society.

The scope of redemption assumed by Gina Mae is far more modest, though none the less decisive. To be sure, she undertakes the conversion of one of two thieves (Rolly) while damning the other (Stevie), but we should not make too much of that. Though Gina Mae claims that her message, "the simple ugly truth," is "metaphysical" (267), the redemption she purveys is ultimately humanist. The principal beneficiary of her efforts, dramatically speaking, is Paul, whose sickness is diagnosed as follows: "You've been living like a fool ... You've lost touch with the genuinely complex nature of reality. All your friends think alike, talk alike, want the same things. [...] You're dying from a kind of simplicity ... It's like you've taken the huge throbbing life force and turned it into a piece of thread ... and it's not enough to hold you together (266). In short, Gina Mae declares: "the simple ugly truth" Paul is missing is that "there's life right here on earth and you're not a part of it!!" (267). Accordingly, Paul's impending marriage to Gina Mae represents not only personal rejuvenation but the invigorating promise of social integration. The implicit possibility is that through marriage to Gina Mae, Paul may become the architect of a better society. Naturally, the sentimental optimism inherent in such an idea is enormous, so much so that the characters themselves retain their skepticism, shrugging awkwardly even as they decide to hope.

Walker's own optimism returned undaunted in *Nothing Sacred* (1988), his adaptation of Turgenev's *Fathers and Sons.* This play, notwithstanding any purist objections Turgenev's admirers might raise, is a beautiful piece of work, perhaps Walker's finest. Here the suggestion of faith in charitable socialist humanism that had been creeping into Walker's work emerges in full flower. Where the intentions of Turgenev's Bazarov had been dubious even to himself upon his deathbed, Walker's Bazarov is able to articulate a much more coherent view, and his legacy is less ambiguous. In the course of reworking Turgenev's novel for the stage, Walker pushed Bazarov's awakening further and bestowed some of his own new convictions on the character.

In the preface to *Nothing Sacred* (excerpted from his 1988 interview), Walker discusses Bazarov's awakening, saying:

> during the play he somehow comes to understand that [...] the roots of his nihilism are a profound concern. Unless you reconcile the roots of nihilism with the ways in which your actions affect people, you really are a person out of your time, perhaps out of your planet. [Cf Gina Mae's comment about "life on earth."] If you forget that your work, and all your indignation and your anger, comes from the way people are being treated—the so-called victims—then you can't talk to the victims, and your feeling for them is useless. I watched Bazarov make that journey, took it with him; and I tried to lay in that understanding so that he would undergo more than a mental exercise. (7)

As his interviewer, Robert Wallace, observes, Bazarov's journey is "very similar to the overall journey charted by [Walker's] plays," moving from "nihilism—to a type of social commitment, even action, in the face of social problems" (7-8). In effect, Walker changes Bazarov from a nihilist into a proto-socialist.

Therein lies Walker's main departure from his source. Turgenev's Bazarov, however strong his dislike of the aristocracy and real his human sympathy, is no socialist. Indeed, Isaiah Berlin suggests that in Turgenev's view socialism was "a fantasy" (44). If all people have the same worth in the eyes of the Bazarov of *Fathers and Sons*, it is only in so far as they are all more or less worthless. Turgenev's Bazarov is a man who believes at first that his ideas are ahead of his time and, hence, that he stands apart from his countrymen; but he finds out gradually that he has not transcended love and, finally, that (to be brief, at the risk of making a profound discovery sound trite) no man is an island. Whereas in *Fathers and Sons* Bazarov is torn between his urge for disaffiliation from other human beings and his desire to reform, in *Nothing Sacred* he is much more consistent in his inclinations. Walker achieves this by muting the first part of the dilemma, the urge for disaffiliation, and giving it a more rationally consistent basis in an antipathy for society's injustices. Though Walker's Bazarov is at first unable to speak directly to a peasant, he is committed to an abstract love of humanity from the beginning. He frequently uses the word "love," by which he means, of course, not *eros*, but *caritas*—charity.

Naturally, the change makes Bazarov into a much stronger (not to mention more likable) character in *Nothing Sacred* than he is in Turgenev's novel. Indeed, Bazarov is probably the strongest and most independently willed character Walker has written since Zastrozzi or Medeiros [in *Science and Madness*]. Arkady is being hyperbolic, but only a little, when he says of Bazarov, "He's not a man. He's a primal force" (49). We see Bazarov's physical strength as well as his strength of character in the first scene when he handily overwhelms the Bailiff (19), a feat he repeats more spectacularly when the Bailiff attempts to clobber him with a board (37-38). He is similarly able to overcome the much larger Sergei through his wits (49); and his self-confidence in intellectual matters is justified by his persuasive analysis of Pavel's weakly self-delusory obsessiveness (67-68).

Even Bazarov's greatest weakness in *Fathers and Sons*, his relationship with Anna, is turned into another kind of strength. Where Turgenev suddenly undermines Bazarov's posture of rational indifference by having him fall in love with Anna Odintsov, a friend of Kirsanov's, Walker gives the prior friendship with Anna to Bazarov. This he reveals with a device familiar from the movie "Butch Cassidy and the Sundance Kid": Bazarov appears to be taking impertinent liberties with Anna when, with a familiar embrace, they reveal their long intimacy. Accordingly, Bazarov seems more suave and self-assured in his relationship with Anna and far less vulnerable than he had been in Turgenev's hands.[5]

Yet by far the most prepossessing feature of Walker's Bazarov is his robust espousal of charity. Turgenev had created in Bazarov a character who denied the existence and necessity of all moral frameworks whatsoever. Walker, however, in having Bazarov affirm ecumenical love, has created a character who rejects all pre-existing frameworks in favour of one central principle: universal suffrage. One might easily argue that by changing Bazarov's character in this way, Walker has derailed much of Turgenev's story. In *Fathers and Sons* Bazarov considers himself a kind of scientist, ruthlessly regarding all situations with skeptical, rational utilitarianism and therefore free of any transcendent scheme of values; then, having fallen in love, his compassion and instinctive humanitarianism spring forth unbidden. In the novel it is while helping his father—who himself acts with a sense of *noblesse oblige* towards the tenants who were formerly his serfs—that Bazarov receives his mortal infection. In short, Turgenev suggests that Bazarov is infected by caring for others; this is what destroys Bazarov—and, by implication, the nihilist ideas he represents. In *Nothing Sacred* Walker has Bazarov infected by caring for others much earlier in the story. Bazarov dies absurdly in the course of his kindly, albeit reluctant efforts to accommodate the honour ethic of Pavel Kirsanov.

All this makes Bazarov into much more of a linchpin to social history than Turgenev ever could have imagined him to be. For example, in having Pavel and Bazarov duel inconclusively over Fenichka's honour, Turgenev evidently has a vague parable in mind. Russia's future is like Fenichka's child, the offspring of peasants and aristocrats, whose future, depending on whether the parents can bring themselves to marry, will either be legitimate (i.e., a part of civilized progress) or illegitimate (i.e., a rejection of civilization). Walker displaces the question onto the hunt for the elderly brothers, Kirsanov and Pavel, in the woods. "All Russia," says Pavel, "is searching for her wayward son. I am moved by her concern. Worried a bit about her competence" (84). The question has shifted to one about finding a way forward for Russia (and, by extension, for civilization at large) through the cataclysmic onset of modernity, while preserving what is worthwhile in her past. But where Turgenev had left the question open, in Walker's hands the answers are very nearly embodied in Bazarov.

Accordingly, though Bazarov himself dies, what he represents in *Nothing Sacred* is passed on. At the end he sends from his deathbed for the servants; it is to them that he chooses to speak his final words. For Gregor, at least, Bazarov was a kind of messiah. And, as people do after the demise of an alleged martyr, once Bazarov dies, the arguments begin about what he wanted to say, what he represented. Then, in the deeply moving final moments, Gregor begins to teach Sergei the principles of socialism he learned from Bazarov. The Christ-like overtones of Bazarov's virtually superhuman status are affirmed, for his legacy is to be passed on through his disciples.

*Love and Anger* (1989) returns to the idea of a martyr who attempts to pilot the way through the injustices and confusions of the modern world. But it does so by integrating themes from some of Walker's earlier plays. Where *Beautiful City* ended—with the impending marriage of a penitent former adherent of patriarchal corporatism and an eccentric, unprosperous, marginal social reformer—*Love and Anger* begins: with a protagonist in whom all those features are already married. Peter ("call me Petie") Maxwell was one of the city's toughest corporate lawyers until he suffered a stroke, which precipitated a spiritual reformation. Maxwell gave away his money; he now keeps a basement office "on the fringe of the downtown," where, with his strait-laced assistant Eleanor, he serves a marginalized and indigent clientele. His latest client is Gail Jones, a young black woman whose husband has been jailed for his part in a break-in at a newspaper office. It emerges that the break-in was sponsored by Babe Conner, multimillionaire newspaper publisher, who, coincidentally, has retained Maxwell's former partner, Sean Harris, as his attorney.

Because the odds against liberating Gail's husband by legal means are overwhelming, Maxwell decides to proceed outside the law. With the help of Gail and Sarah, Eleanor's schizophrenic sister, he drugs and kidnaps Conner in order to put him on trial, securing the co-operation of Harris with some phony photos that link Harris and Conner to the small-time crooks (Dawson and Moore, though they never actually appear) who were responsible for the break-in. With Sarah serving as judge, Maxwell as prosecutor, and Harris as the attorney for the defence, Conner is charged with "Being … Consciously … Evil" (69) and with knowingly pursuing "a career injurious to the public well-being" (73). But before he can complete his case, Maxwell, upset by the people outside who are rummaging through the garbage for food, suffers another stroke and concedes victory. Gail is not willing to let things ride so easily. She pulls out a handgun, warning Conner that she will murder him if he ever crosses her family again. Conner and Harris leave, and then Maxwell dies, wishing with his last words that he had begun his reformation earlier. As the play ends, the three women concentrate on reviving Maxwell through their combined wills.

The stroke Petie Maxwell has suffered prior to the play's action functions dramatically within the story in several different ways. In the first place, the injury is implicitly a consequence of his previous behaviour: apparently, just as indulging in the luxury of eating fatty, high-cholesterol foods leads to cardiac arrest, so does indulgently profiting from a legal system that neglects the miseries of the underclass lead to collapse. The enemy here is the voracious appetite of instrumental reason unchecked by humanitarian considerations, and Maxwell's stroke brings that syndrome to a halt.[6]

Maxwell's stroke also represents the handicap under which his side of the conflict must labour. But here we see an example of the phenomenon discussed by Edmund Wilson in his famous essay "The Wound and the Bow" (1941): the sense of mutilation seems an inextricable feature of any virtues and strengths Maxwell and his allies may claim, because that mutilation is integral to their full humanity (223-42). The idea is related to the fusion of emotions set out in the title, *Love and Anger*. Gail, the purest embodiment of love in this play (in this, as her name suggests, she is the doppelgänger of Gail Quinn), also turns out to be the most focused embodiment of anger when she threatens Conner. Love and anger are also fully embodied in Maxwell himself. There, however, the two emotions are in constant turmoil: a consequence and a symbol of his broken rationality. In other words, there may be some truth to Eleanor's suspicion that Maxwell is inclined to express irrational, hyperbolic ideas because his formerly rational mind has been injured. More significant is the idea that Maxwell's broken rationality symbolizes a breaking of the covenant with reason formed in the Enlightenment.

There are intimations that this is what is at stake in Maxwell's speeches in the opening scene. He begins with a critique of one of the pillars of enlightenment reason, the law, which, he tells Gail, "is vulgar in its rigidity. Insensitive to the nuance of human existence. Derived and constructed from knowledge within a narrow historical corridor. In short, it's in love with itself" (13). This attack on the law, Maxwell admits, is part of his plan "to undermine the entire institutional bias of our culture" (14). And he begins to sound a little like one of the most formidable critics of the Enlightenment, Michel Foucault, when he declares medicine to be "number four on my hit list. Right after law, religion, government" (17).

Gail's case, then, is merely one specific opportunity for action within Maxwell's overall scheme. Similarly, he tells Gail that "the love you have for your husband is just one arm of a many-armed beast. Full of compassion for everything in the world that needs love" (15). This, of course, is very like the sort of love Bazarov espoused, just as Maxwell's anger at social injustice resembles Bazarov's indignation. In a way, then, *Love and Anger* shows an attempt to realize a part of the socialist hope that Bazarov had introduced in *Nothing Sacred*. Maxwell, Gail, Sarah, and Eleanor form an alliance of seekers after justice, a confederacy of the marginalized who are united in both love and anger. Arrayed against them are the forces of the establishment: law, politics, capitalism, and the media, all incarnate in Babe Conner and Sean Harris. The attempt to bring these forces to a reckoning by staging the trial of Conner reveals a yearning for some kind of higher, more conclusive moral judgment of the injustices of the world. If, in earlier plays, Walker explored the ultimate confrontation between good and evil, Armageddon, then the mock trial at the centre of *Love and Anger* is a sort of parody of the Day of Judgment following Armageddon. The scene is humorous, but the accusations of evil levelled at Conner and his kind are unmistakably real. Thus, though the trial disintegrates, the indictment remains.

Walker contrives to place the apparent perpetrators of evil under the thumbs of his protagonists again in *Escape from Happiness* (1991), the third play to feature members of the Quinn family. Ostensibly a sequel to *Better Living, Escape From Happiness* is in many respects a reworking and expansion of the earlier play rather than a foray into wholly new territory. At the literal level, the setting of the two plays is identical: the Quinn family kitchen. Moreover, the women of the Quinn family are still coming to terms with the return of Tom and, at the same time, are wrestling with the question of how to cope with the violence threatening their family from beyond their walls.

However, where in *Better Living* it was the difficulty in accommodating Tom that presented the primary problem, with external violence a secondary, related issue, in *Escape from Happiness* the ratio of emphasis is reversed; the issue of external violence is now predominant. In part, this is because Tom is allegedly dying of some vague sickness that leaves him docile and unaware, so he poses little threat—though he is still shunned by his two older daughters. The play begins when Gail and Nora arrive home from shopping to find Junior lying on the floor, having been badly beaten. Right away the reliability of any external authorities to cope with the family's problems is questioned. Gail calls 9-1-1, but the women are doubtful of a prompt response; Nora insists that what is needed is for Junior to get himself on his own feet. In the event, the police and ambulance do arrive. Two officers begin an investigation, Dian Black, from *Beautiful City*, and her partner, the plodding, apparently rather backward Mike Dixon.

Unfortunately, Dian and Mike are more interested in investigating the Quinns than in probing the assault on Junior, and they discover large bags of drugs in the basement. Elizabeth tries to take things in hand by kidnapping one of Junior's assailants, Rolly Moore, the pathetic small-time crook from *Beautiful City*, who, despite his terror, can tell them nothing about the drugs. Junior and Tom assume that the drugs have been planted in reprisal for their vigilantism. Tom has been feigning illness to avoid being driven from the house, meanwhile operating a scheme with Junior that involves setting all the local criminals on a path of mutual destruction. As it turns out, Rolly and Stevie were only indirectly connected with the drugs. The real culprit was Dian Black, who is here revealed as not merely unorthodox but dangerously fanatic in her devotion to the police. She has planted the drugs in order to thwart Elizabeth's plans to attack the police with a series of charges of police brutality. Mike, for all his reactionary defence of police methods, insists that they must fight Elizabeth by the book.

Once the police have left, the question of Tom's presence in the house is raised once more, for he and Nora have begun to talk honestly to one another again. Bashfully, Tom declares that all he wants is to express his love for his family in whatever way he can, admitting that he needs the strength their love provides. Elizabeth seems almost ready to relent, demanding that Tom's love should include respect for them all, but in the end she remains implacable, leaving the house without having accepted Tom. Mary Ann is prepared to accept Tom, so long as he follows a list of demands. Gail, however, forgives Tom outright. It appears that, despite the incompleteness of his daughters' blessings, Tom will stay living with his family, trying, as Nora puts it, "to make something positive out of the experience" (126).

Whereas in *Better Living* Tom's return home was Odyssean in terms of his attempt to re-establish order, in *Escape from Happiness* the pathos of Tom's diminished stature before his three daughters is redolent of *King Lear*. The connection intensifies when it is Tom's youngest daughter, Gail, who most readily forgives him, despite having suffered most from his history of tyrannical domestic violence. In so far as his mental collapse and sickness is feigned, Tom perhaps recalls his namesake, Poor Tom, the character affected by Edgar to deflect danger. But the more important comparison is undoubtedly between Tom and Lear, both erstwhile, seemingly omnipotent patriarchs. Tom's fatherhood, symbolic of the authority of the past over the present, is now much diminished, with nothing imperious left in it. The Tom of *Escape from Happiness* shows virtually no signs of the coarsely arrogant and foolish ranter he was in *Better Living*, or that Lear is in the first two acts of his play. Rather, he is like Lear in his last three acts, by then shut out of his daughters' houses and left in the storm; he has been forced to change his self-image, and our sympathies have slipped towards him. Tom is fully penitent and eager to atone for his past. Junior, a younger, humbler man, loyally accompanies and protects Tom, like Kent or the Fool does Lear, helping to guide him through to some kind of redemption.

As we find so often with literary treatments of the theme, the only real path for the redemption of male violence lies through women—or, more exactly, through the humble recognition and honouring of those virtues most often associated with women. There remains some question, however, of what, precisely, atoning for male guilt through women might consist in doing (to paraphrase Leonard Cohen, "when they said repent, [we] wonder what they meant"). Dian's summary of the tensions involved has much validity: "It's big this thing we're engaged in! Big and contradictory. It's new and old. Woman and man. Daughter and father. Smart and dumb. Really, really smart! And really, really dumb!!" (119) And yet, thinking of the problem in terms of polarities like that is of limited usefulness, as the play reveals. Even while evidently accepting the premise of a kind of collective male guilt in need of expiation, Walker seems determined that no purely simplistic, politically correct interpretation of the idea should be allowed to prevail unchallenged.

Thus, as in *Beautiful City*, and to a lesser degree *Criminals in Love* and *Better Living*, a kind of matriarchal power structure has arisen to fill the space left by the played-out patriarchy; but that in itself does not provide a solution. On the one hand there are recurring examples in the play of an immensely positive, virtually mystic power associated with females, particularly in their maternal aspect. The threatening visit of Rolly and Stevie Moore, for instance, is foiled when they see Gail nursing her baby (41-42); the Moores become frantic as their brutality is overwhelmed by innate reverence. Similarly, when Gail goes off to secure Junior's job, she is armed with her baby, confident that it will command the foreman's sympathy (63). Nora uses another kind of maternal power when she defuses Elizabeth's savage temper tantrum by blowing a raspberry on her stomach (89). All these examples are essentially pacific, but in themselves they are enough to intimidate men like the Moores.

On the other hand there are situations in which some of the women reveal a wolfishness as ugly as the patriarchal excesses. Undoubtedly the most disturbing examples of this aspect of matriarchal power come from Elizabeth and Dian Black. As a lawyer, Elizabeth is at least as insanely aggressive in her work ethic as Sean Harris or, prior to his stroke, Maxwell, in *Love and Anger* (81-82). With her family, too, Elizabeth teeters on the brink of a lunatic violence much like Tom's (87-88). She also drifts into her brutalism for virtually the same reasons her father did: a conflicted mixture of familial protectiveness and personal pride. Furthermore, clear parallels are laid between Elizabeth's protection of her family and Dian's protection of the police. For Dian, loyalty to her fellow officers (notwithstanding her personal scorn for Mike) is a paramount value overriding any other humanist imperatives; similarly, for Elizabeth, the bond of family (notwithstanding her open scorn for some of them, such as her sister Mary Ann) justifies any measures she takes.

Even the police brutality that Elizabeth has determined to wipe out is sarcastically put into perspective by Mike: "I mean, who the hell are [the police] to get brutal. All the nice people they get to deal with. All that love and affection they get from that wonderful scum out there" (119). Walker's point is hardly to excuse police brutality by pointing to provocation, but rather to show that the situation is too complex to justify any simplistic, self-righteous moralizing. Earlier, Elizabeth refused to accept that Tom's love for his family could in any way exculpate him for acts of vigilantism that, in the end, endangered the family. "He loves us," she exclaims: "Amazing! Can you imagine what he'd do to this family if he hated us. The mind boggles. I don't know, could be anything … little nuclear devices shoved up all our assholes!" (101). The reference to "nuclear devices" returns us to the larger social dimensions of this issue of protectiveness raised in *Better Living*. The mind-set perpetrating the small-scale vigilantism seen in this play is continuous with that which uses the threat of nuclear holocaust to extort peace and security for a nation. So Elizabeth may well be right in saying that having a pure motive for aggressive actions doesn't change the fact that they are more likely to escalate violence than to decrease it. However, she hypocritically fails to acknowledge how deeply implicated her own behaviour is in this syndrome.

Repentance for male violence, then, is rather more complicated than it first appears to be. Perhaps the most promising line of thought about the problem emerges when Nora at last admits that she has known that Tom is her ex-husband all along, but has been withholding recognition to maintain a modest balance of power (93). She suggests that the time has now come to acknowledge who Tom is and, by implication, how his actions have been an integral part of their family, for better or worse. Such an acknowledgment is essential to make any positive progress. "What this family needs now," argues Nora, "is something more clear. Clearer roles. Lighter burdens for … some of us" (94). The need for repentance, she submits, is far more general than the focus on Tom would suggest:

> I think we believe that we don't deserve to be happy. I know Mary Ann believes it's just fate. But Mary Ann is too distressed to think clearly about these things. My theory is better. We're running away from happiness. We think we need to struggle, and suffer, and work really hard before we can just stay still, and let happiness catch up and surround us. (94)

In the end, then, the difficulties devolve upon the question of how to move from a state of penitence to a state of happiness. Naturally, this involves extending some kind of absolution, and it is with this possibility that the play ends. Elizabeth still refuses to absolve Tom, though Nora's theory suggests this may have to do with an inability to forgive herself. Mary Ann, still too fearful even to trust herself, yearns for the assurance of rules and guidelines. Of the daughters, only Gail is able, from within a realm of love, to extend forgiveness and trust. In her easygoing nature resides the sense of hopefulness—or, as Walker prefers it, possibility—with which the play ends.

The intriguing effect that the accommodation of this kind of optimism has had upon the dramatic form of Walker's work becomes evident when we compare the East End plays to the conventions of Jacobean city comedy. Most obvious of the definitive features shared are that Walker's plays are comedies that also use a city setting, the unnamed Toronto standing in for Jacobean London; and that both depict a variety of social backgrounds that are similarly used to bring class tensions into open dramatic conflict.

Perhaps more significant, however, is the similar sense of the social ethos into which these plays enter. What gives Jacobean comedies an aesthetic distinct from that of their more romantic Elizabethan predecessors is the overtone of cynicism and banal immorality pervading the work. These overtones are related to what Una Ellis-Fermor has pointed to as the predominant metaphysical concern of Jacobean tragedy as well as comedy: "the loss of a spiritual significance from within the revealed world of fact and event" (18). We have repeatedly noted the similar overtones of cynicism and banal immorality present in Walker's plays. One symptom is the postmodern "flatness" of many of his characters. To ascribe purely cynical motives to characters results in a cartoon-like delimitation of their psychological conception. This is true whether their nature is accounted for in terms of a Jonsonian theory of "humours" based in Renaissance science or in terms of Walker's ideas about obsession, which have their basis in a wide-reaching cultural and philosophical analysis.

On those grounds we could consider Walker's City Comedies close relatives of their Jacobean forebears, albeit written for the postmodern age. Yet this is too simple. For the shift that took place in Walker's work with the East End plays makes Walker's postmodern city comedy quite distinct from its Jacobean precursor. The basic difference lies in the degree to which the plays themselves partake of the cynicism of the world therein depicted. However much the East End plays embrace complexity and depict ambiguity, they all finally evince some kind of attempt to move dramatically towards a less morally ambiguous outlook. What should we do about our flawed society? What *can* we do? Of what values can we be certain? These are the questions that haunt the East End plays, and the characters grope their way towards a point at which answers will at least seem possible. Similar questions form a subtext to plays like *As You Like It*, *Measure for Measure* or *The Tempest*. In Jacobean city comedy, however, such questions are left to the side. They can be ignored with impunity as part of a metaphysical mode of inquiry belonging to an earlier age and dealt with by an earlier, more romantic kind of play.

As for the element of trickery endemic to Jacobean comedy, which is focused almost exclusively upon the acquisition of wealth, in Walker's postmodern city comedy a comparable trickery is practised by the protagonists, but it is focused upon tricking goodness out of a cynical world. In the case of Gina Mae in *Beautiful City* this trickery required a kind of magic; and in *Love and Anger* the effects of Maxwell's stroke were a sort of pseudo-miracle, almost a divine intervention. However, with *Escape from Happiness* Walker declines any sort of supernatural element, including any particular extraordinary trickster character. Whatever magic there is must be found among the flawed and suffering collective protagonists.

What Walker moved towards in his earlier plays, then, was a form of comedy in which characters are habitually defined by their obsessive relations to their culture and have accordingly become "flat" and cartoon-like. But in the East End plays these characters struggle to develop more complex relations to their society, and accordingly must reacquaint themselves with the sources of depth. By pressing the moral concerns of his characters, Walker's dramaturgy erupts through the very aesthetic conventions he had previously established.

(2001)

## Notes

1 Earlier in chapter 5 of *The Buried Astrolabe*, in a discussion of Walker's *Rumours of Our Death*, I refer to Friedrich Dürrenmatt's 1955 essay "Note on Comedy," in which he argues that, to come to terms with a world overshadowed by the horror of atomic weaponry, tragedy is a wholly inappropriate genre. The only suitable artistic response, Dürrenmatt suggests, is to embrace the grotesque, a choice which, in his view, is not the work of nihilists but of moralists (see Craig Walker 302; see Dürrenmatt, "Note" 58).

2 In a discussion of *The Art of War* earlier in *The Buried Astrolabe*, I draw attention to Jamie's perception that there is not much to choose between the respective cynicisms of Hackman and Power, as reflected in their views on the function of art. Hackman's is opportunistic ("the leisurely reflection of an elite society"), whereas Power's is nihilistic ("the leisurely reflection of a dying society"). Where the field is so entirely defined by cynicism, the only possible ending is ironic, a point which had already been demonstrated by Walker's earlier plays. Accordingly, I suggest that with *The Art of War* he set out to have Power fail and to show the inadequacy of his hero's attitude (see Craig Walker 314; see George F. Walker, *Art* 162, 159).

3 The term "false consciousness," associated with Marxism, refers to people's belief that their actions are freely chosen, when all the while their environments are so totally pervaded by cultural, racial, or economic forces that they are as incapable of seeing how their behaviour is predetermined as a fish would be of describing water. Hence, any sense of consciousness about social issues is false. Marxism purports to enlighten such consciousness, but Sloterdijk contends that such enlightenment normally only removes the individual mind far enough from its habitual environment to recognize the difficulties, not to effect any change, thus begetting a paralytic sense of cynicism (see Craig Walker 312-13; see Sloterdijk 4-6).

4 Indeed, he anticipates the title character in the 1991 Terry Gilliam movie, *The Fisher King*, who is, like William, an effusively optimistic vagrant.

5 Incidentally, in making "Princess R.," the woman Pavel had been obsessed with in his younger days, into Anna's mother, Walker has picked up on a connection that is apparently latent in the novel. According to Rosemary Edmonds, translator of *Fathers and Sons*, both these characters and their effects on Pavel and Bazarov have their origin in Turgenev's lifelong obsession with the singer-composer Pauline Viardot-Garcia, a married woman (65).

6 Evidently, Walker's conceit of precipitating a lawyer's spiritual rebirth by temporarily destroying a part of his brain had a broad popular appeal; a few years later the idea was also used as the premise of one of the most popular movies of 1991, *Regarding Henry*, in which Harrison Ford plays a lawyer who becomes more humane after being shot in the head.

## Works Cited

Berlin, Isaiah. "Fathers and Children: Turgenev and the Liberal Predicament." Turgenev 7-61.

Dürrenmatt, Friedrich. "Friedrich Schiller." *Essays on German Theater*. Ed. Margaret Herzfeld-Sander. The German Library 83. New York: Continuum, 1985. 235-49.

———. "Note on Comedy." *Writings on Theatre and Drama*. Trans. H. M. Waidson. London: Cape, 1976. 54-58.

———. "Problems of the Theatre." 1954. *Dramatic Theory and Criticism: Greeks to Grotowski*. Ed. Bernard F. Dukore. New York: Holt, 1974. 855-58.

Ellis-Fermor, Una. *The Jacobean Drama: An Interpretation*. 1938. London: Methuen, 1965.

Harvey, David. *The Condition of Postmodernity*. Oxford: Blackwell, 1990.

Sloterdijk, Peter. *Critique of Cynical Reason*. Trans. Michael Eldred. Theory and History of Literature 40. Minneapolis: U of Minnesota P, 1987.

Turgenev, Ivan. *Fathers and Sons*. Trans. Rosemary Edmonds. Markham, Ont.: Penguin, 1975.

Walker, Craig Stewart. *The Buried Astrolabe: Canadian Dramatic Imagination and Western Tradition*. Montreal: McGill-Queen's UP, 2001.

Walker, George F. *The Art of War*. *The Power Plays*. Toronto: Coach House, 1984. 133-84.

———. *Beautiful City*. *East* 225-330.

———. *Better Living*. *East* 119-224.

———. *Criminals in Love*. *East* 9-117.

———. *The East End Plays*. Toronto: Playwrights Canada 1988.

———. *Escape from Happiness*. Toronto: Coach House, 1992.

———. *Love and Anger*. Toronto: Coach House, 1990.

———. *Nothing Sacred*. Toronto: Coach House, 1988.

———. *Prince of Naples*. *Now in Paperback: Six Canadian Plays of the 1970's*. Ed. Connie Brissenden. Toronto: Fineglow Plays, 1973. 61-102.

Wallace, Robert. "Looking for the Light: A Conversation with George F. Walker." *Canadian Drama / L'Art dramatique canadien* 14 (1988): 22-33.

# "Some Kind of Transition Place Between Heaven and Hell": George Walker's Aestetics of Hybridity in *Heaven*

by Marc Maufort

Since his early success in the 1970s with *Zastrozzi: The Master of Discipline*, George Walker has earned the reputation of a bold experimenter with dramatic form. Indeed, his tragi-comedies constantly defy the conventional boundaries of established Western genres. As Ric Knowles has made abundantly clear in his study *The Theatre of Form and the Production of Meaning*, Walker's dramaturgy is characterized by perversions of the codes of traditional linear comic form, especially the expectation of a clearly defined resolution (Knowles 31-32). His plays offer characters, themes, and plots that extend beyond the commonly accepted tropes of comedy, wavering as they do between the comic and the tragic mode. Likewise, the parodic reversals that characterize most of Walker's works transcend the limits of poetic realism. More particularly, in *Love and Anger* and other recent plays, such as the one-act pieces of *Suburban Motel*, Walker develops an aesthetics of transgression, which results in a strikingly innovative dramatic *inbetweenness*, to explore a liminal space of shifting possibilities. Walker's dramatic production thus stands at the crossroads of post-modernism, in its questioning of rigid categories, and postcolonialism, in its concern for what Homi Bhabha would term a third hybrid space, in which the legacy of European literary conventions is radically challenged.

The postcolonial framework of analysis suggested by Bhabha's notions of hybridity and inbetweenness offers an ideal vantage point to examine Walker's evolving concept of dramatic form in his recently produced *Heaven*. With the exception of Reid Gilbert, very few critics have examined Walker's dramaturgy through a postcolonial lens. In *The Location of Culture*, Bhabha refers to mimicry and hybridity as artistic weapons meant to destabilize rigid aesthetic Western categories. Mimicry projects a desire for a "reformed, recognizable Other, *as a subject of a difference that is almost the same, but not quite* [...] mimicry emerges as the representation of a difference that is itself a process of disavowal" (86). Although Bhabha's concepts can be used most profitably for the study of non-Western writers, i.e. ethnic or aboriginal artists, it is possible to extend his notion of mimicry and hybridity to study Walker's modification of the canons of Western dramatic realism. Walker's re-visionary challenges to time-honoured codes of realism involve imitation and yet parody of these codes in a pattern akin to the process of disavowal described by Bhabha.

*Heaven* received its premiere on January 15, 2000 at Canadian Stage in Toronto. While this complex drama echoes some of the themes typical of Walker's early career, such as the melodramatic opposition between the forces of good and evil, it expands this thematic texture to explore the Canadian Other. In *Heaven*, Walker, like ethnic and First Nations playwrights, questions the very foundations of Canadian multiculturalism. This new work revises traditional notions of marginality in a postcolonial context; it deconstructs both the white supremacist attitude and the hypocrisy of the discourses about political correctness. In doing so, it reflects Walker's postmodern desire to debunk the authority of grand narratives. It dramatizes the hybrid fabric of Canadian culture, which is characterized by multiple ethnicities. In addition, Walker re-examines the complexity of the link between ethnic, gender, and class differences, showing the profound inbetweenness which marks the inner lives of his displaced protagonists.

Walker has sought to translate this new thematic concern into an equally innovative sense of dramatic form. The hybridity of the subject matter, as it were, reflects itself in the transgressive nature of the play's structure and realism, both of which subvert the conventions of the comedy genre. The very title of my essay, drawn from one of the play's last speeches, reflects Walker's use of dramatic hybridity to unsettle Western rationalism: indeed, heaven may prove more closely related to hell than is generally assumed. In the discussion that follows I will analyse Walker's aesthetics of inbetweenness in a play that signals his entrance into a new millennium.

The characters of the play, torn as they are between contradictory impulses and motivations, illustrate Walker's hybrid thematics. Jimmy, the central character, embodies the paralysis resulting from this inner division. Actually, the play could be regarded, particularly in view of its fluid structure, as a dreamscape representing Jimmy's distorted vision of the universe. From the start, the setting emphasizes this departure from realism into abstraction, calling simply for a stark bench in an unidentified park, against the drab background of a cityscape. Walker purposely refuses to give any precise location for the play's action, beyond the unmistakable fact that it must take place in a North American city.

The opening prologue between Jimmy and Karl reveals the conflictual nature of their relationship: Karl bluntly accuses Jimmy of indirectly causing the death of their mutual friend Tommy. He destroyed the latter's life by obtaining his conviction in a trial during which he defended a black kid. Indeed, Tommy, in the performance of his duty as a policeman, had killed this young black man. Karl unveils the contradiction in Jimmy's behaviour; that is the hypocrisy of his attitude towards minorities. In fact, Jimmy is torn apart between his moral allegiance to the world of the disenfranchised and his own white background:

> **KARL.** Mr. Protect every asshole in the whole fucking world. Protect everyone except his friends. Mr. Human Rights. What a bunch of crap [...] You're wandering around in a strange world without loyalty. You're disconnected. (10)

Besides highlighting Jimmy's displacement, this speech points to the difficulty of implementing cultural policies that tend to take into account the legitimate rights of every single community.

Scene 1, again set in a non-realistic dusky city park, further illustrates Jimmy's inbetweenness. Metaphorically, this psychological trouble provokes his apparent demise. In a parody of melodramatic action typical of Walker's dramaturgy, he finally collapses from a heart attack after venting his anger against minorities. Ironically, although he is a minority lawyer, Jimmy seems to harbour a profound dislike of ethnic groups, probably because their very existence jeopardizes his emotional and social well-being. In an initial exchange with Judy, his wife, he betrays his prejudice against her Jewishness. He feels hated by her because of his Catholic Irishness: these conflictual feelings even threaten to destroy their marriage. His wife harshly calls him a "lowlife working class anti-Semitic prick" (15). Jimmy resents her decision to have an abortion, feeling that this abortion corresponds to a racist desire to erase his Irishness: "I mean he [the rabbi] didn't say something like it's too bad we can't just abort the heathen Irish part and keep the Jewish part [...] Just in case the little half breed's the fucking messiah" (17-18). Jimmy's obsession with the threat of hybridity makes him paranoid: his wife simply thinks that at forty-two she is too old to have another child.

While we first saw Jimmy as a noble defender of oppressed minorities, his subsequent dialogue with the young black man Derek bespeaks hostility. He provokes the young man, calling him "a stupid fucking Nubian" (27). In addition, he derides multicultural practices, showing only contempt for what he calls the "'How to Survive as a Visible Minority in a Hostile White Culture' class [Derek] took" (27). Jimmy is a hybrid blend of good and evil, and as such he recalls earlier Nazi-like characters in Walker's oeuvre. In a provocative confession, Jimmy himself underlines the linguistic hypocrisy of political correctness, which offers white Canadians the benefit of a clean conscience, without really modifying their racist attitude:

> **JIMMY.** I'm a lawyer with the government. Human rights commission. I'm in charge of minority rights [...] I'm very big in minority rights.
>
> **DEREK.** No way. And you're calling me that Nubian shit. That's a replacement word. I'm sure of it.
>
> **JIMMY.** Hey we're making progress, baby. My father never used replacement words. He used nigger, baby. He used nigger, wop, polack, kike. He used them all [...] If I pass out and you're inspired to kill me, could you place an anonymous phone call to the police. I don't want my kids wondering what happened to me okay? Look I'm sorry I keep saying things like that to you. You know, things that suggest you're a piece of criminal garbage. I don't know what's wrong with me [...] And well I had a serious personal altercation earlier that I think has left some deep emotional scars. (28-29)

Jimmy feels crushed under the pressure of the contradictory exigencies of his personal and his public life. The inflated, indeed somewhat absurdist tone of these lines departs from naturalism to heighten the intensity of Jimmy's crisis. His predicament is a metaphor for the malaise of a Western society that is increasingly becoming multiethnic. Thus, the play can be interpreted as a stylized dramatic fable about the politics of multiculturalism and its discontents.

Scene 2 reveals Karl's burgeoning desire for revenge through his repeated attempts to secure a gun from a member of the community he hates most: the young, black man Derek. The intricacies of the plot to recover the gun highlight Walker's parody of B-movies, while underscoring the profound hybrid link between the members of the two communities. The implication of Walker's plot is that policemen are as corrupt as the people they are supposed to police. Karl turns into the typical Walker monster in a speech marked by a radical transgression of the rules of realistic characterization: "I blame you, Derek. You and others like you. You've turned me into a fucking monster. I'm just almost pure anger. I'm not fit to be with civilized people" (34-35). Karl's speech reveals the grotesque creature into which the evil consequences of multiculturalism have transformed him.

Scene 3 confronts a symbolically invalid Jimmy with David, the rabbi, and his wife. Jimmy emerges as the defender of the rights of civilization against such monsters as Karl, although he obviously feels unable to situate himself. He vehemently rejects the absolutism of faith, which he regards as the cause of his failed marriage. Talking about Catholicism and Jewishness, he exclaims: "[A]ll we heard was this crap coming from these two ancient tribes we were trying to escape" (47). Behind this speech looms Walker's critique of all totalizing forms of social, political, and philosophical discourses. While Judy dismisses Jimmy's campaign to eradicate all the "bullshit" from the world such as the dogmatic thoughts typical of ethnocentrism, through Jimmy, Walker pleads for a return to an improved kind of universalism:

> **JIMMY.** Hey. Some guy comes in and tells me he got fired because of the colour of his skin and I find proof he's right, I try to get that company fined out of existence. But if a guy comes in and tells me I don't understand what he's going through because I'm not the same colour, I'm not "of" his religion, I don't live where he lives, I groan real loud and tell him not to waste my fucking time. (54-55)

Despite his indictment of political correctness and essentialism, Jimmy does not deny the existence of ethnic discrimination. He denounces the ambiguity, indeed the problematic hybridity, of the postcolonial Canadian predicament.

Later in the same scene, he further reveals his sense of uneasy inbetweenness when, as an official mouthpiece for minority rights, he locates the origin of the contemporary disease of Canadian society precisely in the hypocritical promises of multicultural policies:

> **JUDY.** Fuck them? Why, Jimmy. How did we get to fuck them.
> **JIMMY.** Mostly because of what they bring with them. Their tribal conflicts. So fuck the Vietnamese-hating Cambodians. And the Cambodian-hating Koreans [...] and yes while we're at it, Jude, fuck the white European male and everyone he hates. And all the Christian-hating Muslims and Muslim-hating Jews and Jew-hating Christians and gay-hating Christians and Muslim-hating Christians. And black and white and yellow and red and so on and so on. (58)

As a disappointed white liberal humanist, Jimmy implies that excessive attention to the rights of minorities can paradoxically marginalize them. Moreover, such insistence can foster the resurgence of the desire for absolute power these minorities precisely had to suffer from.

Scene 4 further characterizes Karl as a demented monster. Judy's evocation of Jimmy's sudden recovery, of his new zeal in his crusade against evil is strongly reminiscent of Pete Maxwell's quixotic quest in *Love and Anger*. This reversal belongs to the pattern of parodic melodramatic plot events that undermine the linear structure of the play. Even Karl's depiction is marked by these reversals and contradictions. Although he may be a monster, Karl suffers from deep emotional wounds. Ironically, the speech which betrays his softer side is spoken at the same time as he kills Judy, which reinforces the pattern of contradictions portrayed in *Heaven*: "What's happened to our beloved city. To the world. Hey. What's happened to me. I mean I wasn't always a monster. Even you gotta admit that. I mean some people even thought I had a certain amount of charm" (69-70). Karl's behaviour symbolizes the disintegration of the postmodern world at large.

Scene 5 bespeaks a radical break with the conventions of dramatic linearity. Realistic elements are disrupted by the sudden intrusion of the supernatural, when Judy returns from heaven in a helicopter. This episode could be interpreted as the materialization of Jimmy's dream, a form of expressionistic extension of the play's comic framework. However, beyond its dream-like quality and its realistic dialogue, the passage possesses an unmistakably farcical, even grotesque, aspect. The play's mixture of widely divergent styles betrays the hybrid nature of Walker's dramaturgy, which recalls the magic realism so typical of postcolonial literature. This distortion of realism could be described as a comic variant of what the critic Jeanne Delbaere has termed psychic realism, which she considers to be a variation of magic realism, in which the distortion of the real reveals the character's inner turmoil (Delbaere 251). While this magic realism is manifest in the plays of Canadian First Nations and ethnic writers, such as Highway and Quan, this is the first instance of Walker's use of such an extended form of realism. The measure of his originality consists in his ability to recast the codes of magic realism within those of comedy and tragedy in a hybrid attempt to reflect the fracture of Canadian society.

The appearance of Judy's ghost can be understood as a dramatization of Jimmy's desire to be reunited with his wife. However, it certainly extends the realistic framework into a hybrid genre, echoing the characters' inbetweenness. Judy's entrance suggests parodic overtones: she is ushered in by the "sound of a helicopter accompanied by some Wagner" (85). Her very attire, now in military style, is endowed with grotesque features that contrast sharply with her previous appearance: "*JUDY is lowered down by a rope or cable … or … She is wearing commando gear. With a few designer flourishes. She hits the ground, unhooks herself, does a few fancy martial arts moves*" (85). She laments that, as a Jew, she was forced into a Christian heaven, which underscores the state of inbetweenness manifest throughout the work and enables Walker to de-authorize the overpowering structures of Christian religious belief.

In a moment of hesitation typical of magic realism, the dramatist leaves us in doubt as to the reality of this supernatural event. Ironically, it is Judy, the ghost, who herself quite logically declares: "I could be a figment of your imagination. And if you don't know how would I" (87). Such a statement keeps the spectator in doubt as to the nature of the events he is witnessing. In addition, this magic realistic episode functions as a form of epiphany, a kind of revelation. Indeed, Judy urges Jimmy to fight for something in life, to move beyond his state of utter despair. In other words, she encourages him to recreate order out of chaos: "It's not gonna be good enough to be against everything Jimmy. You're gonna have to be *for* something" (88). Sadly, this moment of illumination fails to have any lasting effect.

Scene 7 opposes the very symbols of good and evil: Karl and Jimmy confront each other in a cruel dialogue ending up in Karl's confession to Judy's murder. Interestingly, Karl identifies class warfare as the source of Jimmy's predicament. The dramatist clearly links religion, race, and class as the causes of the disease of postmodern/postcolonial inbetweenness: "It wasn't that she was a Jew. It's just that she was middle class. It's the class thing more than the religion thing … I mean basically you're white trash … I mean your mother went to church a lot but basically she was a whore … " (103). Whereas a number of postcolonial writers would celebrate hybridity, Walker perceives it as problematic.

In a mode of alternation typical of the play's overall structure, scene 8 again explores Jimmy's unconscious in a transgression of realistic dramatic form akin to psychic magic realism. This unresolved tension between realism and the supernatural, in itself typical of magic realism, is replete with farcical, even grotesque overtones. The scene takes place in an imaginary hospital situated in heaven, in which Judy performs the duties of a surgeon. Her lines immediately question the nature of the realistic action that the spectator witnesses: "Of course no one is ever really sick. But they let me operate on them anyway. You know just pretend. Because well … they're kind … And they know I wanted to become a doctor ever since I was seven" (107). The spectator quickly realizes, upon Jimmy's entrance, that the scene takes place in his mind and thus can be compared to a form of dramatized stream of consciousness: "So I'm imagining you both, right" (108). Once again, this magic realist scene is devised to reflect Jimmy's epiphany, his awareness that he needs to transcend his state of psychological hybridity. Were he to persevere in his present attitude, he might become as evil as Karl: "What am I supposed to think. That Karl is just the worst thing anyone can become? That Karl is the worst thing I can become?" (109). This hesitant realization illustrates Walker's grotesque characterization: his protagonists are disguised, demented vampires. Sadly, the end of the scene reverts to a more sombre mood. From the good angel that she appeared to be, urging Jimmy to reject his feelings of anger, Judy transforms into the lover of Derek, who by now has also been killed by Karl. This does not fail to arouse Jimmy's jealousy and bitterness. Jimmy eventually echoes Derek's bitter comment that heaven is a place "where you get to be fucked in a whole new way" (112).

The contrasting realistic, even violently naturalistic, mood of scene 9 creates an irreconcilable tension with the fantastic atmosphere of the preceding section, which suggests the very hybridity of magic realism. Scene 9 can be regarded as the true climax of the play, offering the final and most dramatic confrontation between Jimmy and Karl. Their struggle acquires mythic and universal resonances. It indirectly reflects the eternal conflict between good and evil: each individual human being is a hybrid cross between an angel and a vampire. In a statement that echoes many of Petie Maxwell's in *Love and Anger*, Jimmy articulates his newly acquired and idealistic desire to change the world: "The world is wrong. How can I take care of them [his children] if I don't take care of the world first" (116). Further, Jimmy compares Karl to Satan, which obliquely implies that Jimmy can be compared with Christ. The scene acquires biblical, indeed universal, proportions, that transcend the play's pervasive hybridity:

> **JIMMY.** Are you Satan. Is this a test. Are you Satan and are you testing me. Are we in a state of suspended grace here. Is this some kind of transition place between heaven and hell.
> **KARL.** You mean like purgatory, Jimmy.
> **JIMMY.** Like purgatory, yeah. (119)

The metaphor of purgatory as a stage of transition, of being in between, applies to the play as a whole. It suggests an interpretation of *Heaven* as Jimmy's searing struggle to escape from purgatory. Even Karl points to the initiation process that Jimmy must undergo before becoming the master of his destiny: "That's something you're just gonna have to deal with" (119). The end of the scene culminates in the unexpected murder of Jimmy by Karl, who is then subsequently killed by Sissy. This accumulation of melodramatic acts is endowed with heavy parodic overtones. The last stage direction re-asserts the proximity of both Karl and Jimmy, visually linking them on their way to heaven: "*A blinding white light. Music. JIMMY stands and slowly walks into the light. Music changes and KARL stands and is drawn into the light*" (123). The reintroduction of the supernatural suggests ironic overtones, as the over-emphatic use of light and music indicates.

The play's last scene constitutes the high-point of Walker's experimentation with the boundaries of comedy and realism. Thanks to the complexity of the playwright's transgression techniques, this conclusion becomes a mosaic of naturalistic and magic realist elements, indeed a condensed version of the structure of the play at large. This conclusion confers upon the whole section a fluidity that can hardly be fixed by the labels of traditional literary categories. Thematically and formally, then, *Heaven* plunges the spectator into a form of purgatory, into a liminal space in which the ever-shifting nature of the environment performs a profoundly unsettling role. The scene again offers a parodic description of heaven: an announcer welcomes the spectators, while loud early seventies rock music "*should be heard*" (124). Ironically, Karl finds himself in heaven too. He sarcastically exclaims: "But this is heaven. I'm redeemed. I'm redeemed in the name of Jesus Christ Our Lord" (125). To further drive home his point, Walker gives us Derek dressed as a slave. Clearly, this version of the Christian heaven reproduces the injustices and prejudices of white society: "Heaven is crap. It's a cool place for serial killers" (127) and racists. The following magic realist sub-section borders on metatheatre: Jimmy himself asks whether it is conceivable that he could only be a figment of the rabbi's imagination. If such is the case, this feature can only reinforce Walker's technique of hybridity: what could be more paradoxical than the vision of the Christian heaven springing from the mind of a representative of the Jewish faith?

Sissy gives an improbable title to the encounter of the second sub-section: "The rabbi and the heroin addict" (131). The girl confesses her murder of Karl, which weirdly the rabbi promises to keep a secret, provided she does not reveal his own crisis of faith. While Sissy plainly states that she believes neither in God nor in herself, the rabbi painfully admits that he tries very hard to believe in God: "I try hard to believe. I get by mostly just by trying" (133). Sissy eventually points to the painful hybridity of David's situation: "You said you were thinking about them [Jimmy and Judy] having sex in heaven. You don't believe in God but you still believe in heaven. That's weird, David" (134).

The final sub-section of the concluding scene is a long monologue in the stream-of-consciousness mode. It appears unrelated in any logical way to what precedes and constitutes the play's final assertion of Walker's transgression of realistic codes. Its position in the play, together with its length, recalls Denise's final monologue in *Problem Child*, where she conveys her persisting anger against social injustice. Again, Walker introduces parodic metatheatrical overtones: "*JIMMY in a spotlight. In front of a microphone* [...] *A smattering of recorded applause. Canned laughter fading out*" (135). Walker thus emphasizes the performative component of reality in a truly post-modern gesture.

This long interior monologue recapitulates Walker's attack on totalitarian modes of thought lurking in official religions and multicultural policies. It also restates Jimmy's disturbing inbetweenness, as well as his inability to overcome this hybridity. Jimmy performs a kind of self-analysis in this monologue, trying to come to terms with the roots of his torment. While the cause is eventually identified, Jimmy's psychological instability remains. Jimmy explains how, in his excessive fear of being a racist, he was led to try to become the Other, to lose his own identity in an attempted merger with the predicament of marginals:

> **JIMMY.** Yeah in essence I wanted to be a female Greek immigrant worm-picker and nothing else. But I couldn't tell them that. I couldn't tell anyone. Because no one would … understand. So anyway I'm working away integrating myself, my conscious self,

> and therefore I hope, my unconscious self too, into the entire human family [...] I do legal aid work for any person of colour I can find. I don't care if they're guilty [...] I try my best to fuck the system and get them off. (138)

In his pursuit of the good, Jimmy has become contaminated with evil; while fighting for others' well-being, he has lost his sense of belonging, feeling somewhat schizophrenically divided. At this late point in the play, he has come to the bleak realization that his efforts in favour of minorities have been in vain. This epiphanic realization is couched in bitterly ironic words: "And I was a fucking saint. And the people on whose behalf I worked, the poor, the disenfranchised, they were, well, the inheritors of the earth as far as I was concerned. Except I didn't know shit about the people on whose behalf I worked [...] I wasn't a racist [...] but I wasn't anything good either" (139).

Jimmy points to the failure of the Canadian multicultural dream, to the impossibility of truly acknowledging the Other. In the final section of the monologue, he further denies the transcendental consolation that might be derived from God and heaven: "[W]e'd be able to knock off all that bullshit about redemption and guilt and that other terrifying superstitious garbage" (141). Ironically, in voicing such a nihilistic statement, Jimmy destroys any possibility for his redemption or for acquiring a new balance. The monologue ends on a sad note as he reiterates his helplessness: "I'm ... here in heaven but really am I just supposed to forget that happened [...] I mean I guess we'll take just about any fucking excuse to feel good [...] like that helps or something. Like feeling good is the ... most important thing ... or something" (141). The dark epiphanic final moment of the play merges magic realism with the tragic mode. Walker has moved from the comic mood of his earlier scenes to a concluding tragic statement of man's hybrid existence, trapped between heaven and earth. The ending avoids firm closure, leaving the spectator in an emotional turmoil akin to the metaphysical crisis experienced by the characters.

*Heaven* confirms Walker's talent as an inventor of new dramatic forms, renovating as it does the tragi-comic form at the dawn of a new millennium. Walker's transgression of the codes of dramatic realism is bolder here than anywhere in his previous work because of the degree to which he conflates parodic and comic elements with psychic magic realism. Thematically, as well, Walker breaks new ground, seeking to expand his postmodern deconstruction of social and ethical absolutes into the realm of the postcolonial Other. Beyond the dramatic fragmentation of *Heaven* looms the nostalgia of Walker the liberal humanist who laments the impossibility of transcending the throes of postcolonial hybridity. Thus, at the beginning of a new century, Walker's dramaturgy appears in a state of transition between postmodernism and postcolonialism. His reiterated efforts to extend the limits of dramatic realism may still yield their most fascinating expressions in the years to come.

(2003)

## Works Cited

Bhabha, Homi K. *The Location of Culture*. London: Routledge, 1994.

Delbaere, Jeanne. "Psychic Realism, Mythic Realism, Grotesque Realism: Variations on Magic Realism in Contemporary Literature in English." *Magical Realism: Theory, History, Community*. Ed. Lois Parkinson Zamora and Wendy B. Faris. Durham: Duke UP, 1995. 249-63.

Gilbert, Reid. "Escaping the 'Savage Slot': Interpellation and Transgression in George F. Walker's *Suburban Motel*." *Siting the Other: Re-visions of Marginality in Australian and English-Canadian Drama*. Ed. Marc Maufort and Franca Bellarsi. Brussels: P.I.E.-Peter Lang, 2001. 325-45.

Knowles, Ric. *The Theatre of Form and the Production of Meaning: Contemporary Canadian Dramaturgies*. Toronto: ECW Press, 1999.

Walker, George F. *Heaven*. Burnaby: Talonbooks, 2000.

## Equal Before and Under the Law: Rethinking the Marginality in *This Is Wonderland*

by Amanda McCoy

> Yes even this piece of half-eaten garbage might have people who love him and might want to seek their own kind of justice. Love comes quickly to the wretched. Sometimes. I'm beginning to love him myself. I'm beginning to love him quite a lot. (Walker, *Nothing Sacred* 173).

George F. Walker is no stranger to despair; his plays are filled with the poor and the downtrodden, and Walker refuses to volunteer easy answers to their dilemmas merely in order to bring his storylines to a tidy ending. He forces theatre audiences to contend with what are sometimes unfamiliar (or at least distant) concerns: political, economic, and social disadvantages that leave characters powerless to enact change in their lives. A recent project by Walker and his writing partner Dani Romain has brought tales of the marginalized to an even wider audience: the television drama series *This Is Wonderland.* This paper reads the carnivalesque elements of the first season of *This Is Wonderland* as politically transformative; the seeds of revolution are planted by a show that asks us to take steps towards a world in which everyone has fair access to food, shelter, clothing, and medical treatment, and no one is driven to the desperation that leads to crime in the first place. Again, there are no easy answers, but by giving a name and a face to each of the so-called criminals who move through the court system, *Wonderland* demands that its audience consider the circumstances that drive people to break the law, and insists that each individual case be approached with compassion and empathy. In keeping with the carnivalesque spirit of the show, *Wonderland* not only gives a voice to those who are normally silenced, but it also destabilizes hierarchies, erasing the barriers between the affluent and healthy and the poor and sick. Everyone in this world is just trying to get by; *Wonderland*'s mission is to erase the "us and them" mentality of the television audience and engage in serious dialogue about how a broken system—or more to the point, a broken society—can begin to address its most marginalized members.

Episode 101[1] of *Wonderland* has Alice De Raey (played by Cara Pifko), a newly-minted criminal lawyer who has yet to set foot in a court room, thrust into chaos on her first day in the lower courts in Toronto's Old City Hall. When her emotionally fragile boss, James Ryder (Michael Healey), fails to show up for work, Alice is left alone to navigate the crowds of desperate people who pack the halls, the courtrooms, and the jail cells. This particular Wonderland, which is paradoxically both more sinister and more hilarious than Carroll's own, brims over with drug addicts, petty criminals, confused immigrants, single mothers, the homeless, the poor, and the mentally ill. As Alice makes her way down the rabbit hole, she also discovers a colourful cast of lawyers and judges (the cast includes Michael Riley, Siu Ta, Michael Murphy, Eric Peterson, Tom Rooney, and Kathryn Winslow) who have found their own ways of coping with the bedlam—while some have become emotionally detached in order to deal with the pressures of their jobs, others have become just as eccentric and unhinged as the parade of people who are hustled through the courts each day.

Both Ed Nyman and Chris Johnson have identified elements of Bakhtinian carnival in Walker's work, an observation that seems particularly apt to a discussion of *Wonderland*. The comparison isn't flawless; *Wonderland*, which airs on the CBC, is necessarily somewhat restrained in its language and its depiction of violence. The ideological underpinnings of the carnival, though, are very much at play: humour is used to underscore social injustice, the "upper classes" interact with the "lower classes," the status quo is parodied, and those who are not normally in a position of power are given a forum for open discussion. In keeping with the carnivalesque atmosphere, there are no patriarchal authority figures to oversee the action in *Wonderland*; the aforementioned James Ryder may have once acted in such a capacity but a nervous breakdown has incapacitated him—at the end of episode 101, he is literally caught with his pants down, a symbolic stand-in for the disintegration of the institution as a whole. The Crown prosecutors, who are most determined to uphold the law regardless of circumstances, are continuously lampooned as compassionless bullies, whereas a few recurring "criminals" are ultimately the most human, and consequently the most sympathetic, characters on the show. Carnival provides a space to criticize and destabilize the establishment and to achieve equilibrium through chaos; with its DVD tagline, "Law and order without the order," this is precisely what *Wonderland* seeks to accomplish.

There is an excessive number of legal dramas on television (this show's precursors include Canada's *Street Legal*, as well as *Law & Order*, *L.A. Law*, *The Practice*, and even *Night Court*), but Walker and Romain make a unique contribution by highlighting the humanity of those who are largely nameless and faceless in a city like Toronto, particularly the homeless and the mentally ill. Whereas other legal dramas tend to focus primarily on the lives of lawyers and judges, this program spends a great deal of time fleshing out the characters who come before the court. The effect, in essence, is to give a voice to those who are rarely heard from, and to explore the desperation that leads to "criminal" behaviour in the first place. This television show sets up a carnivalesque space where society's downtrodden get to speak out (if only as mediated through Walker and Romain's writing) and share their disdain for the impersonal, indifferent legal system. Defense lawyers—particularly Elliott Sacks (Michael Riley), who seems to attract some of the more eccentric defendants—spend the better part of the season begging their clients to be quiet and let them do the talking. In a sense, by virtue of the courtroom setting, the lawyers and Crown prosecutors all try to mediate the experiences of the marginalized through their own perspectives, and using their own specialized legal terminology. But the accused reject this mediation and refuse to be silent; though they may further incriminate themselves, break the rules of conduct in the court, and maybe even insult the judge along the way, their sense of injustice wins out and *Wonderland* has them speak their minds.

During these outbursts and similar disputes, the show has a tendency to implicitly side with the most disadvantaged party. One such case occurs in Episode 106, in which sixty-year-old Ellie Germaine is in front of the court for using crack cocaine. Her sister Marilyn arrives to bail her out, but changes her mind when Ellie admits that she fully intends to continue her drug use once she is released. The Germaine sisters begin to bicker in bail court, where the prim and proper Marilyn proves to be increasingly disagreeable. Later, when Alice goes to speak to Ellie in her cell, she discovers her client has a lot to say about her use of crack cocaine:

> You know, this is where the real drug violence happens. Getting strip-searched and thrown in jail because the substance you happen to be using is on some list that society hasn't gotten around to recognizing as suitable for use by adults. No one's forcing me to take drugs. If people are poor and desperate they're either going to use it or sell it. Make it legal and deal with the addiction later. They do it for alcoholics. (106) [2]

Ellie goes on to jokingly describe a world in which drugs are sold the way that liquor is, in "nice, brightly-lit boutiques with friendly staff pointing out your drug of choice" (106). Any preconceived notions we might have about drug users are suddenly challenged by Ellie, who seems entirely capable of making her own decisions and who *Wonderland* imbues with extra credibility by virtue of her age. Ellie lives in a world where change seems possible; she doesn't have to be a criminal if society can change its ideas about her life choices.

Although *Wonderland* humanizes and even celebrates the people who move through the lower courts, this carnival is not without its dark side. A number of the accused must await their court appearances in the city jail. Some of the mentally ill and homeless defendants find the jail their best option for living arrangements, given the guarantee of food, warmth, and shelter, inadequate though they may be. The jail's deplorable conditions are described in the first episode—the cells are so overcrowded that prisoners are forced to sleep up against the toilet bowl, where they are urinated on during the night. Prisoners turn up for their hearings starved and dehydrated, without their medication, and having been infected with diseases, beaten and raped by the other prisoners (101). As for Old City Hall itself, the setting is intensely claustrophobic; throngs of shouting, weeping people appear in tightly-framed close-ups. Everybody wants to be heard. The immense, chaotic dissatisfaction of the crowds is a revolution in the making—what happens when these crowds have had enough of their lot in life, grow tired of the legal system's inability to deal with the complexities of their problems, have had enough of not being seen or heard? Although *Wonderland* provides a forum for discussing the legal system's most pressing issues, there is evidently a long way to go before the marginalized members of society are given their due. The atmosphere of *Wonderland* is one of anticipation; the institutional structure is simply incapable of dealing adequately with the cases that come before the court, and the conditions in the overcrowded jail cells violate the basic standards laid out by the U.N.'s *Standard Minimum Rules for the Treatment of Prisoners.* Something *must* be done if Canada wants its legal system to be able to cope with addictions, assault, abuse, homelessness, poverty, and discrimination. The chaos inside the court threatens to spill out into the world at large; directly outside the courthouse, crowds are frequently gathered to hear a speaker berate the legal system's failings and express their anger. One unnamed man even points out the ways in which he is forced to be a criminal just to survive: "Everything about this system sucks. Everything about this system is designed for me to reoffend. I have Attention Deficit Disorder. I need medication just to function. And when I leave here, I have no money, I have no job, I have no home [...] so I steal. That's right, I steal!" (107). Later in the episode, this same man shouts, "Are you listening?" a number of times, at the building, at its staff, at the Canadian legal system as a whole. This question fuels *Wonderland.*

A growing sense of unease pervades the series as the audience is introduced to more and more of the problems the legal system is plagued with. In Brechtian fashion, the audience is never allowed to sit back and enjoy the show, but is instead urged to constantly consider the debates raised by each court case, to consider the inhumane conditions of the prison system, and to ask themselves how things could be different. Further tension is caused by cases that remain unresolved at the end of episodes: what happens to the immigrants who cannot find translators, to the juvenile delinquents who refuse help from social services, or to the accused who are jailed indefinitely because of mistaken identity? *Wonderland* challenges our minds to continue to work on these unresolved questions long after the episode has ended. This approach is yet another departure from the typical legal drama; as in the real court system, there is a lack of tidy resolution and cases are suspended for days while a solution is sought out.

We become deeply involved in the cases for another reason, too: *Wonderland* reminds us of the ultimate humanity of the accused, and of their families and friends. We get to know the defendants, we grow to love them and we care about what happens to them. Again, by giving a particular face and a particular voice to issues we usually consider in the abstract (such as the "homeless problem," "substance abuse," or "welfare"), *Wonderland* demands that we think of the marginalized as unique individuals with unique circumstances. While city dwellers may grow accustomed to seeing men and women sleeping on sidewalks, *Wonderland* never lets the audience simply pass them by. By increasing our familiarity with a range of social, political, and economic issues that lead to poverty, illness, and homelessness, *Wonderland* calls into question our preconceived notions that the class system is part of the natural order; things simply do not have to be this way.

*Wonderland* drives its point home with an unsettling reminder: the gulf between the privileged and the marginalized is almost arbitrary, and their fortunes could be reversed at any time. The show poses a constant question to the judges and lawyers and by extension, to the television audience: if this were you—and it *could be you*—

how would you want to be treated? Alice and her colleagues are repeatedly reminded that in some cases sheer luck and a bit of money are all that separate them from the mental and physical illness, addictions, loneliness, and misfortune that beat down their clients. The differences between the privileged and the marginalized are thus eroded, the hierarchies unstable. In Episode 112, Alice sees her former law professor, Professor Montgomery, panhandling in snowy weather outside a bank. His story demonstrates how easy it really is to lose all of life's comforts. He doesn't even seem entirely sure how he came to be living on the streets: "One day I just woke up and just decided to stop trying so hard. That led to the usual sequence of unfortunate events. My family left me, I lost my house, I lost my job, and then, well, here I am." Then, by way of comforting Alice (but comically drawing attention to the feeling of uneasiness that pervades *Wonderland*), Professor Montgomery adds, "Oh, don't be upset, it could happen to anyone. Have a nice day."

The ghosts of these alternate possibilities hover over the entire first season, and over Alice's character in particular. On a number of occasions eerie equations are made between Alice and various women who appear before the court. For instance, in episode 108, Alice walks along the street behind Janice Pells, a homeless woman who is summoned to Mental Health Court later in the episode. Janice walks along singing the African-American spiritual "Sometimes I Feel Like a Motherless Child." She pays no attention to where she is going, and when Alice pulls her out of the path of a moving vehicle, Janice grows furious and turns on Alice with a volley of abuse. Embarrassed, Alice walks away—but she has picked up the tune of the mournful spiritual and begins to sing it quietly to herself as she walks along. In a sense, this is how *Wonderland* accentuates the common humanity between the two women, a humanity that ultimately transcends their separate lots in life.

A similar parallel is drawn between Alice and a schizophrenic woman who appears later in Season One. On her first day, Alice speaks aloud to herself on the way up the stairs to the court, trying to bolster her confidence and remind herself of the proper way to behave at her new job: "Just pay attention. Ask questions when you don't understand something. Look people in the eye, pay close attention to what people are saying, always, always show respect for the system, don't forget to breathe, definitely don't forget to breathe, and then everything will be fine" (101). Later that season, a woman called Ms. Calma waits to see Judge Malone in Mental Health Court. She has wrapped herself in a blanket, believing she has to "stand naked before the judge" (110). And as she stands in her jail cell, she begins speaking to an invisible person, presumably a child, in words that echo Alice's monologue: "Never lie, never cheat, never steal, never hurt anyone's feelings, never brag, never cut corners, never be rude and never talk back. You never, you never talk back" (110). What are we to make of this? Quite possibly the lines sound similar because they are all penned by Walker and Romain. On the other hand, both women are nervous about appearing before the court and need to remind themselves what kind of language and behaviour are acceptable. Both feel like they will be exposed to intense scrutiny, although Alice does not interpret this quite as literally as Ms. Calma. One situation is mirrored in the other; Alice could *be* Ms. Calma under a different set of circumstances. She could still become Ms. Calma. And since Alice is the protagonist and television viewers are likely to identify with her, the reminder is for the audience, too: anyone watching television in the comfort of their own home is susceptible to poverty and illness. There is no "us" and "them". The parallels between Alice and these women throw our sense of entitlement into question. No one deserves to be sick and destitute; why, then, does it still happen?

The culmination of *Wonderland*'s political bent, its humanizing of the disenfranchised, and its appeal to audiences to recognize the arbitrary divide between the rich and poor all converge in one character who embodies the carnivalesque hero of the disenfranchised: Mr. Jackson (Rogue Johnston), a "self-medicated delusional schizophrenic," as Alice notes, and "probably the most coherent person I've met all day" (101). Mr. Jackson is an educated, charming, and well-spoken man, but he is also disoriented, filthy, and impoverished. He sports a dark beard and has pale, unfocused eyes. He stumbles through the courtroom like a blind prophet, mumbling biblical passages and waving his arms, his thumbs hooked into the torn sleeves of his sweater. At the same time, Mr. Jackson brings a kind of calm to the chaos of the lower courts. Whenever he appears characters are riveted to his words. Mr. Jackson's special gift is language: while so many of the defendants struggle to express themselves and make themselves heard, Mr. Jackson once lived in a more privileged world, and he still speaks the language—he is the ambassador that *Wonderland* puts forward to communicate across economic and social barriers.

In his first appearance in episode 101, Mr. Jackson claims to be running for political office in a bi-election in Rosedale, one of Toronto's most upscale neighbourhoods. He has been brought before Mental Health Court for allegedly stealing his political opponent's placards and lawn signs, and refuses to give them back, claiming that he has proof his opponent is a neo-Nazi. Just as we get ready to chuckle at what is surely one of Mr. Jackson's delusions of grandeur—a homeless schizophrenic running for office in Rosedale?—he tearfully recounts how he paid $200 to enter the political debate and another $500 to have homeless people make his posters. The mere thought of Mr. Jackson raising these funds, let alone putting them towards a political cause, calls into question a substantial number of assumptions we might make about homelessness and poverty. Mr. Jackson pleads with the court to let him go so that he does not miss the debate: "I have a chance to win. A chance to win one thing. Please ... please don't take that away" (101).

Shortly thereafter, Alice goes to visit Mr. Jackson in his jail cell in an attempt to convince him to give the signs back so that he can be released. Again, Mr. Jackson shows his unique ability to use language to claim his place in a world where he otherwise has nothing. An interesting inversion of power takes place in this short scene, when Alice is put in her place by Mr. Jackson:

> **MR. JACKSON.** My opponent uses the police force and the justice system to dominate and to ruin the lives of the poor, disenfranchised people of this city.

> **ALICE.** Okay … okay. Well, what if we ask him not to do that? What if we say, "Don't use the police and the courts to ruin poor people's lives." Huh? Then will you give back the signs?
>
> **MR. JACKSON.** It doesn't help when you patronize me. No, I believe I am entitled to a bail hearing, so please, Miss, just do your job.

Mr. Jackson is ultimately bailed out in another playful moment when his two friends, drag queens Rochelle and Tamika, walk into Mental Health Court unannounced to return the signs and secure Mr. Jackson's release. He does not reappear until five episodes later when we see him circulating an apology to God, which he asks the judges to sign "for any injustices we might have done intentionally or otherwise to the indigent of the city" (105). And, it seems, the judges do sign it—a playful Pascalian wager that if there is a God, and Mr. Jackson is his earthly conduit, then the judges are at the behest of Mr. Jackson, and not the other way around. Once again, authority is subverted in a fascinating way; although *Wonderland* does not make any particular argument for the existence of God, Mr. Jackson's own faith fosters the belief that he is equal to everyone else, and as such he intends to make himself heard.

When Mr. Jackson reappears for the third and final time in Season One (109), he stands trial for assaulting a store manager who has refused to give serious consideration to his job application. Mr. Jackson—again demonstrating his ability to challenge hierarchies—refuses the services of a lawyer and chooses to represent himself. Once again, the spirit of carnival is evoked when Mr. Jackson is given leave to criticize the system and to highlight the ways in which society keeps him marginalized. He points out that he has a right to apply for a job in his own country, and that his homelessness cannot be remedied without some form of employment. And he wins his case. Afterwards, Mr. Jackson runs to Alice to tell her that the judge said he was "concise, coherent, and ultimately justified." A subtle parody in this last scene underscores Mr. Jackson's role as *Wonderland*'s carnivalesque champion of the underclasses: his t-shirt has a tuxedo pattern printed onto it.

Terry Eagleton has observed that carnival may be a means of social control; the authorities, by providing a "licensed enclave" (149) where the masses can let off steam, ensure that social order and hierarchical structure are upheld the remainder of the time. This does not seem to be the case with *Wonderland*. The carnival that goes on inside Old City Hall can scarcely be contained; it spills out onto the steps, into the streets, as Toronto's most marginalized residents find ways to express their despair through acts of civil disobedience and law-breaking. Beyond the bounds of television storytelling is an audience that is not only seduced by the humour of the show and enticed by its colourful characters, but also continually prompted to consider issues of social justice in a new way. Walker and Romain's plotlines loosely follow news headlines, but give a voice to the poor, the ill, and the homeless right alongside professionals and authority figures. There are no easy answers to the issues raised by *Wonderland*, but the act of creating a dialogue is in itself politically transformative.

The very first character we see in *This Is Wonderland* is a shirtless busker who has painted himself to look like a silvery statue. He stands silently on the steps in front of

Old City Hall, before a crowd of onlookers, moving only when someone throws him a few coins. By episode 102, the steps have become a soapbox where a woman criticizes the legal system and discusses "the future of our country" through a bullhorn. Almost every episode thereafter includes someone voicing their dissatisfaction on these same steps. This is *Wonderland*: a place where silence is replaced by the clamouring voices of the disenfranchised, bravely speaking out against a system that tries to keep them silent by occasionally throwing a few coins at their problems. Hopefully Canada is listening.

(2006)

## Notes

[1] My discussion is limited to Season One, which is currently available commercially on DVD. The episode numbers here correspond with the DVD numbering (in which, for example, "episode 101" indicates "season 1, episode 1"), although the episodes originally aired in a slightly different order and are listed in yet another order on the program's website, <thisiswonderland.com>.

[2] In the absence of print versions of the scripts for *This is Wonderland*, I have provided my own punctuation for quoted lines.

## Works Cited

Bakhtin, Mikhail. *Rabelais and His World.* Trans. Helene Iswolsky. Bloomington: Indiana UP, 1984.

Eagleton, Terry. *Walter Benjamin, or, Towards a Revolutionary Criticism.* 1981. London: Verso, 1987.

Johnson, Chris. *Essays on George F. Walker: Playing With Anxiety.* Winnipeg: Blizzard, 1999.

Nyman, Ed. "Out With the Queers: Moral Triage in George F. Walker's *Theatre of the Film Noir.*" *Australasian Drama Studies* 29 (1996): 57-66.

*This Is Wonderland: The Complete First Season.* By George F. Walker and Dani Romain. Dir. Keith Behrman, Bruce Macdonald, Scott Smith, and Anne Wheeler. Prod. Indian Grove Productions and Muse Entertainment, in association with the Canadian Broadcasting Corporation. DVD. Video Service Corp., 2005.

United Nations. Congress on the Prevention of Crime and the Treatment of Offenders. *Standard Minimum Rules for the Treatment of Prisoners.* Geneva: U.N. Economic and Social Council, 1977.

Walker, George F. *Nothing Sacred. Somewhere Else: Four Plays.* Burnaby: Talonbooks, 1999. 169-256.

## Suggested Further Reading

This is merely a selection of the vast quantity of critical writing and reporting on Walker and his works. A wealth of pertinent material is available in the Archives and Special Collections Division of the University of Guelph Library, especially in the George F. Walker Collection, the Factory Theatre Lab Archives, the Toronto Free Theatre Archives, CentreStage Archives, the Peter Blais Collection, the Steven Bush Collection, the Mary Kerr Collection, and the Eric Steiner Collection.

Adilman, Sid. "The Playwright Who Never Was." *Toronto Star* 27 May 1981: C5.

Andrews-Leslie, Coral. "Chaotic Justice: George F. Walker's *This is Wonderland*." *Take One* 13. No. 48 (December 2004-March 2005): 11-13.

Armstrong, Gordon. Rev. of *Tough!* By George F. Walker. At Green Thumb Theatre, Vancouver. *Theatrum* 33 (1993): 44-45.

Baldwin, James Earl. "The Space Between Voices: Dialogics in the Late Plays of George F. Walker." MA Diss. U of Guelph, 1994.

Beaupré, Thérèse. Rev. of *Three Plays.* By George F. Walker. *Canadian Theatre Review* 22 (Spring 1979): 115-16.

Benson, Eugene, and L.W. Conolly. "Three Alternate Playwrights: David Freeman, George Walker, David French." *English-Canadian Theatre.* Toronto: Oxford UP, 1987. 89-95.

Borkowski, Andrew. "Theatre of the Improbable: George F. Walker." *Canadian Forum* 70 (September 1991): 16-19.

Brissenden, Connie, ed. *Now in Paperback: Six Canadian Plays of the 1970's.* Toronto: Fineglow Plays, 1973.

Chapman, Geoff. "Mostly Non-Stop-Fun." Rev. of *Criminal Genius.* By George F. Walker. At Factory Theatre. *Toronto Star* 17 November 1997: C5.

———. "Walker's Dramatic Return." Rev. of *Problem Child* and *Adult Entertainment.* By George F. Walker. At Factory Theatre. *Toronto Star* 27 October 1997: E5.

Conlogue, Ray. "Flaws Show in *Beautiful City*." Rev. At Factory Theatre. *The Globe and Mail* 1 October 1987: D5.

———. "*Nothing Sacred*: Best Play the City Has Seen in Years." *The Globe and Mail* 15 January 1988: D8.

———. "Playwright Plies Trade in U.S.—But Not for Free: Public Taste Catches Up with George F. Walker." *The Globe and Mail* 5 November 1988: C3.

———. "A Triumph of Gothic Comedy." Rev. of *Zastrozzi.* By George F. Walker. At Toronto Free Theatre. *The Globe and Mail* 14 May 1987: C3.

———. "The Unquenchable Sizzle of Carole Laure." *The Globe and Mail* 16 October 2000: R3.

———. "Walker Has Left the City but the City Hasn't Left Him." *The Globe and Mail* 19 September 1987: C1, C4.

Conolly, L. W., ed. *Canadian Drama and the Critics.* Vancouver: Talonbooks, 1987. 207-16, 297-301.

Crew, Robert. "New Play a Good Omen for New Home." Rev. of *Criminals in Love.* At Factory Theatre. *Toronto Star* 8 November 1984: E3.

Dafoe, Chris. "Talkin' 'bout Their Generation." Rev. of *Tough!* Green Thumb Theatre, at Vancouver East Cultural Centre. *The Globe and Mail* 9 February 1993: C2.

Duchesne, Scott. "Our Country's Good: The Export Market Favours Walker, Tremblay and Thompson." *Theatrum* 38 (April/May 1994): 19-23.

Filewod, Alan. Introduction. *The CTR Anthology: Fifteen Plays from* Canadian Theatre Review. Toronto: U of Toronto P. 1993. xi-xx.

Fraser, John. "*Ramona* Kinky, But a Clinger." *The Globe and Mail* 16 January 1976: 14.

———. "Walker Turns to Murder with Comedy." *The Globe and Mail* 19 April 1977: 16.

Galloway, Myron. "George Walker—Resolving the World's Chaos." *Montreal Star* 3 March 1979: D9.

Gass, Ken. Introduction. *The Factory Lab Anthology.* Ed. Connie Brissenden. Vancouver: Talonbooks, 1974. 7-10.

Glassco, Bill. Introduction. *Nothing Sacred.* By George F. Walker. Toronto: Coach House, 1988. 9-12.

Gravestock, Steve. "Investing in *Nothing Sacred.*" *Theatrum* 41 (November-December-January 1994/95): 4-5.

Haff, Stephen. "The Brave Comedy of Big Emotions: An Introduction." *Shared Anxiety: Selected Plays.* By George F. Walker. Toronto: Coach House, 1994. xi-xvii.

———. "George Walker." Interview. *Bomb* Spring 1997: 36-39.

———. "Just Say It." Rev. of *Nothing Sacred.* By George F. Walker. At Atlantic Theatre Company, New York. *Village Voice* 3 November 1992: 112.

Hallgren, Chris. "George Walker: The Serious and the Comic." *Scene Changes* 7 (March-April 1979): 23-25.

Harrison, James. "Reporting a Criminal Act." Rev. of *Criminals in Love.* By George F. Walker. At Factory Theatre. *Theatrum* 1 (1985): 11-14.

Johnson, Bryan. "Self-Effacing Playwright Walker Looks to the Criminal Mind." *The Globe and Mail* 31 December 1977: 38.

Johnson, Chris. *Essays on George F. Walker: Playing with Anxiety.* Winnipeg: Blizzard, 1999.

———. "George F. Walker." *Post-Colonial English Drama: Commonwealth Drama Since 1960.* Ed. Bruce King. New York: St. Martin's, 1992. 82-96.

———. "George F. Walker Directs George F. Walker." *Theatre History in Canada/ Histoire du théâtre au Canada* 9 (1988): 157-72.

———. "'I Put it in Terms which Cover the Spectrum:' Mixed Convention and Dramatic Strategies in George F. Walker's *Criminals in Love.*" *On-Stage and Off-Stage: English Canadian Drama in Discourse.* Ed. Albert-Reiner Glaap with Rolf Althof. St. John's: Breakwater, 1996. 257-67.

———. Rev. of *Shared Anxiety: Selected Plays.* By George F. Walker. *Theatre Research in Canada/ Recherches théâtrales au Canada* 18 (1997): 111-15.

———. "Walker, George F." *The Oxford Companion to Canadian Theatre.* Ed. Eugene Benson and L.W. Conolly. Toronto: Oxford UP, 1989. 586-88.

———. "*Zastrozzi: The Master of Discipline.*" *The Oxford Companion to Canadian Theatre.* Ed. Eugene Benson and L.W. Conolly. Toronto: Oxford UP, 1989. 598-99.

Johnston, Denis W. *Up the Mainstream: The Rise of Toronto's Alternative Theatres, 1968-1975.* Toronto: U of Toronto P, 1991.

Kaplan, Jon. "East End Escapade: George F. Walker's Escape From Happiness, Set in a Big City's East Side, Moves Beyond Anger." *Now* 23-29 March 2006: 78.

Kareda, Urjo. "*Bagdad Saloon*: Young Playwright Leaps Forward." *Toronto Star* 29 March 1973: 46.

———. "*Sacktown Rag*: A New Play with a Creaky Past." *Toronto Star* 6 April 1972: 35.

———. "Theatre Lab's 'Rehearsal' Was an Involving Experience." Rev. of "open rehearsal" of *Prince of Naples*, by George F. Walker, and "preview opening" of Steve Bordenuk's *Gin Rummy.* At Factory Lab Theatre. *Toronto Star* 21 June 1971: 24.

———. "To Begin With, There's this Mad Doctor." Rev. of *Beyond Mozambique.* By George F. Walker. At Factory Theatre. *Toronto Star* 13 May 1974: D6.

———. "Too Much Talk for Theatre." Rev. of *Prince of Naples* and *Demerit.* By George F. Walker. At Factory Lab Theatre. *Toronto Star* 10 April 1974: F16.

Kirchhoff, H. J. "Bare Emotions in the Park." Rev. of *Tough!* At Factory Theatre. *The Globe and Mail* 12 February 1994: C15.

———. "Weird Tangents and Wham-Bam Surprises." Rev. of *Theatre of the Film Noir.* At Factory Theatre. *The Globe and Mail* 19 June 1993: C2.

Knelman, Martin. "The Enigma of George Walker." *Saturday Night* 97 (February 1982): 59-60.

Knowles, Ric. "Reading Material: Transfers, Remounts, and the Production of Meaning in Contemporary Toronto Drama and Theatre." *Essays on Canadian Writing* 51-52 (Winter 1993-Spring 1994): 258-95.

Lacey, Liam. "A Fragile Refuge From a Hostile World." Rev. of *Escape From Happiness.* By George F. Walker. At Factory Theatre. *The Globe and Mail* 24 February 1992: C1.

Lane, William. Introduction. *The Power Plays.* By George F. Walker. Toronto: Coach House, 1984. 9-14.

———. Introduction. *Zastrozzi, the Master of Discipline: A Melodrama.* By George F. Walker. Toronto: Playwrights Co-op, 1979. 3-6.

Leiren-Young, Mark. "Walker at the Wheel." *Theatrum* 12 (February/March 1989): 37-38.

Mallet, Gina. "*Film Noir* Blackly and Absurdly Funny." *Toronto Star* 15 May 1981: D8.

———. "Misfire at Free Theatre." Rev. of *Filthy Rich.* By George F. Walker. At Toronto Free Theatre. *Toronto Star* 21 January 1979: B2.

———. "Navel-Gazing Days Are Over for Theatre." *Toronto Star* 21 November 1981: F3.

———. "Need for Controlled Voices Permeates Toronto Theatre." Rev. of *Gossip* and Jean Barbeau's *A Binge. Toronto Star* 25 April 1977: D6.

———. "Theatre Finds Strength with Style." Rev. of *Zastrozzi.* By George F. Walker. At Toronto Free Theatre. *Toronto Star* 3 November 1977: F1.

Maufort, Marc. "George Walker's Aesthetic of Hybridity." *Transgressive Itineraries: Postcolonial Hybridizations of Dramatic Realism.* Bruxelles: P.I.E.-Peter Lang, 2003. 41-49.

Messenger, Ann. "Canajun, Eh?" *Canadian Literature* 86 (1980): 89-93.

Mietkiewicz, Henry. "Respectability Hasn't Spoiled Renegade Writer." *Toronto Star* 18 May 1986. G1.

Nunn, Robert. "Marginality and English-Canadian Theatre." *Theatre Research International* 17 (1992): 217-25.

Ryan, Andrew. "And Justice for All: *This Is Wonderland* Dispenses Legal Drama with Social Conscience." *The Globe and Mail* 19 November 2005: Television 6

Smith, Catherine Mary. "Parody in the Plays and Productions of George F. Walker." Diss. U of Toronto, 1989.

Taylor, Kate. "Falling Deeper into Motel Hell." Rev. of *The End of Civilization*. By George F. Walker. At Factory Theatre. *The Globe and Mail* 4 May 1998: D6.

———. "*Heaven* Works Best When It Stays on Earth." *The Globe and Mail* 22 January 2000: R6.

———. "Motel Cycle a Gritty Triumph." *The Globe and Mail* 27 October 1997: C3.

———. "Playwright Shoots from the Gut." *The Globe and Mail* 3 February 2000: R4.

———. "*Suburban Motel* Finale Is More Raucous Than Risky." *The Globe and Mail* 19 June 1998: C10.

———. "Theatre for Theatre's Sake." *The Globe and Mail* 18 June 1993: D9.

Wagner, Vit. "Curse of the Shopping Class." *Toronto Star* 25 September 1987: E1, E3.

———. "Drawing Us All into One Fleabag Room." Rev. of *Suburban Motel*. At Factory Theatre. *Toronto Star* 20 June 1998: M3.

———. "*The End of Civilization* Best Yet of Cycle." *Toronto Star* 1 May 1998: D15.

———. "Never Write Another Play? Here Are Six More." *Toronto Star* 18 October 1997: J1, J16.

Wallace, Robert. "George F. Walker." *Profiles in Canadian Literature* 6. Toronto: Dundurn 1986. 105-12.

———. Introduction. *Love and Anger*. By George F. Walker. Toronto: Coach House, 1990. 5-10.

———. Preface. *Shared Anxiety: Selected Plays*. By George F. Walker. Toronto: Coach House, 1994. vii-x.

———. *Producing Marginality: Theatre and Criticism in Canada*. Saskatoon: Fifth House, 1990.

———. "Walker, George F." *The Oxford Companion to Canadian Literature*. Ed. William Toye. Toronto: Oxford UP, 1983. 819-20.

Wasserman, Jerry. "George F. Walker." Introduction to *Problem Child. Modern Canadian Plays*. 4th ed. Volume 2. Vancouver: Talonbooks, 2000-01. 371-74.

———. "George F. Walker." Introduction to *Zastrozzi. Modern Canadian Plays*. 4th ed. Volume 1. Vancouver: Talonbooks, 2000-01. 257-59.

———. Introduction. *The East End Plays: Part Two*. Burnaby: Talonbooks, 1999. 7-8.

———. Introduction. *The Power Plays*. Vancouver: Talonbooks, 1999. 5-6.

———. Introduction. *Somewhere Else: Four Plays by George F. Walker*. Vancouver: Talonbooks, 1999. 5-6.

Whittaker, Herbert. "*Bagdad Saloon*: Cheerful Final Note." *The Globe and Mail* 3 April 1973: 15.

———. "*Beyond Mozambique*: A Lightweight Trying Hard." *The Globe and Mail* 13 May 1974: 12.

## Notes on Contributors

**Carole Corbeil** (1952-2000) was raised in Montreal and moved to Toronto in the early 1970s, graduating from Glendon College (York University) in 1977. In the late 1970s and through the 1980s she became one of Canada's most admired cultural journalists, writing for *The Globe and Mail*, the *Toronto Star*, *Saturday Night*, *This Magazine*, *Canadian Art* and many other publications. She published her first novel, *Voice-Over*, in 1992 and *In the Wings* appeared in 1997. *Voice-Over* won the City of Toronto Book Award in 1993 and was short-listed for the W. H. Smith First Novel Award and the Trillium Book Award. *In the Wings* was short-listed for the 1998 City of Toronto Book Award and Nicky Guadagni's dramatization of the novel, directed by Layne Coleman, was a hit at Theatre Passe Muraille in Fall 2002. Carole Corbeil died of ovarian cancer in October 2000.

**Ken Gass** is the founder and artistic director (1970-79; 1996-present) of the Factory Theatre, and has been responsible for the premiere of hundreds of Canadian plays, including many of the works of George F. Walker. His own plays include *The Boy Bishop* (1976); *Winter Offensive* (1978); *Claudius* (1993) and *Slip Knot* (2002). Gass has also written and directed for radio and television, and teaches at the University College Drama Program at the University of Toronto.

**Reid Gilbert** has taught English at Capilano College, Vancouver, since 1971. He has been Acting and Associate Dean of Arts, Chairperson of Humanities, and Coordinator of English as well as an instructor. His genre specialty is drama, particularly Canadian drama. Among his publications are more than 60 critical articles, reviews and entries on drama and Canadian studies. Most recently, he has co-authored *A Short Guide to Writing about Literature* (Pearson-Longman), now in its second edition (2004). He is a co-editor of *Canadian Theatre Review* and a member of the Editorial Board of *Theatre Research in Canada.* His interests include literary theory, scenography, and social iconography.

**D.A. Hadfield** completed her PhD at the University of Western Ontario in 1999. She currently teaches Drama and English at St. Jerome's University and the University of Guelph. Her book on the politics of feminist theatre production and historiography, *Re: Producing Women's Dramatic History*, is forthcoming from Talonbooks.

**Stephen Haff** has published a whole bunch of articles about George F. Walker's work, directed about ten of his plays, and benefited from years of the playwright's generous mentoring. He is the Founder and Artistic Director of Real People Theater (<www.realpeopletheater.org>) and is currently the Crake Fellow in Drama at Mount

Allison University. For years, Stephen taught English and Drama at Bushwick High School, in Brooklyn, New York, of which he is very proud. He is an MFA graduate of the Yale School of Drama.

**Chris Johnson** teaches theatre and directs plays for the Theatre Program in the English Department at the University of Manitoba, where he has worked since 1979. He has directed a number of Walker's plays for the U of M, and has published numerous articles and book chapters on Walker's plays since "B-Movies", as well as a book, *Essays on George F. Walker: Playing With Anxiety.*

**Denis Johnston** holds a PhD in theatre history from the University of Toronto, and spent 13 seasons as a member of the Shaw Festival. His many publications include *Up the Mainstream*, an award-winning book about the origins of Toronto's alternative theatre movement.

**Ric Knowles** is Professor of Theatre Studies at the University of Guelph and editor of the journals *Canadian Theatre Review* and (from 1999-2005) *Modern Drama.* He is author of *The Theatre of Form and the Production of Meaning*, *Shakespeare and Canada*, and *Reading the Material Theatre*, and co-author (as part of the Cultural Memory Group) of *Remembering Women Murdered by Men: Memorials Across Canada.* He is editor of *Theatre in Atlantic Canada*, *Judith Thompson*, and *The Masks of Judith Thompson*, and co-editor (with Joanne Tompkins and W. B. Worthen) of *Modern Drama: Defining the Field* and (with Monique Mojica) of *Staging Coyote's Dream: An Anthology of First Nations Drama in English.*

**Harry Lane** is a Professor Emeritus of Theatre Studies at the University of Guelph. He has published in the fields of Canadian, Scandinavian, and contemporary British drama and theatre, and has co-edited the journals *Essays in Theatre/Études théâtrales* and *Canadian Theatre Review.* Among the plays he has directed are George F. Walker's *Escape from Happiness*, *Problem Child*, and *Criminal Genius.*

**Marc Maufort** is a professor of English, American and postcolonial literature at the Université Libre de Bruxelles (Belgium). His most recent publication is a monograph entitled *Transgressive Itineraries. Postcolonial Hybridizations of Dramatic Realism* (2003), a comparative study of selected contemporary Canadian, Australian, and New Zealand dramatists.

**Amanda McCoy** is currently a PhD candidate in Drama in the School of English and Theatre Studies at the University of Guelph.

**Mary Pat Mombourquette** is the Managing Director of Symphony Nova Scotia, one of the twelve major orchestras in Canada. After completing an MA in Drama at the University of Guelph and before entering the world of orchestral music, she worked in a variety of positions in theatre, including those of director, stage manager, dramaturge, producer, and general manager.

**Ed Nyman** is a writer and consultant in the City of Toronto. He did his graduate work at York University under the direction of Dr. Kym Bird and Robert Wallace. He is currently working on a book-length study of George F. Walker.

**Craig Stewart Walker** is Professor of Drama and English at Queen's University (Canada) and Artistic Director of Theatre Kingston. He is the author of *The Buried Astrolabe: Canadian Dramatic Imagination and Western Tradition* (McGill-Queen's UP, 2001) and co-editor (with Jennifer Wise) of both the two-volume and the concise editions of *The Broadview Anthology of Drama* (Broadview Press 2003, 2005).

**Robert Wallace** is Professor Emeritus of English and Drama Studies at York University's Glendon College in Toronto. Among his many publications are *Staging a Nation: Evolutions in Contemporary Canadian Theatre*, *Theatre and Transformation in Contemporary Canada*, *Producing Marginality: Theatre and Criticism in Canada*, and *The Work: Conversations with English-Canadian Playwrights* (with Cynthia Zimmerman). As an editor, he has published more than 20 volumes of Canadian plays including *Quebec Voices: Three Plays*, *Making, Out: Plays by Gay Men*, *Shared Anxiety: Selected Plays of George F. Walker*, and *This Unknown Flesh: A Selection of Plays by Sky Gilbert.*

**Jerry Wasserman** is Professor of English and Theatre at the University of British Columbia and editor of *Modern Canadian Plays*, now in its 4th edition. He has published widely on Canadian theatre and written introductions for four of George Walker's play collections. Wasserman is also an actor and critic, and has fond memories of drinking beer with George during the year he spent in Vancouver writing the *Suburban Motel* plays.